THE POETRY OF ROCK:
THE GOLDEN YEARS

Other Books by David R. Pichaske:

Beowulf to Beatles: Approaches to Poetry. Free Press, 1972.

A Generation in Motion: Popular Music and Culture in the Sixties. Schirmer Books, 1979.

Beowulf to Beatles and Beyond: The Varieties of Poetry. Macmillan, 1981.

THE POETRY OF ROCK

the golden years

by

David R. Pichaske

THE ELLIS PRESS
PEORIA, ILLINOIS

The Ellis Press
P. O. Box 1443
Peoria, Illinois 61655

This book is for Deanne Banta, Billy Allison, Tony Mansell,
Fred Haberle, John Stewart, Bonnie Hausman, Linda Teetsel,
the Governor, Harry Lefever, Bob Buhlmann, Jim Roosevelt,
Judy Cooper, Carol Tinsman, Judy Elbert, James Super House,
Ken Norman, Nancy Fischer, Matthew Great Marin, Jeannie
Shoemaker, Frank Marmello, T, Dean Rauch, Suzie Taylor,
Roger Libby, George Blunt, Uncle Phil, Suzie Nature, Bob
Wark, Jan Banks, Dick Shilts, Jan Peters, Perk, Eldon Miller,
Claude Elmer Graves, Ruth Seeh, Bob Lyren, Marilyn Babler,
Kristie Towner, John and Mary Lohr, Mary Jo Coyle, Ruth
Seeh, Bob Cherry, Chuck and John Kindesvatter, C B and L S,
R. Martin Smith, Wade O'Brian, Mike Metzger, Dave Larson,
the Hunk, Peggy Albright, Tod Needham, Doris, the Fox, Sue
and Chuck Green, Jim Updegraff, Red Maurer, Susan Blackburn,
Ted Thompson, Elaine Ezekian, Bill Fischer, Joe Cahill, Craig
the Bird Scobie, Kristin Jensen, Smarty Marty, Bob Peterson,
Bill Coyle, Kool Kurt, Bob Hartje, Suzie McKinstry, Dwaine
Holt, Dave Recker, Thomas Lamert Wolf, Yong Ahn, John
Krause, Paul Yuckman, Gaby and Gordon Jones, Karen McElhenny,
Bob Lysciak, Larry Gearhart, Jack Carey, John Nemo, Peter
Heidtmann, Dennis McInerny, Old White-bearded Satan, Simon
Alwan, Peter Dusenbery, James Ballowe, Wayne Tuminello, Ed
Kaizer, Don, Martha, Ann, Sue, Jo, S & K, and a lot of other
friends of mine.

> May your heart always be joyful
> May your song always be sung
> And may you stay forever young
>
> —Bob Dylan

"The silence of their sinking is all that they reply;
Some have chosen to decay, and others chose to die . . . ."
—Phil Ochs

THE POETRY OF ROCK

PREFACE, 1980

The following essays grew out of a course I was teaching at Bradley University back in 1974 and 1975 called, like this book, "The Poetry of Rock." The course, in turn, had developed out of a Free Press book titled *Beowulf to Beatles: Approaches to Poetry,* in which rock lyrics were subjected—for the first time in a textbook—to the close examination literary critics lavish on poems and short stories. I also wrote a few articles at the same time—something between pseudo-scholarship and unconscious parody, I now realize—and taped a series of radio broadcasts and got a grant from the Illinois Humanities Council for another series of radio forums, and had this manuscript off at Indiana University Press and an outline for another book at Schirmer Books in New York, and was generally pointed toward writing the first essay on Bob Dylan to be printed in *PMLA* when a sabbatical leave caused me to drop everything and head for Germany, France, Italy, England, Scotland and Wales.

Half a year on the other side of the Atlantic gave me a brand new perspective on life. I noticed, while wandering the foothills of the Italian Alps outside of my great-uncle Ernesto Stella's villa at Bisuschio, that them there mountains did not give much of a fat fart about Bradley University, *PMLA,* books, or even rock-n-roll. I lived intimately with my kids—for the first time, really—and they taught me the joys of blowing the day off lounging around some kiddie play park. (I became quite an expert on the parks of Europe that year—not much in the way of museums, but very heavy into parks.) My pulse slowed by about 50%. I was just about to wire home "sell house and send money" when word came from Ken Stuart at Schirmer that yes, they'd be interested in doing a collection/anthology of rock lyrics, and we'll talk about it when you're in N.Y.C. again.

So I returned to the States, matured, a bit half-heartedly, and we talked. As things developed, Schirmer did not do the anthology, and U. of Indiana Press had turned down my collection of rock criticism, and the *PMLA* article was but a fleeting vision, and I returned to Bradley University purged, very mellow, not an iron in the fire and not much caring. In that pleasant state of mind I continued for some while, writing poems, stories, a novel, gradually involving myself in a variety of new projects, most of which had very little to do with rock music. I thought I had grown up.

Then came a hankering and a hungering, and a glance or two over the shoulder. In the perfect vacuum that was disco, I found myself nostalgic for the good, solid rock of the 1960s. In my middle thirties, with shortness of breath and a balding head to remind me of my age, I started looking back and wondering what had happened. The poems, the stories, the novel were largely retrospective. When Phil Ochs committed suicide, I wrote Ken Stuart a short note suggesting "here is a book: the man was the decade, and in his career lies the story of the birth and death of a generation." Ken wrote back, "If America doesn't want Phil Ochs, we can't sell it Phil Ochs. Why don't you write a book about the whole sixties thing, using music as a focus? I'll even make up the prospectus myself."

This book that walked in and sat down became *A Generation in Motion* (Schirmer Books, 1979), and it brought me back to rock—it and the second edition of *Beowulf to Beatles,* which Macmillan commissioned also in 1979. And at length I found myself pondering the manuscript of *The Poetry of Rock,* which had lain unattended in a file drawer for better than half a decade. And I began to wonder.

Nobody likes to throw away a book, and I am no exception. This group of essays, I believe, has something to say—dated though it is—that makes it even in 1981 not a bad book. I tried out one of the essays, part of the chapter on Bob Dylan, at a conference on popular culture held at Bowling Green in 1979, and found my vanity flattered and my judgment reassured when five people asked for photocopies of the paper. *A Generation in Motion* was beginning to seep into college classrooms in history, sociology, music and literature, and one of the orders came from Cal-Berkeley. So I said to myself, . . .

The immediate question was, of course, whether to revise or not, and if so how extensively and in what directions. As will be obvious to the most casual reader, I revised very little: the book is printed in 1981 a good six years out of time. The style remains—too much of it—that turgid pseudo-lit. crit. jargon I used B.S., Before Sabbatical. The stories of Dylan, the Who, the Rolling Stones, the Beatles, Paul Simon, the Jefferson Airplane/Starship are truncated, cut in mid-flight. Some chapters announce the end of careers that have since taken off again; others ignore important developments in pop history. I think the book needs a chapter on Joni Mitchell. (I seem to recall one somewhere, or a lecture, on Joni, and one on the Band, and one on Leonard Cohen. But who knows where they have disappeared.) I think the book needs some attention to/explanation of Bob Dylan, the born-again Christian (although I would refer readers to Paul Williams' *Dylan—What Happened?* which says lots). Ochs is not only buried but forgotten (there *was* a biography, incidentally, just about the time of *A Generation in Motion,* but it was not well received, and I have not heard a Phil Ochs song on the radio in five years). The Rolling Stones are breaking up, but not before giving the 1970s one final flying finger in their brilliant, maybe even best-ever album *Some Girls,* which I have worn clear through the grooves with replaying. The individual Beatles continue to produce, although I think they have fulfilled my prediction that four divided by four equals nothing.

At the very least I was strongly tempted to add postscripts to each chapter, to make myself current, to correct myself, to point out that I was often right in my predictions, to point out that people *are* in 1980 burning rock-n-roll records in the streets.

I did not, however. In the first place, I think there's enough in the essays as they stand to justify the book: it could have been better, but—in light of the little, really, that was done in the seventies—not much better. Most of 70s rock just isn't worth talking about. A second reason was that other matters command my attention: this world is so Big, I keep telling friends, and we have so little time! The third reason I left the manuscript untouched was that in rereading it at five year's remove I discovered in it—not in the analyses of songs and the discussions of artists, but in the spirit which pervades the whole— a sense of where we all were in the mid-seventies, a kind of ingenuous reflection of my own and my generation's lostness, which I did not wish to destroy. "This book is about an art form not much in evidence these days," the preface began, as if on rock-n-roll hung the whole world. How very right those words were, and how revealing of the child of the sixties, lost in the seventies, lamenting his own lost innocence, unable as yet to discover what's going down in the present. Even the style—stiff, pretentious, analytical—reminded me of a part of myself that I had forgotten: the old analyst of the New Left, who would argue a fine point all night, shave close to the bone, endure the most time-consuming and frankly boring analysis, just to make sure. I've gotten away from that tedious closeness, mentally and stylistically, and I think I'm better off for it, but it's nice to remember.

So, with such disarming self-criticisms and admissions, I offer *The Poetry of Rock* to whatever public picks it up. I'm going small press (the small presses inherited, I think, the energy and vitality of sixties' rock—but that's another story), and small press means not many ads, and you probably didn't buy this book at B. Dalton's Booksellers. It means that all the lyrics have been trimmed to what might be fairly used in a critical book—none of that "quote the whole song and let's have a look at it now" I could get away with in *Beowulf to Beatles*. No nice pictures, no four-color cover. We shall see what reviews appear. We shall see whether *The Poetry of Rock* follows its predecessors into the college classroom. If it doesn't happen, at least the book will have broken free of my file drawer and had a chance to run for it, eh?

Somewhere over the past decade I have misplaced the list of persons to be thanked for this book. I can't remember them all, but let me try: Wayne Tuminello, my engineer at WCBU, and Frank Thomas, also of WCBU; Mary Arney, student, and Terri Symonds, student; oh, and Robert Bernstein, who wrote that incredible paper on the Beach Boys; the Illinois Humanities Council for their grant; Ken Stuart and Abigail Meyer for their encouragement and support; the anonymous reader at Indiana who caught the Buddy Holly/Buddy Knox confusion; kids, wife, friends, all listed in the dedication; the people who wrote these songs, poets all of them, of a very high order.

—David Pichaske
October 28, 1980

CHAPTER I
THE POETRY OF ROCK

This book is about an art form not much in evidence these days, about a moment fast submerging into the recesses of a new generation's collective subconscious. Oh yes, record companies continue to crank out gold disc after gold disc: recession, depression, oil shortage or what, "product" is there. And yes, pop music on the AM radio is as profitable as ever; few stations have reverted to "easy listening" formats, and nobody's breaking rock-n-roll records one by one over the air as some stations did in the late fifties. And yes, there is even a more or less vibrant rock underground on the FM networks. But since the arrival of Richard Nixon in 1968, some fundamental changes have occurred in rock music which make the seventies qualitatively different from the sixties and even the late fifties. Let's face it: Harry Chapin is not Bob Dylan, and the Osmonds are not the Beatles. More important, Chapin does not promise to become another Dylan, and there is absolutely no hope that the Osmonds will blossom as did the lovable Moptops. *Most* important, there is really nobody producing the quality product generated in the sixties by the Beatles, the Stones, and Dylan, a product which turned lyrics into poetry and music into fine art. Even Dylan, the Stones, and the dissociated Beatles don't produce the way they used to, although all have their moments. "Rock is dead, really," says Dan Fogelberg, rising pop performer, in an interview.

This everybody knows: the middle seventies finds pop music stagnated in a high tide of promotion-propelled mediocrity, and reviewers search at times frantically for the "new Stones," the "new Beatles," the "new Dylan." Paul Nelson, introducing one Elliott Murphy to *Rolling Stone* readers as "the best Dylan since 1968" observes, "a majority of our overcivilized band of Dylan-Beatles-Stones dispairados have long championed the belief that, while there are some interesting newcomers, there are no new heroes (nothing, really nothing, to turn off)"; nobody since the Who has entered the rock-n-roll pantheon, and nobody will. If there is truth to this accusation, perhaps it's because a disconcertingly high percentage of today's top tunes are revivals—usually inferior—of sixties and fifties songs: "Locomotion," "Please Mr. Postman," "Lucy In the

The Poetry of Rock

Sky," "You Won't See Me," and on and on and on. There *is* good music, but it's frequently instrumental and jazz or country-and-western oriented. It's not a dominant breed, either; the best is not the most popular, the most popular songs lack the consistent thematic weight and poetic subtlety (to say nothing of the musical drive) you need to find in sixties rock lyrics. The Village, San Francisco, Mod, the Movement—they're all dead, and the ashes of the dreams can be found in the magazines. With them died the particularly arty, heavy, substantial kind of music they generated. And not only is today's rock qualitatively different from that of the sixties, the older heritage is rapidly being lost to a new generation of listeners. While fragments of the past find their way into occasional AM consciousness, much of the greatness of the fifties and sixties remains buried on lp's not often played even on the FM stations. Granted that time colors the past, I can't help thinking that today's youth have lost both a heritage and—more important—the very notion that rock can at times rise to art, to poetry. I can't recall hearing "I Am the Walrus" or even "A Hard Rain's A-Gonna Fall" in the last year, let alone any of Phil Ochs' or Leonard Cohen's work. Worse, AM oldies selections have a way of leveling everything, so that the Stones and the Airplane and the Creedence Clearwater Revival all seem equally heavy. You can't help getting the feeling that not only is a moment over, it's well on its way to oblivion.

I've been speaking of a moment; in fact there was a series of contiguous moments: the original rock-n-roll rebellion of the middle fifties, the folk flowering of the early sixties, the flower-power psychedelic explosion of the middle sixties, the radical political movement of the late sixties. But if you read the right books, you will discover that these moments are all related: rock-n-roll was a social and political rebellion as legitimate as the protest movement, the drug scene was responsible for the political activism of the later sixties, and so on. Curiously many of pop music's greatest auteurs—the Beatles and Stones and Airplane, Dylan and Ochs and Simon—moved easily from one moment to another. In one sense Mod and San Francisco and Lincoln Park and even the Alan Freed rock-n-roll concerts of the fifties had one thing in common, for all expressed a visceral impatience with socio-political norms and an expanding consciousness that pushed whatever music they fathered to remarkable achievements of sound and sense. Tremendous intellectual and artistic (not mention sexual) energies were released in the best of rock-n-roll, folk music, and the rock of the sixties, energies which turned music into a fine art and lyrics into poetry, energies which have not for the most part been carried into the pop music of our time.

2

We are not accustomed to thinking of rock, folk, and rock-n-roll this way; in fact, we like to relegate all of it to the subculture or the counter-culture, where we can depricate it and forget it. The fact is, though, that the best of all these moments has been of a quality unsuspected by much of today's audience and many of today's commentators. The ironic truth is that exactly those finest moments of rock, folk, and rock-n-roll are those most denigrated by many rock critics as pretentious, contrived, overly arty rubbish: *Sgt. Pepper, John Wesley Harding, After Bathing at Baxters,* the lyrics of Leonard Cohen or Paul Simon, the content of a Chuck Berry lyric. Taken together these works form a single explosive, radical instant reaching from 1955 (in Chuck Berry's case) to (in the case of the Who) 1973. It is the purpose of this book to examine that moment, the composer-performers who contributed most to it, and—if by nothing more than implication—the vacuum that followed.

In beginning, let me admit that we have seen flashes and glimmers of late from a number of directions: Dylan's *Blood on the Tracks* is a first rate album, Joni Mitchell a first rate performer. Some youngsters show promise: Harry Chapin, Bruce Springsteen, Cat Stevens, Jesse Winchester—you can name your own favorite. McCartney, Harrison, Paul Simon—these have produced competent, even memorable lyrics within the past five years. I do not want to be put in the position of saying nothing lyrically compelling, nothing poetic is going on these days. I most certainly don't want to be put in the position of arguing flatly that today's music isn't worth a damn. Some is. But the moment of rock as a socio-political force and as poetry is ended. Significantly, most of what's good these days is retrospective: the Who's *Quadrophenia,* the Band's *Moondog Matinee,* McCartney's "Band on the Run," even *Blood on the Tracks.*

Let me further admit that not everyone is going to agree with my own lament for the makers, because not everyone wanted pop music to develop into fine art in the first place. Some have argued that the Beatles weren't so very good for rock-n-roll because they mired it in artsy-craftsiness. Some welcomed the turn of the decade as an end to kitsch-masquerading-as-art (the stuff which fills this book). To some the Beach Boys and the Jackson Five are closer to what rock is all about than Paul Simon or Phil Ochs ever will be, and thank god for a return to normalcy. I take a decidedly literary approach to my rock, and not everyone is willing to be all that arty about it. Nik Cohn, an old-fashioned good-beat-you-can-dance-to-it rock-n-roll fan, accused mid-sixties rock of "third-form poetries, fifth-hand philosophies, ninth-rate perceptions" and viewed most of what I call rock poetry—both in the qualitative and descriptive sense—as pretentious, self-conscious nonsense. Jon Landau and Mike Jahn and Robert Christgau have proclivities in this direction too. And for their part, the music profs have been as reluctant to grant rock status as an art as the lit. crit. boys have been reluctant to grant it status as poetry. Said one University of Vermont English instructor in 1965 -- after both the great "Mr. Tambourine Man" and the nearly great "Sad-Eyed Lady of the Low Lands" had been released -- "Anyone who calls Dylan 'the greatest poet in the United States today' has rocks in his head. That is such an irresponsible statement as to deserve no attention. Since his appeal is (apparently) to irresponsible teen-agers, I can't take him seriously. Dylan is for the birds—and the bird brained."

Remarkably similar, these judgments, coming at the issue from opposite sides of the fence: rock is strictly for the teen-aged subculture, and since the subculture has nothing to do with art, poetry, or mainstream culture, rock (Cohn would probably qualify that to read "true-fine rock-n-roll") also has nothing to do with art, poetry, or mainstream culture. All A is not B, C is A, therefore C is not B. Your classic, airtight syllogism. Trouble is, the major premise of that argument just won't stand up, and with it falls the whole syllogism. Because while there *is* a strongly anti-cultural strain in the subculture, that anti-culturalism is not a peculiar quality of rock. Nor is anti-culturalism incompatible with art and poetry, since it can be found in a great deal of what everyone calls, without much reservation, modern art and poetry. Furthermore, the anti-culturalism of pop is not always reflected in rock. Nina Simone, Bob Dylan, John Lennon, Paul Simon all called themselves and each other poets, assuming without either presumption or apology that's just what they were. Blood, Sweat, and Tears copped an album title from Wordsworth; the Jefferson Airplane and Phil Ochs turned to an Irish novelist and an Irish poet respectively for material on which to build songs. The documented influences on Bob Dylan range from Blake to Eliot to Ginsberg to Rimbaud. Tony Scaduto's *Bob Dylan: An Intimate Biography* gives the lie to any romantic notions of a James Dean-type unlettered minstel fresh off the train from Kansas. Dylan, Lennon, Simon—they all meant business, the kind of business I can't find in pop music of the present moment. All this may not *make* rock an art, but it certainly suggests much.

A more sophisticated argument against the kind of literary analysis I propose is advanced by Robert Christgau, who wrote in an early essay on rock and poetry, "Poems are read or said. Songs are sung." While he himself qualified the statement with an admission that perhaps he was being "too strict," the distinction between singing and saying lies at the root of many people's objections to rock as poetry. After all, these *are* songs, and except for a few eccentrics like Vachel Lindsay or perhaps Dylan Thomas, twentieth century poets have had precious little to do

4

with music—at least until Ginsberg, Ferlinghetti, and the Beats. Most modern poets have discarded the regularities of stanza and meter imposed on poetry by its early association with music and virtually discarded all vestiges of poetry as an oral art: refrains, incremental repetition in lines or stanzas, the music of alliteration and consonance. Which just may explain why modern poetry has fared so poorly and rock so well, and which of the two is closer to traditional poetic art.

Wilfred Mellers, critic and composer, has stated the logical answer to Christgau's argument, which is probably more historically and theoretically valid:

> We talk nowadays as though the relationship [between words and music] . . . constituted a problem; even as though there were a natural antipathy between them which composer and poet must overcome as best they may. Yet the separation of the two arts is comparatively recent, and the link between them would seem to be rooted deep in human nature.

Here is the crux of the matter: only recently—since well after the invention of the printing press—have music and poetry gone their separate ways. The history of that unfortunate dissociation is well known and needs no repetition here; the point is that we have short memories indeed if we draw a distinction between poeticizing and singing. When we realize that *Beowulf* originally had some sort of music accompaniment, that the border ballads and Shakespeare's songs came attached to tunes, that a lot of what we consider poems were once songs, we begin to realize a couple of other things. First, we realize that rock lyrics may survive surprisingly well even when stripped of their music (an eventuality which certainly ought not to come to pass in this McLuhanesque age of audio paraphernalia). And we realize second that rock lyrics may be closer to the true poetic mainstream than other forms of twentieth century poetry which, like much culture of this century, prove on close examination to be neurotic, grotesque, abnormal. This in turn suggests that maybe, just maybe we are justified in applying a literary analysis to rock, and that we have some right to expect rock to measure up literarily. The cry "But they're songs, not poems" is really not a valid excuse.

The dissociation of music and poetry is more than an historical curiosity, however, for as Mellers suggests, there are logical interrelationships between the two which disappear when they're separated, much to the detriment of both. I wouldn't go so far as to say music *needs* poetry or vice versa; it does seem to be that each inhibits the other's excesses, and when they are separated each tends toward eccentricities of technique and content. More to the point of this book, which emphasizes

5

The Poetry of Rock

as it does the words as well as the sound of rock's heavies, might be a brief survey of the ways music and poetry interact on each other when they do co-exist.

Certainly, for example, music can be said to carry a meaning of its own, vaguer and less easily defined than that of words, but a meaning understood by both the heart and the head. You could call a melody plaintive or exaltant, a tempo nervous or languid, a performance electric or lethargic. Music has in the past been made to paint pictures and tell stories. Words, of course, paint pictures and tell stories too, and when you bring words and music together, the messages of each can be made to act upon each other in a variety of ways. I would say that the lyrics of "Eleanor Rigby" border on the sentimental . . . especially on a naked page. In the Beatles' own performance of the song, however, whatever potential sentimentality the song contains is counterbalanced by the nervousness of its music and uptempo performance. In this case music and poetry comment ironically on each other, rescue each other. A MUZAK type performance loses the nervous edge, and the song degenerates into mush, gush, and sentimentality. Another Beatles' lyric, "She's Leaving Home," works quite differently, using an instrumentation and melody that emphasize the sentimentality of its lyrics. This is a risk, for depending on your audience you come off with two very different reactions. One casual listener hears something as drippy and self-indulgent as Bobby Goldsboro's song "Honey," while a sharper soul suspects that the excess is a parody, a satire. Or, to use yet another example from the Beatles' work, you can use music to expand the range of lyrics' meaning: "All You Need Is Love" uses music motifs to expand the ambiguity of love developed in its words—"She loves you, yeh, yeh, yeh," "Greensleeves," "In the Mood," "What Child Is This?" A good rock singer-composer-arranger knows not only how to write words and music that mean, but how to make them work with or against each other. That, my friends, is art!

There's another side to the coin. The voice may be turned into an instrument, thereby making it for all practical purposes a part of a song's music instead of a conveyor of cognitive meaning. Blues and rhythm-and-blues and rock-n-roll were at times very good at this, from B.B. King to Elvis Presley to Janis Joplin. While pop music before 1955 carefully segregated solo and accompaniment, using one to set off the other or engaging in a dialogue between the two, rock brings words and music together, sometimes at the same time and at the same volume and—in stereo—on the same track. The commingling is total, resulting in the old complaint about lyrics being obviously irrelevant because you can't understand what's being sung. At times you can't, you know, not that it

6

matters much. We all know what Elvis and Janis and the great blues singers from Blind Lemon Jefferson to B.B. King had in mind when they slurred lyrics. And we all know what "a wop bob a loo bob a wop bam boom" means. There are times when denotative meaning just isn't that central to a song's message.

Words and music alter as well as complement each other, thereby providing both a tension within which a good rock artist could work and opportunities he could explore. Although I can think off hand of a few free verse lyrics (the Doors' "Horse Latitudes," and "Duke of Earl," both printed in Goldstein's *The Poetry of Rock*), music usually imposes a certain order on lyrics. This is one reason, I suspect, that the jazz-rock fusion did not prove as successful as the folk-rock and country-rock combinations: jazz is too loose a musical form for the resultant lyrics to achieve poetic coherence, whereas folk, country, and even blues provided their lyrics with standard, almost rigid patterns. Words seek form; form has to be reckoned with by your artist. One mark of sixties' rock's greatness was its refusal to take form for granted, its willingness to experiment in musical and poetic form.

Music affects more than a rock poem's stanzaic pattern; it influences rhythm and meter as well. Traditionally, from the sixteenth to the twentieth centuries at least, poets have tried to produce more or less regular patterns of accented (/) and unaccented (o) syllables—something like "Once upon a midnight dreary" (/o/o/o/o) or "Half a league, half a league, half a league onward" (/oo/oo/oo/o). But music counts *duration* of sound, not accent, and thereby disrupts this neat pattern of accentual measure. Eight syllables, four syllables, even one syllable can fill a measure, because two eighth notes will do for one quarter note, or four eighths for a half, or eight eighths for a whole, and it's all the same. While repeated musical patterns like stanzas and refrains, or calls and responses tend to regularize a rock lyric's form, music loosens its rhythm and meter. Again, the very best of rock's heavies seem consciously or unconsciously to have been aware of rhythmic and metrical subtleties in their lyrics.

It's possible, then, to come to pop music of the fifties and sixties expecting a certain sophistication of form and content, both musical and poetic. It is this sophistication, combined with a very definite thematic weight, that makes the work of the heavies so qualitatively different from that of today's lightweights and from much of their own recent material. You can draw the distinction quite simply: in the sixties we got poetry, in the seventies we've been getting a predominance of shlock, trivia, nostalgia, promotion, fluff, goodtime music, rubbish—anything but poetry. The particulars of that generalization are to be found in the pages of this book and on the AM and FM airwaves of the 1970's. By the same token, my assumption that pop music could aspire to poetry colors the content of these same pages, for I've chosen to write not a history of rock (a couple excellent such histories are on the market already) or even an aesthetic of rock in the broadest sense, but a careful detailed examination of what has been called "the poetry of rock." A distinction is thus drawn: however important Elvis may have been, he did not produce work comparable to that of Chuck Berry; however much you like the Beach Boys (and I do), you have to admit that "Surfer Girl" and "Little Deuce Coupe" will never make it as poetry in any qualitative sense of the word (on the contents of *Pet Sounds* I admit to ambivalence); and no matter how much you admire Harrison and Lennon and McCartney, you have to admit that their work alone is not qualitatively on a par with their work together and does not, thus, deserve extended consideration. If you want your rock-n-roll pure, if you aren't willing to draw qualitative distinctions, if you just can't feature rock as poetry or part poetry, then all this emphasis on middle Dylan, high art Beatles, Cohen and Ochs and Simon, the artier aspects of the Stones and Airplane is gonna bug you. Join Nik Cohn, flip the Yardbirds on your stereo, and read a good rock history. If you do, however, you run the risk of missing a point, losing the moment I spoke of earlier.

Ultimately the judgment is posterity's, if a music so intent on the moment manages to transcend its own self-imposed temporarily. I can't help thinking that twenty years from now the wheat and chaff will have been separated and a final judgment will have been made on qualitative, not quantitative grounds. What will matter will be who was good, not who sold most. And when such judgment is in, I can't help thinking that those artists seen to be most important to rock's terrific influence and vitality will be precisely those heavies I've included in this book: Chuck Berry, Little Richard, Joni Mitchell, the Beatles and Stones, Bobby Dylan, Slick and Kantner, Pete Townshend, Jim Morrison, Ochs and Simon and Cohen.

CHAPTER II
SOME BASIC HISTORY AND A FEW MIDDLEWEIGHTS

The many roots of what is loosely called rock reach deep, very deep into virtually every tradition of America's musical past. The tangle of influences and evolutions and convolutions has been traced in a number of recent books, several quite good, each providing a part of a composite whole. Charlie Gillett's *Sound of the City* is extra good on rhythm-and-blues and soul; Carl Belz' *The Story of Rock* provides good basic history of 1954-68 pop; Paul Oliver's *The Meaning of the Blues* is a comprehensive and interpretive study of some 350 blues lyrics; Mike Jahn's *Rock: From Elvis Presley to the Rolling Stones* provides a year-by-year recapitulation of pop musical developments from 1954 through the seventies; R. Serge Denisoff's *A Great Day Coming* is a sound sociological treatment of a folk music tradition handled less academically by Oscar Brand in *The Ballad Mongers*. Other bits and pieces are there for the taking in Tony Scaduto's biography and Michael Gray's analysis of Bob Dylan and his work, in Lillian Roxon's *Rock Encyclopedia,* in anthologies like Jonathan Eisen's *The Age of Rock,* in old *Billboard* lists of hot 100's. It is a long, complex, and in many areas still unwritten story to which this book may make its fair contribution.

But surely no single book, no single chapter of a book is going to lay out schematically and in great detail the evolution of pop music from the thirties through the seventies. What follows is oversimplified basics. It is, more important, filtered through my own literary prejudices and bent to my own literary aim: an explanation of the great moment of rock poetry, its development, and its demise. To the greatness of blues, of soul, even of Tin Pan Alley, I can only glancingly allude. Those scenes are for others; what is presented here is intended partially to provide a context in which to place the heavies who follow, and partially as an opportunity to discuss briefly the work of a few middleweights whose work cannot receive extended treatment.

Rock, a phenomenon largely of the middle and late sixties and a form distinct from folk, rhythm-and-blues, and mid-fifties rock-n-roll, grew directly out of all three of these musical movements. Each, in turn, had its antecedents. The Folk Revival of the early sixties has a long and important history reaching through the Weavers and the Almanac Singers

9

The Poetry of Rock

to white balladeers of the union struggles and the Great Depression, and to black blues singers of the twenties and before. Rhythm-and-blues has its origins in jazz, swing, and the blues of the twenties. Rock-n-roll, by the classic explanation, grew from a fusion of white country-and-western music with black rhythm-and-blues somewhere in the early fifties. The wellsprings of rock, then—blues, folk, country-and-western—lie deep in the American musical underground, and rock's history begins with names and places familiar in their day to only small segments of the American populace. The incredible popularity of rock has obscured the fact that the best pop music was really not very widely known for most of the twentieth century; where rock blew classical and "easy listening" music nearly off the air (and out of record catalogues) during the sixties, rhythm-and-blues, folk, country-and-western, even rock-n-roll spent most of their lives in the shadow of both classical music and easy listening schlock.

Easy listening music, which dominated air programming in the forties and early fifties, is actually a debased form of the so-called Tin Pan Alley music of the thirties and forties. Because the Tin Pan Alley publishers derived their songs initially from Vaudeville and later from Broadway musicals, most hit tunes through the thirties reflected a Broadway musical influence: they were occasionally witty, frequently sentimental, almost always inconsequential. Hoagy Carmichael, Cole Porter, George Gershwin—these names dominated the industry and produced urbane, sophisticated lyrics that set the upper limits of the form:

Birds do it, bees do it,
Even educated fleas do it,
Let's do it,
Let's Fall in love.
(Porter, "Let's Do It")

Toward these limits other composers, now consigned to oblivion, strained unsuccessfully; the standard Tin Pan Alley lyric is infinitely less clever, less suggestive, and more forgettable than Cole Porter.

Around the end of the thirties the big bands made their appearance, promoting not so much a new breed of lyric but a musical style in which band dominated lyric: swing music, ripped off like so much American music from black blues bands, had developed into a style during the late twenties; by the late thirties it became a rage. Count Basie, Duke Ellington, Glenn Miller, Tommy Dorsey, Harry James—the names that predominate are not composers but band leaders and instrumental stylists. The sheet music companies of Tin Pan Alley had fallen on hard times. But with the end of the War, vocalists were back in style: Perry Como, Tony Bennett, Bing Crosby, Frank Sinatra, Dean Martin, the McGuire Sisters, Eddie Fisher—some of the names are still around today, return-

10

ing in rock's demise to prominence on network television. Tin Pan Alley, with its bland conservatism, was back in business. It roared into the fifties hale and hearty, producing hits like "Vaya Con Dios", "Doggie In the Window", "Oh, My Papa", and "Three Coins in the Fountain." Columbia Records will sell you a two-disc LP labeled *The Fifties Greatest Hits* that includes "Wonderful! Wonderful!" "Tennessee Waltz," "I Believe," "Come On-a My House," "My Heart Cries For You," and "The Little White Cloud that Cried." Of the bunch, only "Come On-a My House" ("I'm gonna give you candy") sounds vaguely interesting today.

In the other half of the world, however, significant musical developments had been taking place which were to lead to rock-n-roll, rock, and the blues revival of 1968, and which surfaced occasionally before 1954 in something like the big band sound of the War years or a cleaned up version of Leadbelly's "Goodnight, Irene." It was these developments which produced the vitality of rhythm-and-blues, of folk music, and ultimately of rock-n-roll and rock. Much of this development took place in black music and was thus not widely known to white audiences until heavies like Dylan, the Beatles, the Stones, and Eric Clapton began owning up their sources. It is white America's loss that people like Blind Lemon Jefferson, Leadbelly, Howlin' Wolf, Billie Holiday and Elmore James were better known after their most productive years, usually after their deaths, than at the peak of their careers.

Blues, of course, was a going proposition in the twenties and thirties, despite the dominance of Tin Pan Alley, a vital counterculture of, by, and for the black market, both north and south. In fact, blues by this time already had a history of some thirty or so years, an oral history now lost like most folk musical history of any race or culture. In the twenties, however, blues appeared on record—total "Race Music" sales ran to five or six million records a year, almost all from small independent record companies—and subsequent blues history can be reconstructed with some accuracy. Generally blues of the twenties fell into one of two categories: largely instrumental blues with a marching or dancing rhythm (later to subdivide into jazz and band blues styles), and banjo or guitar folk blues (a style developed in the South but later to migrate to the urban North). A highly individualistic form, blues flourished from the Mississippi Delta to the northern ghetto, from New Orleans to Chicago. By the end of the twenties, blues was beginning to seep above ground, especially in the speakeasies and honkey tonks. But the Great Depression, while providing more cause than ever to sing the blues, dealt recorded blues a severe blow: most of the independents who sold to the black market either folded or sold out to the majors; they would not reappear until after the second world war. Blues ducked underground again, although not before producing among other giants Blind Lemon Jefferson, a legendary, vaguely country stylist from Couchman, Texas whose influence extends ultimately to Dylan and the Stones via persons like Leadbelly, Lightning Hopkins, and B.B. King.

With the close of World War II, "race music" had evolved to "rhythm-and-blues," a term first coined by RCA-Victor (which, having bought out a number of failing independents in the early thirties, found itself in the black music market and needed some term other than "race" to distinguish white from black), and made official when given the blessing of *Billboard* magazine in 1949 (*Billboard* kept separate but equal ratings for country-and-western and rhythm-and-blues markets). At this time rhythm-and-blues covered a multitude of styles: dancehall blues, a very rough Memphis-Chicago style bar blues, west coast club blues (closer to jazz than to band blues), even gospel singing. The dancehall blues ranged from singer-oriented ensembles backing up blues shouters like Joe Turner (the original "Shake, Rattle and Roll") and Roy Brown to steaming equivalents of swing bands, which ran a regular circuit through every city with a black population large enough to support a dance hall (the *Johnny Otis Rhythm and Blues Caravan* toured until well into the rock-n-roll era). The right band, heavy on sax and horns, could blow dancers right out of the dance hall with sophisticated boogie rhythms and long saxophone solos:

> "Showtime!" people would start hollering about the last hour of the dance. Then a couple of dozen really wild couples would stay on the floor, the girls changing to low white sneakers. The band now would really be blasting, and all the other dancers would form a clapping, shouting circle to watch that wild competition as it began, covering only a quarter or so of the ballroom floor. The band, the spectators and the dancers, would be making the Roseland feel like a big rocking ship. The spotlight would be turning, pink, yellow, green, and blues, picking up the couples lindy-hopping as if they had gone mad. "Wail, man wail!" people would be shouting at the band; and it would be wailing, until people would be shouting at the band; and it would be wailing, until first one and then another couple just ran out of strength and stumbled off toward the crowd, exhausted and soaked with sweat.
>
> (Malcolm X, *Autobiography*)

Here was energy and drive unmatched in even the best of the swing bands.

The forties were filled with other important rhythm-and-blues artists. T-bone Walker, west coast progenitor of Bo Diddley and Elvis Presley, developed the "jump style" set by Louis Jordan's Tympanny Five back in the early forties, a style which, because of its cool stance and boogie rhythms, had perhaps more effect on rock-n-roll than any other rhythm-and-blues form. Bill Haley, Chuck Berry, Fats Domino, even Little Richard all drew on the jump blues style. Second in importance was the bar blues of Mississippi, Memphis, and Chicago. It was a raucous music, born in the Delta and transplanted into Chicago by Muddy Waters, Howlin' Wolf, John Lee Hooker, and Elmore James. The sound turned Chess records into one of the country's major independents and, especially in the bottleneck guitar style of Elmore James, had a major impact on such giants of British rhythm-and-blues as Eric Clapton.

Lyrically blues reflected the honesty, the vitality, and above all the pain of black life. Sex was an open mystery; hard times were honest-to-god hard times; jail and poverty, booze and dope were basic facts of everyday life:

If your house catches on fire and there ain't no water 'round;
If your house catches on fire and there ain't no water 'round'
Throw your trunk out the window and let that shack burn down.

. . . .

Some people like to love in the parlor, others go down lover's
lane;
Some people like to love in the parlor, others go down lover's
lane;
But I like to love in the wee wee small hours of the morning.
When it's pouring down with rain.

. . . .

I was standing on the corner with my reefer in my hand,
Up steps the sergeant, took my reefer from my hand,
"My brother used a needle and my sister sniffed cocaine;
I don't use no junk, I'm the nicest boy you ever seen."

. . . .

This sort of earthy honesty, of course, seldom left the ghetto, which is one reason that rock-n-roll appeared so real life when compared with early fifties mainstream pop, despite the fact that it's earthiness was a debased, adolescent form of R&B.

The story of rhythm-and-blues, independent of its co-option into rock-n-roll and its influences on rock is not unlike the story of baseball's Negro leagues. It's another world, complete with names and legends of its own, with a quality perhaps superior to the big leagues that got all the attention during the thirties and forties. It is a story that no white is really qualified to chronicle. Some indication of rhythm-and-blues' vitality

13

could be had on the radio if you listened to just the right stations very late at night; some indication may be had from Malcom X's or Le Roi Jones' descriptions of black blues band performances; scratchy records preserve a part of the heritage. But much is legend to which white audiences were not a part and will never be a part, which reached WASP audiences, in fact, in only watered down, second hand form with the rock-n-roll revolution of the fifties.

Almost as unfamiliar to middle class Americans as blues history is white American folk music of the earlier decades of this century. American folk music received its first real public notice in 1933 with Macmillan's publication of John Lomax' *American Ballads and Folk Songs,* and the radio series "Back Where I Come From" produced by his son Alan. Carl Sandberg hyped folk, and Lomax took people like the folk-blues singer Leadbelly on the university circuit, but for the most part folk—like blues, much of which is for all practical purposes a form of folk music—lived an underground existence until the emergence of the Weavers in the late forties. Names there are, many again more familiar after than before their deaths: Leadbelly, Joe Hill, Woodie Guthrie, Aunt Molly Jackson. And again there are the faceless hundreds and thousands of Spanish Civil War partisans, IWW protesters, Depression minstrels, men who never achieved the reputation of a Hill, a Guthrie, or a Leadbelly. Thematically, of course, white folk dealt with white institutions and white problems, although there was much interchange between black blues and white folk music. Many songs in Lomax' collections are attributed to black folk-blues singers; many more come in the blues calls-response form. A song like Blind Blake's "No Dough Blues" knew no race in the Depression:

> It's a hard, hard times; good man can't get no dough.
> It's a hard, hard times; good men can't get no dough.
> All I can do for my baby don't satisfy her no more.

Still, folk encompassed more than the blues, and more than songs about hard times during the Depression. Formally folk music preferred the ballad form or a series of stanzas and refrains to the blues form, and thematically it had a political edge that blues usually lacked. Aunt Molly Jackson, for example, produced these lines in "I Am a Union Woman" (1931):

> The bosses ride fine horses
> While we walk in the mud.
> Their banner is a dollar sign
> While ours is striped with blood.

Woody Guthrie, Okie Poet, sang these lines:

California is a Garden of Eden,
A paradise to live in or see;
But believe it or not, you won't find it so hot
If you ain't got the Do Re Me.

And the "Boll Weevil Song," popularized in the heyday of rock-n-roll by Brooks Benton, had a certain bite to it in the 1934 original:

The Farmer said to the Finance Man,
I'd like to make out a note.
"Go to hell, you rascal you,
Gotta Boll Weevil on your coat!"

Social protest of the Depression and the labor movement, the crusade against Franco in the Spanish Civil War, the injustice of being poor or black or both—these themes came to color folk music during the twenties and thirties, so much so that the genre became politically suspect. This reputation for radicalism and subversion killed the first folk boom of the late forties nearly as soon as it began. The Almanac Singers—Lee Hayes, Pete Seeger, Woodie Guthrie, Millard Lampell, and at times the likes of Cisco Huston and Josh White—had achieved a certain popularity around the country in the late thirties, singing for supper and gasoline money, but it wasn't until the Weavers—Hayes and Seeger with Fred Hellerman, Greta Brodie, Jackie Berman, and Ronnie Gilbert—that folk music first reached the consciousness of most Americans. Reaching back to Leadbelly, to Guthrie's early works, to John Lomax and the union songs of the Almanac repertoire, the Weavers made it as no folk singer or group had to that time. "On Top of Old Smokie" and a cleaned up version of "Goodnight, Irene" (I'll *see* you in my dreams" replaced Leadbelly's "I'll *get* you in my dreams") made the hit charts, and the group played Carnegie Hall. The Weavers even had success with essentially country songs like "Darlin' Cory" and "Lop-Eared Mule," although in this respect their audience had probably been prepared for them by Hank Williams and the "Grand Ole Opry" show. In any event, the Weavers—and with them the first folk boom—had their careers aborted by the attacks of *Counterattack of Red Channels: The Report of Communist Influence on Radio and Television* (first published in June of 1950), of the Birchers and the blacklisters. Folk disappeared quickly, not to be resurrected until the end of the fifties by the Kingston Trio, Peter, Paul and Mary, Joan Baez, . . . and a scruffy impersonator of Woodie Guthrie named Bob Dylan.

Country-and-western music, another form of folk, did not suffer the fate of the Weavers, just as it did not suffer the same repression endured by black rhythm-and-blues. In the first place, C&W was white; in the which it did not aspire and rarely aggressed. Pseudo-country (Gene Autrey, Frankie Lane) may have made it in the big time, Davey Crockett may have turned country into a momentary rage, but basically C&W was Southern and/or shitkicker music. Grand Ole Opry, a name synonymous with C&W up through the sixties, may be popular in Evansville, Indiana and Peoria, Illinois, but until C&W producers began the great sixties exodus to L.A., country meant Nashville and Nashville meant country.

The audience was narrowly defined, but it was loyal. This is not to say it was orthodoxly white. Bill Malone has written, "Perhaps one of the reasons that rising black country artists Stoney Edwards and Charley Pride feel so at home in country music is because of the receptivity to black music and musicians shown by such men as Hank Williams and Bob Wills. Wills and the Playboys have been dipping into the black repository for many years, a circular process of borrowing and retransmission typical of the southwestern cultural interchange . . . ." One of the paradoxes of C&W is its concurrent conservatism and multiracialism. But country—basic country, not to be confused with a slicker, urban C&W coming out of L.A. these days—had a very dedicated following: a good country hit of the fifties could expect immediate sales of several hundred thousand discs; Hank Williams, star of Opry until his death in 1953, rang up eleven million-sellers. Most C&W was and remains formulaic, stylized, very much of a piece both lyrically and most of all musically, temperate, even in its many cheatin' and drinkin' songs. In the hits of a man like Williams, however, you see a flash of energy, a hint of sex, and not a little pure talent: "Your Cheatin' Heart," "Jambalaya," "Ramblin' Man," "Hey, Good Lookin'." In the wake of Williams' success, a host of fry, including Carl ("Blue Suede Shoes") Perkins, made it big in C&W. Many of them, Carl Perkins included, returned quietly to country after the rock-n-roll honeymoon ended.

What brought the attention of middle class white Americans retrospectively to folk, rhythm-and-blues, and C&W was the revolution in taste began by rock-n-roll. The standard line runs something like this: blend the rhythms and just a touch of the earthy sexuality of rhythm-and-blues with the form of country, tempering black radicalism with white conservatism, and you'll get rock-n-roll, a music just right for the youth of the fifties. In fact, however, rock-n-roll is an amorphous music and resists such formulas. Charlie Gillett (*Sound of the City*) actually identifies five varieties of rock-n-roll: northern band rock-n-roll (Bill Haley and the Comets), New Orleans dance blues (Fats Domino, Little Richard), Memphis country rock (Elvis Presley, Carl Perkins, Johnny Cash), Chicago rhythm-and-blues (Chuck Berry, Bo Diddley), and vocal group rock-n-roll (the Orioles, the Penquins, the Platters). Gillett himself may be overly schematic; the point is that rock-n-roll was, second it was, or had become, a conservative, relatively innocuous style of music. Most important, it had staked out its own audience beyond at the beginning at least, a pretty eclectic sound.

The man most responsible for the rock-n-roll revolution was not a musician at all. In 1951 Leo Mintz, owner of Cleveland's Record Rendezvous, happened to mention to a friend of his that for some strange reason white teenagers were buying black rhythm-and-blues. The friend, Alan Freed, a television personality at the time, talked WJW, an above ground radio station, into giving him a late night spot which he christened "The Moon Dog Show" and devoted to rhythm-and-blues. By 1952 Cleveland had not only the radio show but live dance concerts promoted by Freed. By 1954 Freed had himself a job with WINS, New York. It was the concerts which provided the best indication of growing white interest in rhythm-and-blues: featuring performers like Joe Turner, Fats Domino, the Moonglows, and the Drifters, playing to predominately white audiences, they drew heavily, often turning into riots or near riots, incuring much displeasure from established authority and thereby doubling and redoubling their popularity with kids. If a non-performer could aspire to the title "Father of rock-n-roll," Freed was just that: not only did he introduce rhythm-and-blues to the white teenaged masses, not only was he the original fast-talking d.j., not only did he suffer a martyr's death (accumulated establishment hostility culminated in attacks on rock-n-roll in general and Freed in particular which drove him off the air in 1959); consistently he stuck with rhythm-and-blues originals, both on the air and in his shows, when other stations opted for prettier, cooler "cover" recording.

Other factors were important in the birth of rock-n-roll of course: the vacuity of "Doggie In the Window," a vague but very palpable dissatisfaction especially obvious in youth with that sort of vacuity and rock-n-roll's early association with social rebellion through movies like *Blackboard Jungle.* When Bill Haley's "Rock Around the Clock" knocked "Cherry Pink and Apple Blossom White" out of the numero uno spot on 1955 pop charts, rock-n-roll had its first number one record and its first star. Folks at the time considered it all a fad, to be endured as was the Davey Crockett thing. They were wrong. Though it's been going in and out of style, one thing is clear: rock-n-roll is here to stay.

An honest appraisal of rock-n-roll requires a dual perspective: from the point of view of rhythm-and-blues or folk music of the Depression, rock-n-roll is almost unbearably amateurish, adolescent, trivial. Many rock-n-roll hits were in fact cover versions of rhythm-and-blues songs (Haley himself made a fair piece of change covering Ivory Joe Hunter's "Shake, Rattle, and Roll" in 1955), and as covers they invariably bowdlerized originals. The standard example of covering is that of Hank Ballard and the Midnighter's "Work With Me Annie":

Work with me, Annie,
Let's get it while the getting is good.
Annie, please don't cheat,
Give me all my meat.

This piece of hard-core rhythm-and-blues was cleaned up by Etta James in "Wallflower":

Roll with me, Henry,
You better roll it while the rollin's on.

But even this was not clean enough for Mercury Records, which covered the cover with Georgia Gibbs:

Dance with me, Henry,
Let's dance while the music rolls on.

One could argue that what's lost in direct statement is gained in metaphor, but the laundering of the original is unmistakable. Even Elvis "The King" Presley looked like a cleaned up cutie pie version of a rhthym-and-blues original. Not only was rock-n-roll sexually impotent in comparison to rhythm-and-blues, it was pretty thin poetically, especially looking back from the perspective of the sixties. It lacked the wit of Cole Porter, the directness of rhythm-and-blues, and the imagery and metaphor of sixties' rock. Musically rock-n-roll was thinner than rhythm-and-blues: rhythms settled to a standard 4/4 beat, emphasis on the backbeat; chord progressions were simple and minimal (Shirley and Lee's "Let the Good Times Roll", 1956, made do with only two notes of two chords!); musicianship was amateur.

Looking at rock-n-roll from the other side, however, you get another picture. After the easy listening vacuity of 1950s mainstream pop, rock-n-roll sounded vital, exciting, sexually stimulating, almost revolutionary. I'm not sure this is a matter of rock-n-roll's adoption by an adolescent subculture; I rather suspect all of middle class America was pretty adolescent in the fifties, that the whole WASP establishment saw rock-n-roll in pretty much the same terms (raw, sexual energy and social disruption), that only teen-agers were flexible enough to deal with rock-n-roll and to rise to its challenge. Coming at rock-n-roll from this direction offers a more charitable, if perhaps naive view of its music and poetry.

Formally, thematically, artistically, poetically rock-n-roll was, for all its show of rebellion, a conservative music. You can count its major themes on the fingers of one or two hands: invitations to love (but not necessarily to marriage, and frequently disguised as invites to dance), celebrations of love (sacred and profane), complaints and I'm-gonna-be-all-right-now songs, car songs (sometimes love songs in disguise), high school songs, descriptions of one's girl or of a girl, very muted social protest songs (sometimes disguised as high school songs or lyrics of parentally frustated love), and finally rock-n-roll songs about rock-n-roll. To these may be added a handful of novelty songs, ranging from David Seville's chipmonk records to the Trashmen's "Surfin' Bird" to the infamous "Stranded In the Jungle" (which popularized that catch phrase of American adolescence, "meanwhile back in the States"). Occasionally a song from country, rhythm-and-blues, or even Dixieland ("Quarter to Three", "Midnight in Moscow") broke into the rock-n-roll market, but for the most part, having revolted against the strait jacket of Tin Pan Alley, rock-n-roll settled quickly into thematic conventions of its own.

Formally rock-n-roll was just as conventional, usually settling for one of three elementary forms. One was the stanza-refrain form of elementary folk. Another was an AABA pattern of melodies adopted from Tin Pan Alley, which produced lyrics with first, second, and fourth (A melody) stanzas slightly different from the third (B melody) stanza: Phil Spector-written, Teddy Bears-recorded "To Know Him Is To Love Him." The third dominant form of rock-n-roll was the AAB series of calls and responses borrowed from the blues: Leiber & Stoller-written, Presley-recorded "Hound Dog." The blues form seems to have been more prominent in the earlier days of rock-n-roll; as its energies dwindled, as its stars were co-opted, jailed, or killed, as networks opted for safer and prettier songs, the Tin Pan Alley form and the simple stanza-refrain favored by country-and-western music came to predominate.

Generally we think of convention as stultifying, and there is no denying that especially toward the end of the sixties that was indeed the case with rock-n-roll. But convention doesn't have to be suffocating, and some of rock-n-roll's best work was done within rather narrow limits. One of my favorites has always been Felice and Boudleaux Bryannt's "Bye, Bye, Love," popularized by Don and Phil Everly and resurrected by Paul Simon and Art Garfunkel on *Bridge Over Troubled Waters*. The sparseness of detail in this common enough teenaged tragedy is one of its strengths, restraining tone and achieving much needed universality. The rhetorical balance of some of the lines, the clean rhymes, the largely undistorted syntax, the careful use of colloquialisms and trite phrases ("I feel like I could die") all combine to make the song work by providing a sense of formalism at odds with the speaker's personal emotion. The phrase "I feel like I could die" creates a tension between the uniqueness and intensity of personal problems and the awareness, suggested by the cliche, that everybody goes through this once or twice in his life. Emotion is sublimated into convention and rhetoric, which become important elements of the lyric. The tension, moreover, is emphasized by the light, moderately fast tempo of the song. People who are genuinely miserable don't sing this way, except to cover their unhappiness. "Bye, Bye, Love" makes convention work and has nothing to apologize for either as a song or a poem. It represents the best of rock-n-roll.

Similar moments of uncharacteristic brilliance are managed in several other rock-n-roll lyrics. The understatement and smooth, flat, prosy language of "Love Letters Straight from Your Heart" and its dead, rigid stanzaic form strain against the obvious emotion of its meaning to create a lyric almost as impressive as "Bye, Bye, Love." The song is admittedly more mature than most rock-n-roll ballads, but an example of what might be and actually was done.

The use of the popular dance metaphor in "Do You Wanna Dance?" is delicate in its ambiguity, reflecting a conflict between the need to speak frankly about sex and proscription against speaking out that resolves itself into metaphor:

> Do you wanna dance and make romance
> Squeeze me all through the night,
> Oh baby, do you wanna dance?
> Bobby Freeman

The imagery of "A Rose in Spanish Harlem," a late rock-n-roll ballad by Jerry Lieber and Phil Specter, is impressive. (The rose reappears in rock-n-roll, incidentally, in "Sally Go 'Round the Roses," where it is used rather uniquely to suggest untrue love.) And then there was the elementary, elemental, Romantic imagery of Nelson and Burch's "Tragedy," released in 1959:

> Like smoke from a fire of love
> Our dreams have all gone above,
> Blown by wind,
> Kissed by the snow;
> All that's left is the dark below.

"O Westron Wind" this may not be, although it resembles that early English poem (also probably once a song) very much in its stark, simple, natural imagery. This imagery reflects a problem rock-n-roll never faced squarely: the desire to be romantic and even literary without being cultural, arty, or intellectual. Here the problem is solved by resorting to safe, conventional images: roses, wind, smoke, fire. Written poetry, faced in the fifties and sixties with a similar problem, turned to brutal images and flat prosody, a more successful solution.

Another rock-n-roll lyric that has always impressed me is the Coaster's hit "Yakety Yak," a song which broke artistic rules by making its title a functional part of the song instead of a simple repetition of one catchy line or phrase. "Yakety Yak" is the kid's portion of this dialogue, a sarcastic back-talk to the parental gas he's getting; its use as a title tips the lyric's hand even before we hear it and alerts a listener to what's going on. There is a certain verbal facility in that lyric which, it seems to me, elevates it to the ranks of a minor pop classic. It scans, for example, as nearly perfect iambic tetrameter:

> Take out the papers and the trash
> Or you don't get no spending cash;
> If you don't scrub that kitchen floor
> You ain't gonna rock-n-roll no more.

The monotonous rhythm is intentional, functional, perfectly in keeping with youth's views of parental absolutism. The rhymes are easy, the word order undistorted. It also featured a mean sax.

The quality as well as the variety of rock-n-roll is most easily seen in its three most original auteurs, Little Richard, Buddy Holly, and Chuck Berry. Little Richard came to rock-n-roll from a gospel and rhythm-and-blues background which he never forgot during his many years as a performer and composer, celebrity, and theology major at Oakwood College in Huntsville, Alabama. He mishandled form outrageously and represents, more than anyone else, with the possible exception of Jerry Lee Lewis (who sounds much more like Little Richard than any other rock-n-roller), the drive and manic energy rock-n-roll drew from its black roots. Buddy Holly came to rock-n-roll from a country-and-western background. His work exhibits tight form and much control, breaking only occasionally into Little Richard-Elvis Presley style emotion. And then there's Chuck Berry. Berry managed both the drive of rhythm-and-blues and country-and-western's facility with form. He is *the* great rock-n-roll artist, perhaps the only man who can be legitimately said to have influenced virtually every rock artist who came after him.

"Wherever you're going, I've been," Little Richard proudly proclaimed in one live performance long after a flambouyant and showy rock had supposedly made his rock-n-roll obsolete. "There is nobody else, only Little Richard," he has raved on television talk shows. Some folk think he's vain and a bit stagy. I think he's probably right. Because Little Richard, beautiful child of Macon, Georgia, was the original pop showman. The wild, shrieking, hip action that seems just a bit manneristic in Elvis Presley or Jerry Lee Lewis seemed organic to Little Richard. He was doing the showy costume thing long before Sly and the Family Stone, the heavy make-up thing long before Mick Jagger and David Bowie. Accustomed in the early days to having his records "covered" by the cleaned-up releases of cleaned-up white singers (including Pat Boone and Bill Haley), in 1956 he went one-on-one with both Boone and Haley, outsold both with versions of "Long Tall Sally" and "Rip It Up" respectively, became the first black to break into rock-n-roll, and put an end to the cover rip-offs. Little Richard was there firstest, and more often than not he was there with the mostest. Not without cause does he call himself the father of rock-n-roll.

Vitality, energy, drive, frenzy—that's what Little Richard is all.about. Most often that energy is sexual and very explicit:

> Good golly, Miss Molly, sure like to ball.
> Good golly, Miss Molly, sure like to ball.
> When you're rockin' and a-rollin', can you hear your mama call?
> ("Good Golly Miss Molly")

Then there were titles like these: "She's Got It" ("and I can't do without it"), "Slippin' and Slidin'," "The Girl Can't Help It" ("she was built that way," from a movie by the same name), and "Whole Lotta Shakin' Goin' On."

Two things about Little Richard's rock-n-roll, however. First, his music is so sexually driven, and possibilities for sexual release in rock-n-roll are so limited that his songs inevitably resolve themselves into nothing more than nervous exhaustion. That kind of dissipation is really no release at all, however, and Little Richard resurrects himself almost immediately into new drive and more rock-n-roll. His concerts were exhausting but not liberating the way a Doors' performance could be. Poetically the effect is not unlike that of certain mystical and religious verse, which can manage only to repeat itself in various forms and images, always searching for ways to express the inexpressible, always coming away unsatisfied. Probably Little Richard found this exhaustion unsatisfactory too, since he threw over rock-n-roll (along with his costume jewelry and public concerts) for gospel music with his *Coming Home* album in 1963. It contained favorites like "Just a Closer Walk With Thee" and "Precious Lord." Ultimately Little Richard found his salvation not in sex or religion, but in music, although the songs continue to ring with that peculiar sacred-profane, sexual-celestial fervor so peculiar to fundamentalist gospel singing. "My music is the healin' music," he proclaimed. "It makes the lame walk, the blind see, and the deaf hear!"

Lyrics were for Little Richard something to hang a performance (not even a tune in the strict sense) upon. Most of the time you couldn't even hear them—they got lost in whoops and hollers and oohs and aahs. When you could make them out, they just might turn out to be something like this:

> Gonna have some fun tonight,
> Gonna have some fun tonight,
> We're gonna have some fun tonight,
> Well, everything will be all right.
> We're gonna have some fun tonight.
> ("Long Tall Sally")

22

or this:

> a wop bob a loo bob a wop bam boom
> ("Tutti-Fruitti")

The words may not be much, but even today the music heals.
And such frenzy!

Buddy Holly was Little Richard's alter ego; indeed, it's hard to find much these two shared as rock-n-rollers. Holly's work was all form, almost pure country-and-western. He had none of Little Richard's earthiness where sexual matters were concerned, and in his heavy glasses and delicate curls he looked a real sexual peacenik. How nitty gritty can you get, rhyming on *turtledovin'* (with *lovin'* in "That'll Be the Day") and singing lines like "piddle-de-pat, I know that new love thrills be" ("Heartbeat") in a slightly rococo falsetto? Even the boogie-woogie of "Heartbeat" sounded stiff, formal, controlled, innocuous.

Holly's strength lay in tight form, easy rhyme (frequently two or three syllable rhyme), smooth word order, and almost effortless movement within the confines of couplets or stanzas. No matter that Holly himself frequently had little or no hand in the composition of his own hits, that they were often written by persons like Bobby Darin ("Early In the Morning"), F. and B. Bryannt ("Raining In My Heart"), and Paul Anka ("It Doesn't Matter Anymore") . . . Holly imposed his style on his lyrics, so that they were as much his as if he had in fact written them himself. He is the sort of rock auteur described by Mike Jahn (*The Story of Rock*) as one who imposes himself on his lyrics instead of letting his lyrics impose on him.

Most striking about Holly's lyrics is the rhyme: *sensation, fascination,* and *destination* in "Moonbeams", or all the internal rhyme of "It Won't Matter Anymore." All that rhyme helps this sprightly, competent, purely conventional I'm-all-right-Jack farewell to love in the tradition of "Bye, Bye, Love" and the rhythm runs right alone too, helped by unnecessary *wells* and *babys* and *whoopsedaisy,* accentuating the rhymes and adding to the tune's bounce.

There is little imagery in Holly's lyrics (in fact, "I love you, Peggy Sue, Peggy Sue, I love you" is precious slender content), but there is a rhythmic proficiency you don't find in Little Richard's material, a technical proficiency that carried into the Beatles' early work, and from there into rock of the sixties. The trick of running a quick line or two into one very short, heavy, end-stopped phrase is one Holly gimmick that stands out in particular:

> You don't know what you've been missin',
> Oh boy.
> ("Oh Boy!" Sonny Wert, Bill Tilghman, Norman Petty)

For the benefit of Mr. Kite there will be a show tonight
On trampoline.
("Being For the Benefit of Mr. Kite," Lennon-McCartney)

Whatever sexuality existed in a Buddy Holly lyric came from a drive sunk deep in Holly's subconscious (perhaps from the days when he was covering rhythm-and-blues hits, including one of the "Annie" songs), a drive that battled futilely against the forms he borrowed from blues and Tin Pan Alley. Occasionally the former breaks loose in an unguarded image, a peculiar vocal nuance, a riff that tears off out of control just long enough to maintain the song's vitality, to break the prettiness of Holly's form and pattern.

Chuck Berry was the one undisputed rock-n-roll heavy. About Little Richard or Buddy Holly you may get some argument, especially if you go preferring them to Elvis Presley, but about Berry there is no dissension. Richard Goldstein called him "America's first rock poet"; Carl Belz called him "the folk rock poet of the fifties"; John Lennon called him "one of the all-time great poets, a rock poet." "It Goes to Show You Never Can Tell," "Too Much Monkey Business," "Sweet Little Sixteen," "Rock and Roll Music," "Johnny B. Goode," "Roll Over Beethoven," "Too Pooped to Pop," "Maybellene," "Back in the U.S.A.," "Brown-Eyed Handsome Man," "School Day" and a fistful of other first rate rock-n-roll songs indicate a major creative talent at work over a prolonged period. And with roots deep in the rhythm-and-blues tradition and a real facility with non-blues form, the man is certainly the obvious choice for representative rock-n-roll poet of the fifties. Moreover, he did his own stuff; he was a legitimate rock auteur.

The tensions that underlay much early rock-n-roll, between *is* and *ought,* between societal restrictions and individual needs, between release and restraint were especially pressing to Berry, a black artist making it in what was essentially a white world. Rock-n-roll was, for all its ripping off of blues and rhythm-and-blues, essentially a white music; blacks have never gotten much into it, and right from the start major record companies preferred to cover black originals than promote straight "race music." The restraints may have let up after Little Richard KOed Pat Boone, but whites remained suspicious, hostile, always looking for a chance to bust Berry's black ass. (The opportunity presented itself in the early sixties, when Berry was hustled off to the cooler for "violating the Mann Act" with a fourteen-year old prostitute. The whole business stank like a bottle of greasy kids' stuff.) Berry's songs, circumspect even in their brashness, strike a balance between Richard and Holly and express themselves most often in metaphor. Most central, of course, are rock-n-roll's two major metaphors—dancing and cars—which fill Berry lyrics: "All the cats want to dance with sweet little sixteen." "Maybellene," a forerunner of "Nadine", is the classic rock-n-roll fusion of woman and car (or woman as car, or whatever you want to make it), juxtaposing the Cadillac-Ford rivalry with sexual slippin' and slidin'. Berry managed the same ambiguity with the dance as metaphor in "Too Pooped to Pop" (and too old to stroll) and the great "Reelin' and Rockin' "

Well I looked at my watch, it was 9:32,
There's nothin' I'd rather do than dance with you,
Reelin' and rockin' . . .

Berry was a master of form as well as metaphor. More controlled than Little Richard, less sophisticated in his stanzaic patterns than the country-and-western school, Berry preferred the couplet. In fact, that's all he used in his classic "School Day." Metrically the song may be a bit rough, but it has its moments, like "You gotta hear something that's really hot" or the rather inspired "round and round and round yoo go."

Implicit in "School Day" is a social protest. The same protest is more explicit in a song like "Too Much Monkey Business," from which Bob Dylan undoubtedly drew both form and content for his great "Subterranean Homesick Blues." Berry is harassed by bills in the mail, smooth-talking salesmen running him up the creek with installment plan autos, and a good lookin' blonde trying to latch onto old Chuck, get him married, settled down into a home, busy writin' a book. "Too much monkey business for me to get involved in," Berry concludes.

The best of Chuck Berry's protest, however, was "Almost Grown," a pre-folk statement of the generation gap and a very un-rock-n-rollish awareness of the temporality of youth. "I'm doing all right in school," broken no rules, never been in trouble, doesn't cruise around like the hoodlums my mother always warned me about, a good kid—but "leave me alone, anyway, I'm almost grown." Being good, clean, decent, wholesome is mainly . . . dull. Especially in his protest, understated and even-tempered as it is, Chuck Berry looks forward to the sixties. Perhaps it is this as much as his technical skill that makes him the folk poet of the fifties.

So what happened? Elvis joined the army, got his hair and his balls cut off, turned into an All-American Nice Guy; Buddy Holly died in an airplane crash; Little Richard got religion; Alan Freed was harassed and hounded right off the air and died in 1964; Jerry Lee Lewis was drummed out of rock-n-roll for marrying his thirteen-year-old cousin (although like many former rock-n-rollers of country origins, he's returned to C&W to become a big star), Chuck Berry was jailed (he is now a free but extremely reticent man). Meanwhile the Eisenhower-Nixon-

The Poetry of Rock

Dick Clark forces of sobriety and propriety responsible for the demise of Berry, Lewis, and Freed had radio stations breaking their rock-n-roll discs one by one on the air and worked gradually to replace jailed blacks or debunked hillbillies with well scrubbed, white pseudo-rockers of the Buddy Holly school: Rick Nelson, Paul Anka, Gene Pitney, Bobby Rydell, Tommy Sands, Neil Sedaka, and a host of South Philly-via-American Bandstand nonentities. Rock-n-roll went soft, resolved itself sexually into masturbation fantasies for adolescent girls (the phrase is George Melly's in *Revolt Into Style*), and metaphorically into teenangels, wedding bells, and marriage rings. Cheap music drove out dear music, aided and abetted by the D.A.R. and the John Birch Society.

My own suspicion is that all of this would not, could not have happened were it not for fundamental changes in rock-n-roll's audience. It grew up. What was revolutionary to the middle class masses in 1955 was not revolutionary in 1960. The youthful rebels of the mid-fifties either got a job and found themselves co-opted into the "adult" establishment or matured. Rock-n-roll was left to the softies.

American Graffiti catches the moment perfectly. It's 1962 and we're living in a world of rock-n-roll, young love, and cars. But the symbol of youthful rebellion is a hot-rod king already graduated from high school, soon to lose his first drag race ever, and sentimentally chauffeuring around somebody's kid sis as his teen queen-for-a-night. Scratch him off your list. The apparent hero and heroine are two incredible dullniks, student council prexy and captain of the cheerleaders types respectively; as the flick ends, he goes off to sell insurance and she to bear his children. Scratch them. Then there is this other guy, a quiet fella who's wandered his way through the film from one episode to another. Finally he wanders his way off to college . . . to become a writer. By 1960 the old cars-and-dancin' rock-n-roll rebellion was on its last legs, over the hill, ready to lose its race. But somewhere, off in the coffee houses of college campuses and the heart of Minnesota a new music had been born, a music nourished, like rock-n-roll, by roots deep in American musical past, but a music very much different from rock-n-roll. The folk movement was about to mature.

The early sixties folk revival began just where interest in folk music might have been expected to be centered: the nation's colleges and the coffee houses associated with them. It was Ivy League folk at first—the Kingston Trio, the Chad Mitchell trio—but the first Newport Folk Festival (1959) brought old timers like Odetta, Pete Seeger, Lester Flatt, and Oscar Brand together with new timers like the Kingston Trio, and a rage for authenticity set in. All of these artists, of course, had a glamor not found in those faithful of earlier decades from whom they drew much of their material, but generally "the genuine" (or the apparently genuine) was valued over the artificial. What made the Kingston Trio appear authentic in the late fifties was the artificiality of most debased rock-n-roll; but Peter, Paul, and Mary soon made the Trio sound contrived. Then fresh, honest, pure Joan Baez made Peter, Paul, and Mary sound too slick. Finally Bob Dylan, with a harsh voice and raspy delivery, made Joan sound overly mellow, smooth, inauthentic. As to Dylan's authenticity, Jack Elliot could only remark,

> Some of the people around were turned off a little bit because Bob was playing the hobo role. I thought that he was maybe a little too young to pull it off in the style in which he was doing it. He was trying to sound like an old man who bummed around eighty-five years on a freight train, and you could see this kid didn't even have fuzz on his face yet. . . . I thought sometimes he had a lot of nerve trying to get away with that bullshit.

Very quickly the folk movement dissociated into three different factions. First there were the purists who, like most purists, ducked quickly underground and cultivated in an almost academic fashion the old and the genuine: they wanted old tunes and authentic folk (i.e., unlettered) originals done in an authentic folk (i.e., unprofessional) style. These had little effect on the subsequent history of popular music, except insofar as they prepared the way for late sixties English folk groups like Pentangle and the Fairport Convention. Then there were the descendents of the Kingston Trio, clean cut madras shirt types who took their own guitars and the *Joan Baez Songbook* and did hootenannies across the country. This was perhaps the largest of the factions, although in imposing on all music their own narrow stylistic range (pure, lyric female solo or full, wholesome group sound), they were as kitsch in their own way as Frank Sinatra or Dean Martin. Moreover, hootenanny music was material sung out of historical context, performed out of sociological context, and adopted by people who had no legitimate claim to the material. Unlike rock, folk does not admit of acting.

The third faction opted for new, original songs in the old style, frequently with a bit of the old folk radicalism, often allied with the various protest movements of the early sixties. This group most influenced subsequent pop music, perhaps because it included the most important singer-composers: Tom Paxton, Dave Von Ronk, Joan Baez, Phil Ochs, Paul Simon, and grand master Bob Dylan. Protest folk was more legitimate than hootenanny folk because it integrated itself more with the social and historical movement. While protest songs did not generally break into the top ten (Peter, Paul, and Mary's recording of Dylan's "Blowin' In the Wind" and Barry McGuire's "Eve of Destruction" being the obvious exceptions), both the songs and the move-

27

ments to which they belonged influenced the shape of rock in the later sixties. In fact, it could be intelligently argued that rock was but a more sophisticated form of protest and folk music.

What precipitated the decline of folk has never been properly determined. Legitimate folk was never a strong force anyway, and needed little to kill it. Hootenanny folk was probably a fad to begin with. As to folk protest, perhaps the shallow apocalypse of things like "Eve of Destruction" did it in. Perhaps establishment hostility was to blame; perhaps the inherent temporality of topical songs. Perhaps the assassination of John Kennedy was in some way relevant. In any event, the folk experience left pop with two great legacies: analytic songs treating serious political and social issues in which words were as important as music, and—just as important—the pre-eminence of the lp album over the 45 single.

Into the power vacuum created by folk's demise stepped the Beatles. But that misstates the case some, for the hurricane that was Beatlemania would have created its own vacuum anywhere, any time. Fads there had been and would continue to be: the twist, surfin' music of the Beach Boys and Jan and Dean, the Davey Crockett and Elvis Presley todos of the fifties. But nothing matched the arrival of the Beatles in America. I have one top ten listing from April, 1964 that shows Beatles songs holding down the number one, two, three, four, five and seven positions! Suddenly, very suddenly, American music (Beach Boys excepted) was *out* and British music was *in:* the Beatles were followed by the Dave Clark Five, the Searchers, Peter and Gordon, Gerry and the Pacemakers, Chad and Jeremy, the Zombies, the Yardbirds, Herman and his Hermits. With these good-time "Mersey Beat" groups came British rhythm-and-blues in the personage of the Rolling Stones and the Animals, the more aggressive, uglier, side of the British Invasion. Between the Beatles on the one hand and the Stones on the other, pop music of the sixties was drawn to increasing pitches of artiness and aggressive honesty unmatched in earlier American pop.

The American pop music scene, reinvigorated by folk and the British groups, needed yet one stimulus to coax it into full bloom. The Byrds—Jim McGuinn, David Crosby, Chris Hillman, Gene Clark—brought together such diverse elements are rock-n-roll, folk, bluegrass, Dylan, the Beatles, and the Stanislavski method of acting to produce progressive rock: electrified rock-n-roll with the thematic weightiness of folk and a musical sophistication borne of self-conscious awareness and deliberate borrowing from other, often classical, models. All this and not a little bit of showmanship. "Folk rock" some critics called it, perhaps because so much of the Byrds' material came from folk sources, the main one being Bob Dylan. All the public knew was that the Byrds' "Mr. Tambourine

Man" and "Turn, Turn, Turn" (lyrics compliments of Ecclesiastes 3:1-8) were dynamite songs. They exploded on the consciousness of Dylan and even the Beatles and helped propel pop music into rock. Meanwhile The Lovin' Spoonful (with John Sebastian right out of the village folk scene), Simon and Garfunkel ("Sounds of Silence"), and the Blues Project (Donovan's "Try and Catch the Wind") began developing various potentialities of the new music and turning rock lyrics into conscious poetry. Lyrics came to be printed on album jackets, songbooks became increasingly popular, and progressive teachers started using lyrics in their Eng. Lit. classes. Not far in the future anthologies like Spinner's and Goldstein's collections of "rock poetry" and textbooks like *Beowulf to Beatles* were in the offing.

A sense of the multiplicities of rock—and it was an enormously ecletic music, capable of almost infinite mutation and variation—is fundamental to the remaining chapters of this book, which examine in detail the greats of the sixties. Conversely, the story of rock is largely the story of the Beatles and the Stones, the Doors and the Who. So vibrant was the music scene of the sixties, though, that even the middleweights made important contributions which, in fairness to their composers and in the interest of a fuller vision of rock's breadth and depth, ought not to be ignored. How can you talk about rock, for example, without mentioning everybody's darling the Buffalo Springfield; or Mr. Imagery, Donovan Leitch; or the Association; or Procol Harum and Cream; or Joni Mitchell? For a split second, even the Beach Boys turned serious/artsy with *Pet Sounds,* and how can you finish the story of rock's birth, development, and demise without Blood, Sweat and Tears, Pentangle and the Fairport Convention, the Band, James Taylor, Sha Na Na, Alice Cooper, the Osmonds, David Bowie, and the Carpenters?

Two minor groups that played significant roles in rock's early development were the Association and the Buffalo Springfield. Both were slightly anomolous, in that both were "soft" when rock was "hard." The Association—headed by Terry Kirkman, a former English major from UCLA—was essentially a clean-rock group that got its head together long enough to produce "Along Comes Mary" (a drug song), "Requiem for the Masses" (an anti-war protest song), and "Windy" (a Paul Simon-like throwaway). "Along Comes Mary" leapt right into the middle of the drug-song controversy of the sixties ("Puff, the Magic Dragon," "Lucy in the Sky", the Byrds' "Eight Miles High," Dylan's "Rainy Day Woman No. 12 and 35"), found itself attacked in print, played on the air, and taken to the hearts of millions of right-thinking collegians. More verbose than the Beatles' "Norwegian Wood", less imagistic than Dylan's "Mr. Tambourine Man," the song has its virtues: heavy internal rhyme reminiscent of early Dylan, a quick and regular meter, an appropriate sense of confusion assisted by rhyme and tempo.

The Poetry of Rock

"Requiem for the Masses" managed to be a rock protest song long after protest songs were supposedly dead. Mothers of America, forget your apple pies, Kirkman suggests, and have a look at the bloodshot skies, at the flag flying at half mast "for the matadors who turned their backs to please the crowd and fell before the bull." In uncharacteristic bitterness he characterizes the flag's red, white and blue as "the color of his blood flowing thin," "the color of his lifeless skin," and the color of the morning sky, last thing seen by the dying soldier. Then red, white, and blue are contrasted to black and white: the figures that recorded him, the newsprint that mentioned him, the questions that bothered him but remained unasked and, certainly, unanswered. A final "kyrie eleison" and appropriate bugle call, and soldier and song disappear from sound . . . but not from memory.

From such weighty considerations the Association moved on to the relative trivia of "Cherish" and "Windy" . . . and to oblivion.

The Buffalo Springfield endured for a moment (1966-68), then disbanded into the myriad of relations formed subsequently by Richie Furay, Neil Young, Jim Messina, Dewey Martin, Stephen Stills, and Doug Hastings. It produced an album (the group's second, *Buffalo Springfield Again*) that started rock thinking in terms of good *studio* albums (as distinct from live material); it produced a single prophetic of rock's return to the country after the end of the sixties (Stills' "Go And Say Goodbye"), and it produced the masterpiece of folk protest, actually an anti-protest song, "For What It's Worth." "There's something happenin' here," began Stephen Stills; "What it is ain't exactly clear." A lot of noise and a lot of naked power and a lot of heads being cracked. But most dangerous of all is the paranoia that begins creeping into your head after it's been whacked and whacked and whacked again. This is certainly no live to live! What bothers Stills most of all is not the causes and the "Hooray for our side," and not the field day for the heat; it is living in a police state, the constant fear that when you step out of line they take you away, the conformity bred by this kind of paranoia.

Then Stills throws this ultimate protest away with a title as casual as "For What It's Worth."

Buffalo Springfield went on to father groups like Crosby, Stills, Nash and Young, the country-rock group Poco, Loggins and Messina, and Manassas. A soft, country, mellow sound dominates the work of Buffalo Springfield and its progeny, a sound which betrays its origins in C&W and folk music and makes for exceptionally comfortable listening. In terms of form, Stephen Stills has proven the most interesting of the group, developing the suite form used in things like "Suite for Judy Blue Eyes," on his Manassas album, in Van Dyle Parks' song *Cycle* and by the Jefferson Airplane on *After Bathing at Baxter's.* Lyrically Neil Young was probably the Best of the Buff.

Donovan Leitch, kitsch poet of the new rock, began his career as a Scottish version of Bob Dylan. As a junior Dyklan he produced "Catch the Wind" (a lovely enough love poem), but little audience enthusiasm, especially in the U.S. of A., where he was but one of a hundred pseudo-Dylans. Between 1966 and 1967 Donovan transformed himself into the high priest of the drug-hippie culture ("Mellow Yellow," "Sunshine Superman" and "Sunny Goode Street"). When the San Francisco-hippie-flower power scene faded, Donovan turned himself into the high priest of transcendental meditative rock, "a product of success, the Maharishi, and Mickie Most," as Lillian Roxon described him in her *Rock Encyclopedia*. Through all this, Donovan made himself a name, built himself a following, and produced much pseudo-poetry akin in spirit and style to that of Rod McKuen. At his best, Donovan was pleasant, melodic, visual, delicate. His work will not stand careful analysis, however, and degenerates easily into richly imagistic but overripe pretention.

What the Stones were to British rhythm-and-blues, what Donovan and the Airplane were to psychedelic rock, Joni Mitchell and Paul Simon were to folk rock: her early work—including "The Circle Game" "Woodstock" and "Michael from Mountains"—was popularized by other artists: Ian and Sylvia; Crosby, Stills, Nash and Young; Judy Collins; and Tom Rush. But with "Both Sides Now" (1968) Joni made the top ten listings herself. The preponderance of her early work is pure folk marked by a richly poetic imagery, much of it simple or not so simple love songs in the introspective Dylan tradition. "Cactus Tree" is particularly interesting, with its two-edged depiction of the whimsical lady in the city who "loves them all," but rallies her defenses against them because she's afraid "that one will ask her for eternity, and she's so busy being free."

In more recent albums, Joni has turned to a jazz-rock featuring very heavy themes, loose poetic and musical forms, and chord structures impossible on a normally tuned guitar. The old undercurrent of topical protest songs has developed a series of sharp celebrations of the redeemed generation (her famous "Woodstock"), and harsh critiques of the damned: "Fiddle and Drum" on American militarism (Joni is Canadian), "Banquet" on twentieth century escapism ("Some turn to Jesus, and some turn to heroin. Some turn to rambling 'round looking for a clean sky"), and her popular song on heroin, "Cold Blue Steel and Sweet Fire." Lyrics full of imagery and music full of complexity: Joni Mitchell is now recognized as the female genius of rock poetry, equal in some respects to Bob Dylan, one of very few individuals who emerged during the sixties and continued to develop artistically during the seventies.

The Poetry of Rock

The Procol Harum and Cream, two lesser known groups of the sixties, were perhaps most reflective of all middleweights of pure rock's enormous eclecticism and range. Procul Harum is now best remembered for its "Whiter Shade of Pale," the music for which was derived from J. S. Bach's contata "Sleepers Awake," the lyrics to which represented a pure imagistic poem. It was a pure art song from a pure art group: the Harum, in the tradition of the Beatles circa *Sgt. Pepper,* was essentially a studio group, used extensive studio production on all cuts, and admitted frankly to mainstream literary and musical influences. Cream, one of the early supergroups, drew more from English blues than did Procul Harum and featured a heavy full sound, but was just as arty as the Procul Harum in its execution and poetry: the group purged rock of the cheap flash that had marked earlier British blues, producing hits like "Sunshine of Your Love," "White Room," and "Tales of Brave Ulysses," which was imagistic and literarily allusive in the style of "Whiter Shade of Pale":

> You thought the leaden winter
> Would bring you down forever,
> But you rode upon a steamer
> To the violence of the sun.

> And the colors of the sea
> Find your eyes with trembling mermaids,
> And you touch the distant beaches
> With tales of brave Ulysses.
> (Eric Clapton and Martin Sharp)

"With Cream, rock finally grew up," writes Lillian Roxon; other critics have been more reserved in their pronouncements, but clearly Cream was important to rock's history. It initiated the blues revival of 1968 and gave the rock world its finest guitarist in Eric Clapton.

Whatever became of rock? You get as many answers as people you ask, as performers you ask about. Some rockers kept right on cookin': the Stones (the good old steady Stones), Joni Mitchell, the Who. Some of the sixties' great rockers went into retirement early: Dylan's last great album was probably *John Wesley Harding* in 1968; the Beatles' was the white album of that same year. In 1969 Phil Ochs released *Rehearsals for Retirement;* Simon and Garfunkel's *Bridge Over Troubled Water* (1970) was a fine album but overripe. The concensus is that somewhere around 1970 rock went into a protracted decline from which it has not rescued itself.

By 1970, of course, a lot had happened: all major rock auteurs were approaching or already past thirty. Many were married or about to be married. Rock is a young music, demands terrific sexual energy and perhaps a bit of adolescence, and just may be uncomfortable to stable, married, familied men over thirty. The times were different too: the radicalism of the sixties had given place to the retrenchment of the seventies, the movement against Vietnam crested, deposing Lyndon Johnson and Hubert Humphrey but electing Richard Nixon and failing to effectively stop the Vietnam War. Perhaps people were simply weary of rock's sociological, thematic, and musical radicalism and were looking for something soft, comfortable, conservative. Theories are cheap; you pay your money and talk your choice. My own suspicion is this: rock was by nature a sophisticated music, capable of consciously assimilating virtually any musical and poetic style. Its natural tendency was to expand—you can see this expansion in the work of every major rock auteur, including the "good old steady Stones"—and when something expands overly much, it explodes. Rock exploded—or, to change the metaphor, it popped. It lost its center and flew outward in a dozen different directions at once. High rock art was continued by groups like King Crimson and lyrically by the Moody Blues. (The further this stuff went, the less sure you became: was it art or a put-on? Sure was obscure.) Low rock reasserted itself in the rock-n-roll revival begun around 1969, and lead by Sha Na Na. In the wake of the revival we've gotten a dozen or so top ten hits that are in fact revivals of fifties tunes, done by everyone from the Osmonds to the Carpenters, and fresh composed music that *sounds* like fifties materials (Elton John's "Crocodile Rock," for example). Chuck Berry released an lp; Little Richard took to t.v. The trouble is, most of the rock-n-roll revival chose to revive the vacuity of the late fifties; thus the Carpenter's sweet "Please, Mr. Postman." Tony Orlando and Dawn returned to prominence in a network t.v. show. Soon folks ceased to take the rock-n-roll revival with any degree of seriousness; perhaps it never was serious to begin with. Certainly the early 70s betrayed a bankruptcy in rock, however, for a music that looks back is obviously not going to move forward.

Other shlock movements included the mindless show-rock of Alice Cooper and Iggy Stooge, the fag-rock of David Bowie and the Cockettes and the New York Dolls, female-rock of Suzie Quarto and the group Fanny, a pre-fifties revival lead by Ringo Starr and Bette Midler, the wholesome sound of the Partridge Family, women's lib rock (Helen "I Am Woman" Reddy, perhaps Carly Simon). More significant to good music, if not to simple music history, was the emergence of a new school of legitimate folk music (Pentangle and the Fairport Convention), the "soft sound" of Tim Hardin and James Taylor (this died an early death somewhere in the seventies), jazz rock (originating around 1968 with the first rate Blood, Sweat and Tears, and carried on by the equally good Chicago), a rebirth of legitimate blues begun in 1968 and involving both older (Muddy Waters, Howlin' Wolf) and new singers, and the back-to-the-country movement. Country rock was perhaps the strongest of all these movements. It originated with Bob Dylan's *John Wesley Harding,* was accelerated by the much deserved popularity of the Band (both in content and style the Band conveys feeling for and attachment to good old basic country pie), impacted on such traditional folk singers as Joan Baez, CSN&Y, and Joni Mitchell, altered both style and content of non-folkies like the various Beatles and the once-upon-a-time-San Francisco-sound Grateful Dead, and washed ashore new groups like the Flying Burrito Brothers and new soloists like Kris Kristofferson, Elton John, John Denver.

"Booms and Boomlets" Mike Jan (*The Story of Rock*) calls all this, reeling off schools and individuals in bewildering array. That, of course, is precisely the point: somewhere around the end of the seventies, rock lost what focus it had and shot off not in one or two directions, but in twenty different directions at once. This dissociation diffused rock's energies; no man (or woman) has dominated the scene the way Dylan, the Beatles, and the Stones ran the show back there in the sixties. Nobody could, because nobody can go everywhere at once. It may be that rock's diffusion is explicable in sociological or commercial terms (a surfeit of product and promo); I prefer to think that the explosion of the seventies was but the logical endpoint of rock's development through the sixties. What is lamentable is not that we have come finally to David Bowie and Donny Osmond and Alice Cooper—that was probably inevitable. What is lamentable is that we came here so quickly, and that the many brands of schlock distract attention from people like Joni Mitchell, the Stones, even Dylan and Paul Simon, in whose work the tradition of rock as a musical and poetic art lingers.

CHAPTER III
THE BEATLES

The Beatles, Bob Dylan, the Rolling Stones: rock's big three, the biggest of the big, each with literally millions of devout partisans from Sidney, Australia to Kewanee, Illinois. The biggest of the biggest? No easy choice: Dylan was probably the most intellectual and the truest poet, the Stones the steadiest rockers, the Beatles the most popular. Ultimately, I suspect, one has to acknowledge the Beatles as the prime motivating force behind pop's resurrection in the early sixties and the development of rock later in the decade. Help at home and hands across the water there were, but I seriously doubt that rock could have achieved full flowering or even birth without the moptops from Liverpool.

Not that their early work was all that impressive, especially in retrospect; some of it was not much better than the most trivial kitsch of the early sixties. You don't have to hear Peter Sellers reading aloud "It's been a hard day's night,/And I've been working like a dog,/It's been a hard day's night, I should be sleeping like a log, But when I get home to you/I find the things that you do,/Will make me feel . . . alright" to know just how awful some of them come off as poems. Unrelieved convention, that song, unredeemed by that silly day-night antithesis. Almost as bad, but partially rescued by the metaphoric implications of hand-holding (a later comment about love being "more hand just holding hands" to the contrary) was the Beatles' first American hit, "I Want to Hold Your Hand." The form was basic AABA, and the lyrics featured awkward object-verb inversions like "my love I can't hide." All possibilities inherent in the dance metaphor of "I Saw Her Standing There" are undercut on the one hand by its insistence on a literal dance ("when I crossed that room") and on the other hand by the assurance "I'll never dance with another." What you've got here is that very honest-to-goodness, twenty-four karat love-at-first-sight-forever-and-ever nonsense against which rock-n-roll revolted way back in the fifties. True blue to the one you screw. The this boy-that boy foolishness of "That Boy" is a rhetorical gimmic, promising in light of more sophisticated word play in later lyrics, but certainly the sort of thing done much better in Lennon's prose and later lyrics like "She Said She Said." "It Won't Be Long" represents a real nadir in rock-n-roll lyrics, as the male (who at worst was able to shrug off put-downs, at best rolled through a series of one night stands) waits patiently for his girl's return, promising "I'll be good like I know I should" and "every day we'll be happy, I know."

Well, there you have it: the lyrics of *Meet the Beatles,* the first great American album we all rushed out to buy, the lyrics that held down the number one spot in charts across the nation week after week, month after month, the songs that triggered Beatlemania on three continents. Put that stuff next to Chuck Berry, Little Richard, or even the tight formalism of Buddy Holly, and it certainly looks pale.

But, on the other hand, next to "Goin' to the Chapel and We're Gonna Get Married," it looks pretty good. Add the driving rhythm of "I Want to Hold Your Hand" (a song that bears the clear imprint of those early days on Hamburg's Reeperbahn) or the echoing and re-echoing "yeh YEH yeh YEH" of "It Won't Be Long" and the Beatles sound even better. And consider the potentiality of some of the better early Beatles lyrics, and you see that we are right back where we started in 1955: the drive of rhythm and blues and the formalism of country and western have been joined with more sophistication than in anything since Chuck Berry's work. Moreover, the ironic stance taken toward their art by the Beatles both inside and outside of their songs adds a new and crowning irony—that between creating quality art and throwing it away. Some of those early Beatles lyrics were good—good songs, good poems in the best rock-n-roll tradition—and, had the group never undergone the transformation of *Rubber Soul, Yesterday and Today,* and *Revolver,* the Beatles would still have an important place in music history.

Think, for example, of the facility of "All My Loving": a song that manages regular meter and clean rhyme without a single distortion of word order, a song with a rhyme scheme far more sophisticated than most pop songs. The perfect anapestic feet, the aabaab rhyme scheme, the feminine rhymes of "kiss you" and "miss you" give the song a wit reminiscent of Cole Porter: "Close your eyes and I'll kiss you, tomorrow I'll miss you, remember I'll always be true; And then while I'm away I'll write home every day, and I'll send all my loving to you." Not a bad piece of throw-away poetry. Or consider another piece of technically proficient fluff: "If there's anything that you want, if there's anything I can do, just call on me and I'll send it along with love from me to you." There is a certain ambiguity here between the innocence of holding arms and kissing lips and the desire—later in the song—to "keep you satisfied," but the song's real strength—like that of "All My Loving"—is the technical proficiency of lyricist John Lennon manifesting itself in undistorted word order and rhetorical balance. The sort of lines you find in Buddy Holly, who sang the first song John Lennon learned on the guitar.

36

The dominant influence on early Beatles was the country and western half of rock-n-roll, which the group found more compatible with English skiffle music (remember Lonnie Donegan's "Does Your Chewin' Gum Lose It's Flavor On The Bedpost Over Night?") that originally inspired Lennon, McCartney, and half of Britain's youth, to play pop music. Rhythm and blues was also important, especially Little Richard and Chuck Berry, although less important. A quick glance at the titles of their early albums betrays both influences: songs in the Tin Pan Alley tradition ("Til There Was You") are mingled with early rock-n-roll ("You Really Got a Hold On Me," "Twist and Shout"). The sexuality of rhythm-and-blues based rock-n-roll are very much present in the early Beatles' work, not merely in the dance metaphor previously discussed, but in the drive of their harder songs, in lines like "if this is love you've got to give me more" ("I Should Have Known Better"), and in whole lyrics like "Little Child," with its dance metaphor and its invitation: "If you want someone to make you feel so fine, we'll have some fun when you're mine all mine." I suppose the immediate ancestor of this song is the Coasters' "Young Blood," its progeny is the host of rock lyrics which treat under-aged over-grown jail bait, and its kissing cousin is "I Saw Her Standing There" ("Well she was just seventeen,/You know what I mean . . ."). While "Young Blood" is more explicit in its suggestiveness ("What crazy stuff,/She looked so tough/I had to follow her all the way home"), "Little Child" has the greater sense of proscribed wickedness, even perversion which marks something like the more recent "I'm the friendly stranger in the black sedan" or the Door's rejuvenation of the Brecht-Weil "Show me the way to the next little girl." The tension between sexual urgency and a pretty, light melody is peculiar to the Beatles' lyrics; the perverse combination looks foreward to rock, novels, and films like *Clockwork Orange*.

The same delicate ambiguity is to be found in a number of other early Beatles' love lyrics: "Any Time At All," "Hold Me Tight," "I'll Keep You Satisfied." "I'll Keep You Satisfied" was especially interesting in the ambiguity of its title, the innocence of kissing and missing, the sexual implications of "here I stand." Whatever the song may say about "a simple thing like love," love in this song is obviously complex, the promise of "satisfaction" intentionally ambiguous.

I've spoken thus far about the early Beatles' ability to manage form, their use of ambiguity and irony, and their facility with rhyme and meter—all qualities demonstrated by the great songs of their middle period. Later lyrics evidence two other talents: facility in creating images, and a remarkable and unmatched ability to produce fresh melodies. Music critics are more competent to pass judgment on the latter than I, and many of them have: Cathy Berberian's comment to the effect that "Eleanor Rigby" was one of the most beautiful songs she'd ever heard, Leonard Bernstein's enthusiasm for the Beatles' music, Ned Rorem's statement that "She's Leaving Home" is equivalent to anything Schubert ever wrote, the praise of Wilfred Meller and George Melly all speak to the Beatles' musical talent. The assertion of the *Times* music critic that early Lennon-McCartney songs are formulaic ("submediant switches from C Major to A flat Major") is true only of their very early work, and Richard Rogers' remark that the Beatles bored him represents a minority view.

The quality of later works most obviously missing in their early work (as, with the exception of some of the songs quoted in chapter two, in most rock-n-roll) is imagery. "You've Got to Hide Your Love Away" comes close, with its staring people (suggestive of "A Day In the Life") laughing at Lennon ("I Am the Walrus"), the two foot small personna ("Lucy In the Sky"), and clowns ("For the Benefit of Mr. Kite"). It is not typical of early Beatles. The direct or indirect influence of Bob Dylan on this song is very apparent in its heavy use of end line and internal rhyme—"Here I stand with head in hand,/Turn my face to the wall./If she's gone I can't go on,/Feeling two foot small"—and it may well be that its imagery owes much to Dylan's influence as well.

More indicative of the shape of things to come were a few lines in an especially un-rockish ballad "And I love her": "Bright are the stars that shine, dark is the sky . . .." These visual images, very basic and by now a bit stale, formed the basis of Michael Foreman's illustration of the song in Allan Aldridge's *Beatles Illustrated Lyrics,* because they quite literally overpower the rest of the lyric. Moreover, they demonstrate the kind of ambiguity (between bright and dark, between stars and sky, between mundane and celestial, between our knowledge that the stars are indeed eternal and the knowledge the song tries to deny—that love is, alas, merely mortal) that makes the song work and saves it from self-indulgent sentimentality. However, the lyric is unique, I believe, among early Beatles' music, and without hindsight it must seem more an anomaly than an indicator of the shape of things to come.

"Yesterday," released in the summer of 1965, and their next three albums (*Rubber Soul, Yesterday,* and *Revolver*) through late 1965 and 1966, made it obvious that the Beatles were moving far beyond traditional rock-n-roll music, incorporating a wide variety of musical and literary influences (folk music and straight country and western among them), experimenting and innovating in all aspects of rock-n-roll music. Cello, sitar, baroque trumpets, heavy strings, a pseudo-harpsichord (in "In My Life"), and countless other music instruments heretofore ignored by rock-n-roll are examined for the tonal shadings they will lend music; traditional pop forms are bent nearly out of recognizable shape; new interrelationships between lyrics and music are explored; the range of themes is widened immensely, as is the range of metaphor or anti-metaphor used in dealing with old themes; lyrics become infused with an imagery as splendid as the clothing the Beatles wore or the music they played; and realism yields to surrealism, symbolism, imagism. In short, you discover in abundance the sort of sophistication that manifested itself only sporadically and guardedly in rock-n-roll. As to its causes, one can only speculate: increased possibilities offered by more sophisticated production facilities, the talents of producer George Martin, the influence of Dylan's work, a general heightening of social and artistic awareness in the middle sixties, a drug-related heightening of sensual perception (and we would be both foolish and inaccurate to deny this last), the maturation of two (or three, or four, or five) consummate musicians. About the results, one can say much: rock-n-roll music became rock music, pop became art, poetry became the rule rather than the exception.

You see this revolution most easily in the musical experimentation and in the dramatically widened thematic range which marked the three albums mentioned above (and their successors, *Sgt. Pepper* and *Magical Mystery Tour*). As a rock instrument, the sax had been dead for some time, of course, but its influence was strong enough to make the heavy orchestration of Phil Spector-produced records appear strange anomalies, and to leave a hole in the position it once occupied. In part this was because rock-n-roll had not yet discovered what to do with added guitars, in part it stemmed from the fact that sax-based music is inherently incompatible with most other instruments, especially strings, and musicians simply hadn't taken time to look around. In these songs the guitar work of both Harrison and Lennon developed dramatically, but more significant is the addition of new and frequently exotic instruments never before heard in pop records, a movement which would culminate in the use of full orchestra and the literally dozen tracks involved in producing *Sgt. Pepper*. Rhythms became immeasureably more subtle. Chord progressions became more varied and more sophisticated. Counter-point appeared and all the other musical innovation which make the Beatles' earlier works (indeed, all of earlier rock-n-roll) seem in retrospect thin and artless.

The albums revealed a similar broadening of the thematic range of Lennon-McCartney and George Harrison songs (one ought to draw a distinction). Most of *Rubber Soul,* for example, is love songs, but they are a different breed of love song. We have been used to either sex-on-the-sly or eternal love-and-marriage; here we discover "I'm Looking Through You," which examines the way "Love has a nasty habit of disappearing overnight," suggests that people do not always grow together in a relationship, implies that love is not forever, and—most important—blames no one. "In My Life," technically a love song, really concerns itself with the problems of things past and loss of memory of things past, indicating a clean break with rock-n-roll's implicit insistence on an eteral present. There may be a Dylan influence here, since he had sung about these themes: "We thought we could sit together in fun/But our chances really was a million to one" and again, "To remain as friends and make amends/You need the time to stay behind." The same concern reappears in "Yesterday."

"Wait" signals another development of the love theme, linking slippin' and slidin' love with traditional love-in-marriage: "I've been good, as good as I can be,/And if you do, I'll trust you,/And know that you will wait for me." This is the new morality, finding expression here similar to its expression in Peter, Paul and Mary's "Leaving On a Jet Plane." "The Word" is concerned more with personal freedom than simple love problems ("Say the word and you'll be free,/Say the word and be like me."), and "Think For Yourself" moves beyond lost love to deal with the problem of communication between two radically different people. Similarly "We Can Work It Out" really concerns much more than boy-girl relationships: "Life is very short and there's no time for fussing and fighting, my friend." Heavy philosophy in a rock lyric!

In addition to expanding the possibilities of the love lyric, the Beatles explore several other themes not seen in pop music since the mid-fifties. "Taxman," which leads off *Revolver,* is a timeless topical song (if there be such a thing) on the government's big bite: "If you drive a car, I'll tax the street,/If you try to sit, I'll tax your seat,/If you get too cold, I'll tax the heat,/If you take a walk, I'll tax your feet." It demonstrates the increasing sophistication of both composer and audience with an allusion like "Now my advice for those who die,/Declare the pennies on your eyes," and references to the politicians Heath and Wilson. "Nowhere Man" is social protest, as is "I'm Only Sleeping." "Dr. Robert" and "Tomorrow Never Knows" belong to a new genre, the drug song. "Norwegian Wood" begins a journey into the surreal and "Yellow Submarine" the beginning of a concurrent and not unrelated flight into the world of children's fantasy, both of which will culminate in *Sgt. Pepper.* A number of lyrics treat communication problems, not merely between generations (the theme of rock-n-roll), but between those who see and understand, "the heads") and those who do not ("the straights"): "Think For Yourself", "I'm Looking Through You", "She Said She Said", "I Want to Tell You", "And Your Bird Can Sing", "We Can Work It Out". Much of *Sgt. Pepper* is foreshadowed in these lyrics.

Perhaps more interesting are the developments these albums make within traditionally defined themes, genres, and metaphors. "Drive My Car," for example, takes a standard rock-n-roll metaphor (cf. "Maybellene," "Almost Grown" and some traditional poetry like Cumming's "she being Brand") and drives it in two directions: while insisting on the literal leg so strongly as to construct a narrative on it, it is also unusually insistent on the metaphorical significance of driving: "Baby, you can drive my car,/ and maybe I'll love you." The song *consciously* plays games with standard metaphors, indicating both a sophistication absent in earlier rock-n-roll and a denial of the need for metaphor at all. This denial reaches its ultimate development on the white album in "Why don't we do it in the road?" although it can be seen in these albums in something like "Love you too." What you have here is Andrew Marvel's famous poem "To His Coy Mistress" without its imagery and metaphor. His closing lines suggest very clearly that Harrison feels no need for easily understood metaphors, and has reached a point where he can either do without, or experiment in metaphor for its own sake and run the risk of being misunderstood: "I'll make love to you if you want me to."

"Day Tripper" is perhaps the best example of these middle albums of a new metaphorical approach to an old subject: the fickle woman, subclass two, the prick-tease. "She's a big teaser," the Beatles sing, "she took me half the way there." We have met this girl before in pop music: "First you say you will and then you won't"; "She only wanted some one to play with/And all I wanted was a love to stay." And we will meet her again: "She won't say she will, but there's a chance that she might." The lyric, drawing perhaps on a "Ticket to Ride" and on the emerging drug scene, casts its metaphors in the language of trips: "a one way ticket," "a Sunday driver," ' "Day tripper". One line in particular stands out: "she only played one night stands," perhaps an echo of "Knew it wouldn't be a one-night stand" and a conscious ironic reversal of the usual meaning of the expression. The form of the lyric is a modified blues, although the tune is so up-tempo and the tone so light—this is another of those gonna-be-alright-now songs the likes of "Bye, Bye, Love"—that the Beatles manage irony even in this Aldridge has captured the lyric perfectly in the *Beatles Illustrated Lyrics* with a series of corny sex-joke postcards and a beach honey out of *Clockwork Orange* licking a very phallic pop-sicle.

What is most striking about the songs on these albums, after their new musical virtuosity of course, is the rich imagery and growing surrealism of their lyrics. You had to look very hard to find imagery in the early Beatles lyrics: those lines in "And I Love Her" are just about it. You can't help attributing the advent of such imagery, then, to causes outside what one would have expected to be normal development of Lennon-McCartney talent: either a heavy Dylan influence or the result of experimentation in psychedelics, or (most likely) both. Much of the imagery involves strong impressions of color and taste, and attaches itself to drug songs or lyrics treating the problem of communication between straights and heads. "Norwegian Wood," whatever it is *really* about, is widely held to be about pot; "Dr. Robert," Paul recalls, is about "some fellow in New York, and in the States we'd hear people say 'You can get everything off him; any pills you want . . .' That's what Dr. Robert is all about, just a pill doctor who sees you all right." It is difficult to imagine Paul did not know Nembutals were widely known as "yellow submarines," and his denial to Alan Aldridge is, to me at least, as unconvincing as Peter Yarrow's protestations that "Puff the Magic Dragon" is a clean song and neither he nor had Leonard Lipton (Puff's co-author) had any idea what jackie paper is. Of course both are children's songs, the same way that *Through The Looking Glass* is a child's book. The fact that the book traces a chess match (white pawn Alice to play, and win is eleven moves) in no way detracts from its validity as a children's story, although it certainly suggests an alternative view of things. The same may be said about "Lucy In the Sky." And so on. But Paul and Peter Yarrow and Bob Dylan are all right on one point: as often as not the drug motif is used as a metaphor for something else, which comprises the major theme of the lyric. And certainly whatever heightened sensibility is due to psychedelic experience is easily transferred to other subjects as well: old age and loneliness ("Eleanor Rigby"), the generally vacuous existences led by most of modern man ("A Day in the Life"), the male-female put-down ("And Your Bird Can Sing").

Three transitional lyrics deserve special attention: "Eleanor Rigby", "Yellow Submarine", and "Norwegian Wood". "Eleanor Rigby" is so clean, so tight, so focused that it is almost visual: Eleanor cleaning up after a wedding, Father McKenzie darning socks and writing sermons . . . and then the event which finally brings these lonely individuals together, Eleanor's death. (If you listen closely, you'll note the instrumental correlatives to Eleanor and the good Father join only at the song's close.) These are little vignettes, the sort of thing we all see every day at the greyhound station, the shopping mall, the school. In fact we ourselves have contributed the rice Eleanor sweeps and the boredom Father McKenzie must sense during each sermon. But there is no sentimentality to either the lyrics or the music; if anything the understatement of the words ("Who is it for?" "What does he care?" "Nobody came" "No one was saved") and the music's pointless and somewhat irritating busyness is a pitiless analogue of the empty busyness of their lives. Ironically, both Eleanor and Father McKenzie work within a wall of each other, need each other, remain separated all their lives . . . by busyness! Death brings them together, but Father McKenzie, "wiping the dirt from his hands," neither understands nor cares about Eleanor himself. This complex irony is the difference between this lyric and much of the work of, say, early Paul Simon, who over-sympathizes and overstates, or of Harry Chapin (I'm thinking of busyness and isolation in "Cat's in the Cradle"), whose ironies are always one dimensional. The only line which redeems the song from utter callousness is the incessant "All the lonely people, where do they all come from?" That line is important; it stresses the overwhelming multitudes who share this plight, it juxtaposes the implicit millions to the two very small individuals singled out for description, it interjects a genuine sympathy into the song, it heightens the irony of understatement and sharply restricted visual focus. It is a line similar to Eliot's comment on the crowd flowing over London Bridge, and both Eliot and Lennon are treating the same theme: "I did not think death had undone so many."

"Yellow Submarine" is the opposite side of the coin, a depiction of the redeemed to contrast to the damned. It is to the Beatles' eternal credit that they are capable of describing both companies with equal sympathy. The relationship between the two songs was made clear in the movie *Yellow Submarine,* in which the "Eleanor Rigby" scenes in black-and-white contrasted dramatically with the rich color of the rest of the film. While "Eleanor Rigby" is deliberately baroque, a suggestion of the antique quality of the old guard, "Yellow Submarine" is rock in all its flamboyant eclecticism: the chant of a children's song, the brass band which pre-figures *"Pepper's,"* the rich orchestration which marks the Beatles' new music, all the production tricks of multi-track studio recording equipment, and behind everything the driving 4/4 rhythm of rock-n-roll. The imagery of "Yellow Submarine" is heavily visual: yellow boat, sea of green, sky of blue. They are flat, basic colors in contrast to "Lucy in the Sky," with its tangerine trees and marmalade skies, but the song is, after all, a halfway house between "And I Love Her" and "Lucy in the Sky." It is also a halfway house between the normal, work-a-day world of the Beatles' earlier work and the wild supra-realism of "Lucy." Obviously we're not on anything resembling a literal submarine. We are in Wonderland, on Big Rock Candy Mountain, in Paradise before the Fall. All life a life of ease, everyone has everything he needs. But this life is a metaphor for something, although the song is not particularly clear on whether it is merely a child's fantasy built on memories of an old man, a drug trip, or the life style of the beautiful people. *That* ambiguity, I suspect, is as intentional as the ambiguity of "Puff", and lends the song the charm it unmistakably has.

The Poetry of Rock

"Norwegian Wood" is a very complicated song, offering fewer clues to its meaning than we have to "Yellow Submarine." Regardless of what "yellow submarine" means on Long Island, there is no place where "Norwegian Wood" means pot . . . although, that's what everybody wants the song to be about. I am not so sure. It appears on *Rubber Soul,* the earliest of the transitional albums, an album dealing mainly with women of various sizes, shapes, and relations. Only the unusual behavior of the persons involved in the narrative and the speaker's own uncertainty as to what happened would suggest dope. Most specifically the experience seems to deal with a one night stand, although the speaker does not seem particularly unhappy about the passing of his lady, unless you take line three to mean he's been had in something other than a sexual sense. Certainly the lyric involves intoxication, although it may stem from the wine, or the woman, or something else. That wine is perplexing: is it actual wine, a metaphor for the woman's beauty, or a metaphor for other "controlled substances"? The sitar accompaniment suggests something exotic, this is vague indeed. And the Norwegian wood which we presume, without much real proof I suppose, is what's getting consumed in the fires -- no clues here, either. You can't go automatically linking smoke and pot every time you smell it, or you'll come out with pretty wild interpretations of, say, Jerome Kern's "Smoke Gets In Your Eyes" or "On Top of Old Smokey." Of all possible interpretations the drug trip best fits the events of the song, but there is little internal evidence to support it. Lennon claimed, "I was trying to write about an affair without letting my wife know I was writing about an affair." I find it preferable to think of the song as concerning itself with all temporary states of intoxication: wine, women, hash, a good time. They are here and then they're gone, and you eat the ice cream before it melts.

The experimentation indicated by these transitional albums culminated in *Sergeant Pepper's Lonely Hearts Club Band* and the lyrics of *Magical Mystery Tour, Abbey Road,* and the white album. *Sgt. Pepper* and the white album demand special commentary, since the one demonstrates clear thematic unity and the other is just as clearly a conceptual unity. The same might be said about the first side of *Magical Mystery Tour*—although the coherence of the television film was not transferred to the album—and about the second side of *Abbey Road,* although that album does not come off the way *Sgt. Pepper* did and has not without justification been disparaged (by Lennon himself, no less) as a pile or rubbish. While *Abbey Road* contains some very calm, professional, easy work, it does not measure up to several of the individual lyrics on *Magical Mystery Tour,* and—the historical break-up of the Beatles aside—it is clear that *Abbey Road* is the product of a group already overripe.

44

Sergeant Pepper's Lonely Hearts Club Band has been called everything from a sonata to an opera to a *roman a clef* to a symphony to a collage to the Beatles' "Wasteland." It provoked almost instant enthusiasm, despite a bad review in the *New York Times,* selling over a million records within two weeks of its release in the United States. Richard Goldstein once dismissed it as "an album of special effects, dazzling but ultimately fraudulent," but the current concensus is that the album represents a pinnacle never reached before or since by the Beatles or anyone else. It has everything: a bewildering variety of musical styles ranging from Indian ragas to soft shoe (suggesting, as Poirier has said, "the hippie and the historically pretentious, the genteel and the mod, the impoverished and the exotic, the Indian influence and the influence of technology"), an equally impressive array of musical and rhythmic textures and tones, virtuoso studio production, imagery which is resplendent without being obscure to the point of impenetrability, and most unique of all a definite thematic unity. More than a concept album, *Sgt. Pepper* demonstrates something of a circular linear motion which manages direction in spite of musical variety, reflecting the form of a sonnet cycle more than that of a collection of poems. It was this album that taught audiences to think in terms of album-as-conceptual-whole instead of album-as-collection-of-individual-singles. The analogy to Eliot's "Wasteland" is structurally as well as thematically apt, and accords well with Lennon's recollection of the period: "There I was consciously writing poetry, and that's self-conscious poetry." Perhaps that is the reason that lyrics from this period in the Beatles'—and rock's—development resemble most closely traditional poetry.

"Sergeant Pepper's" sets both the tone and the central metaphor of the album: performance by lonely people as an antidote to their loneliness. On the surface of things, it would appear that the band is having a fine old time of it, playing to this enthusiastic crowd, ripping through its eclectic repertoire, announcing to all who care to listen "It's wonderful to be here,/It's certainly a thrill." In fact the audience is encouraged to join along with the band, to "sing along" as well as to "sit back and let the evening go." This is very show biz and very pleasant, except that there are some things wrong with this performance. The album appears at a time when the Beatles no longer give live performances. The pseudonym they have adopted is Sergeant Pepper's Lonely Hearts Club Band—if we take this at face value we're being invited to join a lonely hearts organization, and that innocent remark "we'd love to take you home with us" suggests deep-seated needs and desires: the desire to be understood, the need for companionship, the need for fellowship which the audience fills collectively for the duration of the performance and is invited to fill even beyond that. The band's loneliness is insisted upon by the repetition of "Sergeant Pepper's Loney," the ambiguity of which is made very clear on the lyrics printed on the back of the album. In the "Reprise" there's a period after *lonely,* which is spelled with a lower case *l:* "Sergeant Pepper's lonely." Or, "Sergeant Pepper is loney." And there are other questions. Is the performance successful ("they've been going in and out of style")? In what terms? They certainly sound high-spirited enough; are their spirits a front, or is all this for real? Is anybody paying attention (the remark "I don't really want to stop the show" indicates otherwise)? What is the band like when the shouting's over?

We have clues, as I have suggested, in the band's name and the formulaic show biz theatricalities in which they posture and speak, but it is Billy Shears' song which really tips us off. "What would you do if I sang out of tune,/Would you stand up and walk out on me?" he asks plaintively, promising he will "try not to sing out of key." Obviously the group is not so assured as it might have first appeared; "the one and only Billy Shears" is a vocalist of modest talents and considerable insecurity. Either that or something else is bugging him: perhaps the show we'll get is not what we expected ("out of key" used metaphorically), perhaps the bond between audience and band is not as close as it appears. Most significant, I think, are the frequent admissions that Billy needs somebody—anybody—to love. He is still lonely and still in need of someone: "I just need someone to love."

"How have you been since your girl left."

"Oh, I get by all right, don't worry about me."

This man is dead on the inside. Love at first sight happens to others but not to him. When he turns out the light there's nothing there (but it's all his!). Which is, of course, what makes him part of the band, Sergeant Pepper's Lonely Hearts Club Band, the band we see performing before us. And it is this loneliness which lies at the root of Billy's acute fear that we will walk out on him, leaving him in the words of a more recent and infinitely inferior poem by an infinitely inferior poet "alone again naturally."

By the time the album's first two songs are finished, then, we have a pretty fair idea of the nature of Sergeant Pepper's ensemble and the reasons for its brave facade. Two questions present themselves: what is to be done, and do other people have these problems? Succeeding songs, beginning with "Lucy in the Sky," answer these questions. "Lucy" is a trip song. There can be absolutely no doubt about it—its music if nothing else should make that fact clear. The image of Lucy may in fact have come straight off a picture drawn by John's son, Julian, just as some of the images of "Being for the Benefit of Mr. Kite" may have come straight off a wall poster. No matter what their genesis, the images here are made to carry hallucinogenic meanings. The song concerns itself with a boat on a river, newspaper taxis, and a train in a station . . . all vehicles for trips. Lines like "sun in her eyes," "head in the clouds," and the title all suggest specific forms of tripping. The action is surreal: ties turn into looking glasses, eyes become kaleidoscopes, actions proceed without logical cause and effect relationships. Normal patterns of time and proportion are distorted: "you answer quite slowly," "you drift past the flowers," "suddenly someone is there," "cellophane flowers . . . towering over your head." The imagery becomes brilliantly visual (something right out of an animated cartoon), and senses of taste and sight become confused: "tangerine trees and marmalade skies." The poetry is heavily alliterative. Some of this is borrowed from the realm of dreams, some from the world of children's fantasy (like "Yellow Submarine"), some from *Through the Looking Glass* (the Beatles themselves admit this much) in which Alice finds herself at one point drifting lazily down stream picking the flowers that grow just off the shore. But the song borrows precisely because dreams, children's fantasies, and Lewis Carroll's fiction provide appropriate metaphors for drug trips.

What I find most important about the song, however, is that none of it really takes place, in the minds of the band or of anyone else. We're asked only to *picture* ourselves on a boat, on a taxi, on a train. We are only considering this avenue of escape as a possible response to the loneliness presented in the album's first two songs. Right now it does not appear a particularly pleasant response, even if it is demonstrably transitory; only within the context of later lyrics do the inadequacies of such escape become apparent.

The same cannot be said of the response to loneliness outlined in "Getting Better" and "Fixing a Hole." The first of these is the brighter of the two, postulating a vague "you"—possibly the drugs of "Lucy In the Sky," possibly the somebody to love of "With a Little Help," possibly something else entirely—which has literally turned the world of the speaker around and made everything better. "You" has done marvelous things: straightened out uncool teachers, made restrictive rules palatable, mellowed an angry young man, cured a confirmed wife-beater. You can take this all at face value, but I get the distinct impression that the man protesteth too much; that in insisting again and again that things are getting better (they are, yes they really are) the speaker is doing little more than attempting with partial success to convince himself. Such delusion, of course, prevents a genuine confrontation with difficulty, and insures that things will not get any better.

"Fixing a Hole" poses a similar solution, in that it involves running away from problems and the people who cause them. It may be a drug song, I do not know; but one thing that is clear is that the central figure of this song has turned inward upon himself to the absolute exclusion of everybody around him, even to the extent that he becomes sole arbiter of right and wrong (it's right if I think it's right) and exhibits self-defensive, derisive disdain for all the rest of humanity. His mind will wander uninterrupted, without the hassle of engaging other people or ideas or outside influences, freed by a self-imposed isolation not significantly different from the isolation imposed on Eleanor Rigby and Father McKenzie by others (or was it their own selves after all?). Again a solution which appears initially attractive loses, after sober thought and in the context of the rest of the album, some of its initial appeal.

"She's Leaving Home" poses the obvious solution: pack it up and leave. "She's leaving home after living alone for so many years." Things will be better elsewhere, we tell ourselves. The major accomplishments of this song, however, are its examination of the causes for this loneliness (the generation gap in melodramatic form), the consummate irony of "free" (which the band knows good and well is not free) and "fun" (which the band demonstrates is the cruelest illusion of all), and in the mocking stance the lyric takes toward its subject. Who, one wonders, will be worse off: the girl, who must inevitably realize the inadequacy of running away and the illusion of fun and freedom, or her parents, self-centered to the last ("How could she do this to *me*?), who will complete their lives never understanding what happened to them, continuing to buy, buy (pun intended) their own emptiness, never even sensing their own loneliness?

"Being for the Benefit of Mr. Kite" closes side one of the album. It brings us full circle, back to the band and its own solution to loneliness, in posing a final antidote to boredom: "In this way Mr. K. will challenge the world." You can go off to the show—better still, you can become the show, join the circus. "John has this old poster that says right at the top, 'Pablo Fanques Fair presents the Hendersons for the Benefit of Mr. Kite' and it has all the bits that sound strange: 'the Hendersons'—you couldn't make that up" said Paul in his now famous interview with Alan Aldridge. And this is not beyond the realm of possibility, although it is difficult to imagine a poster advertising anything like "Over men and horses, hoops and garters" or creating the rhythmic subtitles of the Lennon-McCartney lyric. But the important thing is not the source of these images, it's the use to which they have been put. "Being For the Benefit of Mr. Kite" is in effect a miniature *Sgt. Pepper* or *Magical Mystery Tour* in its brilliant and surrealistic imagery, its splendiferous music, its enchanting performance, and its guarantees of entertainment. "Satisfaction guaranteed" we were told in "Magical Mystery Tour"; "A splendid time is guaranteed for all" we are told here, a line which becomes an epigraph for the entire album (cf. album jacket, bottom right). Moreover, the performance by which Mr. Kite challenges the world suggests both the desperation of the band's performance and the surrealistic trip of the mysterious tour. The performance benefits the performer in the way Sgt. Pepper's band hopes its performance will benefit itself: it is an act of existential defiance against boredom and loneliness. On the other hand, performance annihilates the individual, and this particular performance is strangely grotesque: "the Hendersons will dance and sing as Mr. Kite flies through the ring", "ten somersets he'll undertake on solid ground", "Mister Kite performs his tricks without a sound." The swirl of show biz that marked "Sergeant Pepper's" is there (Mr. Kite is "celebrated" as Billy Shears was "the one and only"), but so are the silences, the loneliness, the isolation of "With a Little Help from My Friends." Make it a drug song if you wish (kiff and hashish, horse and the rest), but the lyric's major concern is the sublimation of personal estrangement and neuroses in the unreal world of circus.

And that concludes side one: a very depressing series of vignettes depicting various responses to loneliness, made the more depressing by the almost irresistable high spirits of the music of "Being For the Benefit" or "Lucy In the Sky" or "Sergeant Pepper's."

Side two begins with a recapitulation: We were talking about the space between us all And the people who hide themselves behind a wall of illusion, Never glimpse the truth. Then it's far too late when they pass away." There in a nutshell is the message of every song on the first side. In some respects this song appears to answer directly some of the previous lyrics: "it's far too late when you pass away" the band tells those parents of "She's Leaving Home"; "it's all within yourself, no one else can make you change" it tells the speaker of "Getting Better All The Time"; "when you've seen beyond yourself, then you may find peace of mind" warns the recluse of "Fixing a Hole." In very straight, unimagistic, unmetaphoric prose the song tells us what the band knows and is trying to communicate: "We were talking about the love we all could share/ . . . With our love we could save the world." This love involves a denial of the ego and an internalizing of the external, the very things all the characters of side one have found impossible. "Within You and Without You" represents the thematic center of the album, although it is scarcely a depressing thematic statement. What makes it depressing is the inability of the audience, directly confronted in a line like "Are you one of them?" to grasp its message even though it has been cast in the simplest, clearest of terms. As the song ends, the band's audience giggles.

The next three lyrics describe the most unlikely, unaware, perverse, self-centered collection of gulls I've ever met anywhere. One proposes a marriage of unsurpassed stultification to what appears to be a mail-order bride: mending fuses, knitting sweaters, Sunday morning rides, summers in a cottage on the Isle of Wight (if we can scrape up the dough), and then asks inanely, "Who could ask for more?" For all the prostestations of "Yours sincerely, wasting away" there is neither love nor life nor communication here: the speaker looks foreward only to his death (obviously he's mentally aged already); the locked door and the postcard emblemize an absence of communication which stems from an absence of genuine feeling. He can think only in stereotypic terms, and acts accordingly. "Fill in a form/Mine forever more." Probably he is insecure ("Will you still need me?"), although he doesn't realize it.

Another jerk attempts to put the make on Rita the Meter Maid, using corny lines like "When it gets dark I tow your heart away." He is apparently unsuccessful despite her obvious acquiescense ("Got the bill and Rita paid it"), and manages only a grotesque parody of the slick seduction he had in mind: "Nearly made it/Sitting on the sofa with a sister or two." As for Rita herself, one does not picture her as "a Liverpool whore who uses her job as a meter maid to help in procuring customers" (Joan Peyser) but as something of a plain, simple girl who is herself searching a bit desperately for either some genuine inter-personal relationships or some recreational sex. The whole scene, with its hot panting and hustling tempo, reminds me a bit of the "Game of Chess" section of Eliot's "Wasteland."

The third gull is perhaps most detestable of all: bored and supercilious, he talks in platitudes and unfelt convention. "Good morning, good morning, good morning . . . How's your boy been? What a day! It's okay." Work is a drag, town is a drag, the wife is a drag, the old school is a drag. His utility is limited to telling us the time. All that sparks him to life is the hope of a purely sexual relationship with another skirt (interesting word, "skirt," in its reification of human relationships). "Go to a show, you hope she goes." Clearly there is nothing to do to save this life, "I had not thought death had undone so many."

Into this morass of mundane stupidity breaks the band, its old high spirited theme now more depressing, more cynical, more ironic than ever: "We hope you have enjoyed the show, We're sorry but it's time to go. Sergeant Pepper's lonely." By this time we're more than a bit lonely ourselves, recognizing as we do the human predicament implicit in these lives and in our own life. The spaces don't seem to diminish, the walls of illusion seem impossible to destroy, even for the band.

"A Day In the Life" stands outside the context of a band performance as delineated by the two appearances of "Sergeant Pepper's." It represents an encore or a coda . . . and it is as bleak or bleaker than anything we've seen before, because it presents life without pretense or illusion, only detachment and boredom. The old tedium is still there, along with all the old spaces . . . four thousand of them to be exact, sit-

50

ting before the band in Albert Hall listening to this concert. People do not recognize people. One man's predicament is another man's joke. Wars are won and nobody really cares. What is important is to get to work on time and sneak a quick escape every now and then. The song demonstrates technically the same concise vision we saw before in "Eleanor Rigby", but now the camera is looking at us, not them. We may throw the rice Eleanor cleans up and yawn in Father McKenzie's face, but it is we ourselves who measure our lives in cups of coffee and smoked cigarettes. The detachment of audience and listeners is more awful than of the illusions of which the band has sung. In light of this the ambiguities of "turn you on" are many: the band would like to show us ourselves, it wants to make us aware of what man has done to man, it would like to introduce us to a new and higher reality, it would like to start our vital juices flowing once again. The fact that after the band's performance we still need turning on, the desperation of this song, and that long last dying chord all suggest the apparent impossibility of this a mission.

Sgt. Pepper, then, its music aside, is a very depressing album, although it certainly offers a penetrating glimpse into life in the modern age. The "Wasteland" comparison is accurate, both thematically and structurally; and given Eliot's apparently deliberate obscurantism and the Beatles' more complicated medium, I don't think they come off second best in the comparison. And you can even push the comparison further: from "the Wasteland" Eliot moved on to spiritual regeneration in "Ash Wednesday"; from their own wasteland the Beatles moved on to an attempt at spiritual regeneration in *Magical Mystery Tour* and the white album.

Magical Mystery Tour, a first-rate album made from a second (although not third, as many critics have claimed) rate television film, may in fact represent the Beatles at the height of their powers. There is not one really bad song or poem on here, although given the kind of imagistic surrealism attempted by virtually every song on the album, the risks are great. Moreover, the Beatles manage both musical and lyrical imagism, complicating problems by multiplying those elements requiring integration. "All You Need Is Love" is a classic, the ambiguities inherent in "love" made all vaguer by deliberately repetitious lyrics, then clarified by the specific suggestions of number of musical motifs. The disjuncture between the vagueness on one hand and specificity on the other is mirrored perfectly in syncopations of rhythm and disjunctures between vocal and accompaniment. "Your Mother Should Know" offers traditional metaphors to a youth generation, rejuvenating what was tired, mixing old and new, bridging whatever generation gap rock may have produced: "Let's all get up and dance to a song/That was a hit before your mother was born"—and "dance" leans toward the sexuality of the fifties, "hit" toward the drug culture of the sixties. Mother knows, though, and the gap is gone, lost in what is really an old-time new-time melody with an old-time new-time arrangement. I might effuse endlessly about the imagery and word play of "Penny Lane" (and the tension between its innocent child's world and its sexual innuendos), about the tensions between literalism and imagism in "Strawberry Fields" (and between its Tin Pan Alley formalism and recurrent melodic disarray), about word play and resolution of communication difficulties in the suggestive repetitions of "Hello Goodbye". These are absolutely first rate art songs. Three deserve special attention, however: "Magical Mystery Tour," "Fool On The Hill," and "I Am the Walrus," all from the television film. The journey is a natural structure on which to build a concept album, and proved very popular with late sixties rock: the Moody Blues' assorted sojourns, the Band's trips into the past, the Jefferson Airplane's trips into the future. The journey into self or into a surreal landscape colored with metaphysical significance is likewise a natural structure for a philosophical concept album—or film. *Magical Mystery Tour* is such a film, such an album. The lead cut, "Magical Mystery Tour," is the barker's call to adventure, a song of promises and invitations. "Satisfaction guaranteed," he claims, and in music and lyrics the song reproduces the vague excitement and satisfaction of a carnival or guided tour: the full circus music of those opening chords, the barker's gallyhoo of the initial lines, the heavy rhythms and jangling rhymes of "invitation" and "reservation". A couple of things strike me as odd about this call, however: first, it is unusually vague, offering only some sort of mysterious magic on which neither album nor film ever really elaborated. And second, there is a curious ambivalence to the tour: in one stanza it is merely hoping to take us away, as if the effect depended more upon our co-operation than its own efforts; then it is *dying* to take us away, an indication of some genuine urgency on its part . . . or a pun or clue of some sort. My own suspicion is that all the Paul-Is-Dead business "discovered" several years ago and so vigorously denied by the various Beatles was a planned hoax, the mystery tour offered in this song. Certainly clues were carefully planted, both on this album and elsewhere—after all, the man does say "dying," and if you listen carefully to the back of this song a vehicle of some sort *does* come roaring out of one speaker and crash audibly into the other—and such a joke would not be beyond the Beatle's fertile imagination. Such a narrow interpretation would, I suspect, adequately explain both the mystery and the dying business of this lyric, and some peculiarities of "I Am the Walrus" and a few other songs, but it leaves the lyrics as pretty flat art. What it forgets is the magic, and the metaphorical possibilities of images of death and resurrection. While I doubt that Paul died, the Beatles may have chosen to write metaphorically about death and resurrection of the spirit, brought to the theme by *Sgt. Pepper* and its wish to turn us on. On to what? Not simply to pot or drugs, but to the magic in life, to the potentiality of human existence so often squandered on the day-to-day mundane busyness that killed Eleanor Rigby and Father McKenzie. To sound like the Bible, you have to die in the flesh to be resurrected in the spirit. That, I suspect, is what the magic of this trip is all about, and why the tour is both hoping (for our sake) and dying to take us away. This song, then, sets the context for what is to follow, and takes its meaning primarily in terms of what follows: the death of normal patterns of perception and behavior, and the rebirth of wonder. Nor is the fulfillment of the lyric confined by the context of a single album, for nothing could more aptly describe the effects of rock music: It's trip, and once you're there you're never quite the same. Dylan says just about the same thing in "Mister Tambourine Man," the Beatles elsewhere in "how does it feel to be one of the beautiful people?"

"Magical Mystery Tour" leads directly into "Fool on the Hill," the way "Sergeant Pepper's" leads into "With a Little Help from My Friends"; obviously important connections exist. The fool is both the prime mover behind the trip, and the personage into whom the trip moves. He has always reminded me of J.R.R. Tolkien's Strider, a suspicious looking fellow much distrusted by the Hobbits who, it turns out, wears one of the all-important three rings and is, along with Gandalf, one of the major beneficent forces controlling the world of *Lord of the Rings.* Goes to show you never can tell. The fool partakes of the paradoxes shared by such incognito deities: he is obviously very powerful although he is called the fool; he sees all and knows all, but is unknown by any; he never gives answers but speaks perfectly loud; he speaks in his own exemplary fahsion, but is heard by none; he is both a part of the world and transcends it. Such a figure is bound to invite comparison with the Maharishi and with Christ, although he is neither. He represents a paradox explored earlier by the Beatles ("Within You and Without You") and by several orthodox theologies: you go out by turning in, you discover magic in the mundane and eternity in the finite. The paradoxes of the song and its imagery ("the eyes in his head see the world spinning round") are to precisely this point: The magical mystery tour is within you. "Maybe you've been on a magical mystery tour without even realizing it," the album's jacket suggests.

"I Am the Walrus" comes closest to failure of any of the songs on this album, probably because it attempts so much lyrically. It is an imagistic song, both musically and poetically, and the images don't always work together. I have found it extremely unpleasant in both respects: the wrenching cacophony of its opening bars wants to saw me in half, screeches of high pitched feedback in its concluding cyclone of noise hurt my ears, and the very heavy beat of "I am the eggman, they are the eggmen, I am the walrus Goo Goo Goo Joob" sounds like Hitler's marching millions tramping up behind me. Similarly there is extreme unpleasantness to an image like "yellow matter custard dripping from a dead dog's eye," or "see how they smile, like pigs in a sty, see how they snied." "Priestess" is polluted by "pornographic", and even the gentile English garden is ruined by rain and a vague but clearly diabolical terror. The walrus, according to John, comes from "The Walrus and the Carpenter" in *Alice in Wonderland:* "We saw the movie in LA and the Walrus was a big capitalist who ate all the fuckin' oysters, if you must know . . . He's a fucking bastard, that's what he turns out to be." Even the words sound ugly: "crabalocker fishwife," or "expert texpert choking smokers." Something very awful is happening here.

And if I listen very closely as the song howls to its conclusion, I hear someone chanting "hunchback, hunchback, everybody's a hunchback," and somebody else reading out of *King Lear:*

Gloucester	Oh, untimely death . . .
Edgar	I know thee well, a serviceable villain,
	As duteous to the vices of thy mistress
	As badness would desire.
Gloucester	What, is he dead?
Edgar	Sit you down, father, rest you.

It seems to me that what we've got here is a song about death and the ugliness of death, and the promise of rebirth which follows death. We are all eggmen (rebirth) and walruses (death) in the process of dying to the values of an old system: policemen, priestessess, clean-shaven lads and virgin maidens, corporate ideals and English gardens. The death involves villainy and badness, sex, vice, and evil: you have to delve deep to hit rock bottom. But when you hit bottom, you're cleaned out and ready to rebuild. What bothers me most about this poem, is that it never fulfills the promise of the egg. If that was the intention, then "eggman" is a bad image because it suggests rebirth that doesn't happen; if not, then like Eliot's "Wasteland" this poem kills without ever really resurrecting. Technically I am not sure the Beatles were up to the sort of poem they imagined, although they had obviously caught a glimpse of something very terrible and something very awe-ful, and tried to express it in this song. Phil Ochs saw it in "Crucifixion," Leonard Cohen in "Teachers." The Stones usually saw it steady and saw it whole. The Beatles return to the vision in other songs on *Abbey Road* and the white album, with even less success. But then, Carlisle was not particularly effective in describing his "Everlasting Nay," and Edgar Allen Poe (an appropriate reference in this song) conveyed his terror in vague, impressionistic prose.

With *Sgt. Pepper* and *Magical Mystery Tour,* the Beatles completed their move from basic rock-n-roll into something new and strange. It might be argued that others preceded them, that they were popularizing or even unconsciously following already pre-determined musical developments, that subsequent musical history would have developed much as it did had they spent the rest of their lives playing "I Want to Hold Your Hand." I rather doubt it, but the issue is really irrelevant. What matters is that the new music is somehow different from rock-n-roll, and to be appreciated it must be viewed from a perspective different from that of rock-n-roll. Disregard the difference and you come out with a statement like Nik Cohn's "I'm not sure the Beatles were good for rock-n-roll," or Lennon's remark that "No group, be it Beatles, Dylan, or Stones has ever improved on "A Whole Lot A Shakin' for my Money." Of course the Beatles were not good for rock-n-roll, because they abandoned it for something very different; and of course it is unlikely that any of the folk music of the early sixties or the rock of the later sixties improved much on some of the early classics of rock-n-roll . . . at least not on rock-n-roll's terms.

It's within the context of rock with all its eclecticism that the Beatles' white album is best appreciated. While rock as a whole was capable of assimilating virtually any number of musical and poetic traditions, certain rock groups (the Beach Boys) chose to incorporate little into their own unique style, other groups (the Stones) chose to restrict severely their experimentation, and even the phenomenal Bob Dylan tended to reflect major influences in succession rather than concurrently. Some few composers and works—Van Dyke Park's "Song Cycle," Sly & the Family Stone, and the Beatles—were capable of producing virtually contemporaneous pieces reflecting a wide variety of musical or literary influences. We see glimpses of this remarkable virtuosity in *Sgt. Pepper* and *Magical Mystery Tour,* but it is most easily demonstrated in the so-called white album, which has been called everything from a history of rock to a pastiche of self-conscious, show off nothing. My own estimation is somewhat tempered: clearly there is genius on this album and even though it doesn't appear to be "Beatle genius" it is a genius that cannot be denied. Just as clearly the album represents a musical tour-de-force unmatched by any other rock auteur. What is annoying is the album's slick proficiency which makes it appear somehow bogus at the very moment it's most impressive. You want a Beach Boys song? O.K., here it is. You want a country ballad? A calypso? An imagistic poem? An anti-poem? Here they are. We will write them long or short for you, we will write them any way you want us to. If there is aesthetic heresy in saying that music has to be genuine to be good, then I suppose I'm committing it here. In any event, I find the white album more technically proficient than anything the Beatles ever did, but for some reason a comedown after *Sgt. Pepper* and *Magical Mystery Tour.*

"They are no longer Sgt. Pepper's Lonely Hearts Club Band, and it is possible that they are no longer the Beatles" wrote Jann Wenner in his review of the album. In fact, a song like "I Will" or "Julia" parodies early Beatles as "Glass Onion" parodies later Beatles as "Back in the U.S.S.R." parodies the Beach Boys and Chuck Berry. In a sense this represents the inevitable end point of the group's (and rock's) eclecticism, an explosion into infinity and infinitesimalism, a dispersion of its nucleus into rays and particles, a dissipation of its concentrated energy in many directions. Perhaps this album was unavoidable, the logical extension of developments begun in those transitional albums. Whatever, it is an end point beyond which there is literally no progression, and in this sense at least the Beatles were bad for rock. That they moved so quickly through the various phases of rock to this ultimate development (three years at most) is unfortunate, since rock was barely born before it was old, scarcely old before it exploded. In fact, in their self-parody the Beatles inadvertently suggested the direction rock would take after its bubble collapsed: back to the roots. I don't find this conscious; that is, the earlier Beatles are not the *subject* of "Julia" or "I Will," or earlier rock and rock-n-roll styles the *subject* of other songs, as Carl Belz would have us believe in *The Story of Rock.* No, the album is not self-conscious in this sense; you would do much better in making *Pepper* such a conscious statement, since it purports to be a concert of in-and-out of favor styles. The return to roots of the white album is no more conscious than rock's voracious appetite for musical and lyric styles. On this album, some of those styles happen to be those which formed part of the original amalgam which produced rock-n-roll way back when: country-and-western, rhythm-and-blues. Others are earlier stylistic mutations of rock-n-roll or rock. But none of the album's songs represents a deliberate return to the roots in the manner of the subsequent rock-n-roll revival. The Beatles are not the Mothers of Invention, and the white album is not *Cruising With Ruben and the Jets.*

What then is the white album? It is a collection of thirty different songs representing every conceivable style of music, both alone and in various combinations. They are not songs about music, but deal with a variety of topics from revolution to love to politics. Some of the lyrics parody their subjects or musical styles, becoming anti-love or anti-revolution or anti-rock-n-roll or anti-metaphor songs. We've seen some of this in cuts on earlier albums ("She's Leaving Home," "Sergeant Pepper's Lonely Hearts Club Band," "When I'm Sixty-Four" to name only a few). As an aesthetic it was implicit in the stance the Beatles took toward their art right from the start: nothing serious here, chaps, no meaning, no art, just a bit of random and fooling around at the old piano. But here the parody and the irony it implies are quite strong and very much on the surface of the album. Other songs sound perfectly straight: "While My Guitar Gently Weeps," "Blackbird," "Revolution Number Nine." The album has no linear movement, although it would appear to be a concept album. I don't see it as a show-off history of pop music, although other people do. Probably it is best considered what I have suggested: the end point of rock's stylistic explosion, an album of amplitudes and infinitudes, an album of dispersion.

It also contains a number of very fine lyrics. The lead cut, "Back In the U.S.S.R.," is as good an example as any. "An imitation of the Beach Boys imitating Chuck Berry" Wenner called it, and of course he's right: the title looks to Berry's "Back In the U.S.A." as the music looks to Brian Wilson's triple-refined cotton candy. Part of the lyric is pulled directly from "California Girls." The jumbo jet that roars in one speaker and lands on the other is pure pop-rock. But the song's significance is not limited to it parody; the Beatles have a socio-political point to make in their own oblique fashion, hitting at a vacuous and stereotyped response which is global ("Man, I had a dreadful flight," "Honey, disconnect the phone," "Been away so long I hardly know the place") in a manner reminiscent of "Good Morning." The lyric plays word games as well, on U.S. and U.S.S.R., Georgia, U.S.A. and Georgia, U.S.S.R. It's all very subtle, but the whole poem sounds suspiciously like a put-down not merely of the Beach Boys or of U.S. Nationalism, but of ideologies on both sides of the iron curtain.

"Dear Prudence", the album's next lyric, is an invitation to wonder reminiscent of "Lucy In the Sky." A much tighter lyric, more delicate and refined, it works off the name "Prudence" the way that other lyric works off the name "Lucy In the Sky." Formally the song is classic Tin Pan Alley; poetically it follows a rather rigid and complex rhyme scheme. Poetically the lyric draws its strength from the tension between an impulse toward childish joy and prudent, mature restraint. The former is present in the lyric's echoes of childrens' songs and nursery rhymes ("Playmate come out and play with me,/Swing in my Apple tree," "Roses are red,/Violets blue/Sugar is sweet,/And so are you"), the pure, "natural" simplicity of its imagery (sun, sky, birds, daisies), and the request for a smile "like a little child." The latter is present mainly in the name Prudence, the girl's reticence, the song's formalism, and the delicate, measured regularity of its music. Reverence for childhood and the importance of "taking time" are common enough themes in pop music (Mac Davis' "Stop and Smell the Roses" is but the most recent of the series; Ray Steven's "Take Care of Business, Mr. Business-man" is probably the most popular). I think what makes me prefer this lyric to the many which have come before and since is its delicate under-statement: how much weight falls on that final word in the second-to-last line: "So let me see you smile again"? How metaphoric is a word like "chain"? How much sadness exists in the wistful whimsy of "Look around round round" and "Open up your eyes"? This song says much: adults lose a sense of wonder and a spontaneity infinitely preferable to the prudence with which they guard their lives. A literal new day means nothing to us (I am reminded of Dylan Thomas' lament for his own lost sense of new creation with each new dawn in "Fern Hill." Thomas is, in-cidentally, one poet Lennon admits to "getting.") When a social or political new day dawns, adults are too cautious to embrace it. I see a lot of the "Eleanor Rigby" -- "Yellow Submarine" tension in this poem, as well as the lessons preached by "Within You and Without You": "You are a part of everything; Dear Prudence, won't you open up your eyes?" But this is an understated poetry, so subtle that we very nearly miss its point. So understated that it tells us without preaching to us. So under-stated that it is, as Archibald MacLeish claimed a poem should be, "motionless in time/As the moon climbs".

"Blackbird" is another lyric which implies much but says little ex-plicitly. It works off paradoxes: death is birth, blindness is sight, night is day, in the midst of darkness is singing. There is something of the Walrus here, or of the philosophy of the walrus: in death is a birth, rejuvenation demands some sort of death. Traditionally the raven emblematizes death, connotations re-enforced in the song by night ("the dead of night" to be specific), blackness, broken wings, sunken eyes. But this blackbird sings, flies, sees. At the very moment of his death, he is born; in fact, he was awaiting the moment of his death to arise anew. In this respect he resembles the mythological phoenix, who dies to be reborn. The myth is old, and it is important. It is also applicable—to man (who is mourned elsewhere on this album in a very fine guitar elegy), to the Beatles, to rock as a music, to social and political institutions. The Beatles have had their say on modern man and his condition in *Sgt. Pep-per*; we all saw the dissociation of their close-knit group not long after to this album; we are watching in this very album the explosive disinte-gration of rock's nucleus; we recall the political and social troubles of the late sixties and the political right's constricting reassertion of itself. Cer-tainly this song speaks to all issues . . . and given the social, political, and musical commentary of some of the other lyrics on this album, I rather suspect the Beatles intended it to.

The theme of death reappears frequently throughout the album. One of its most complex treatments is "Yer Blues": "The eagle picks my eye;

the worm he licks my bones; I feel so suicidal, just like Dylan's Mr. Jones. Lonely, wanna die.'' So desperate are Lennon's straits he even hates his rock and roll. Sources of the song's content are to be found in its blues roots, but sources don't tell us much about the poem. A key is to be found in those early lines "My mother was of the sky./My father was of the earth./But I am of the universe/And you know what it's worth.'' Here are the eagle and the worm that devour him: earth father and sky mother (an interesting inversion of traditional sexual roles). Here also is the tension which is destroying him: not between earth and sky, but between the mundane and the cosmic. Like the fool on the hill, who is also "of the universe,'' this man sits alone, mocked by his more mundane companions. Autobiography aside—and it seems to me there is a lot of John Lennon autobiography in this song—the lyric centers on the self-doubt and periodic sense of alienation and rejection which accompanies all transcendent effort—from that of Henry Thoreau to that of Jesus Christ. John's comments on Christ are used by Alan Aldridge as a gloss on this song in *Beatles Illustrated Lyrics,* and I think he has hit the lyric on its head: "Jesus was all right, but his disciples were thick and ordinary. It's them twisting it that ruins it for me.''

One of the album's heaviest songs is Harrison's elegy for diverted, perverted, unalerted modern man, "While My Guitar Gently Weeps'': it is an absolutely first rate poem full of metrical subtleties, assonances and alliterations, and clever rhymes. I'm reminded vaguely of "Within You and Without You'' on *Sgt. Pepper,* but this lyric is fuller, more structured, more sympathetic with the general human condition than its predecessor. And it is more sophisticated and more mature in its realization that love takes time and mistakes and concentration and learning.

At the other end of the spectrum are "Rocky Raccoon'' and "Don't Pass Me By,'' both pure kuntry korn, one by Lennon-McCartney, the other by Ringo. Of the two I prefer the first, an epic story of Rocky, his fickle woman ("Her name was Magill and she called herself Lil/But everyone knew her as Nancy''), and a third party, Dan. Rocky comes to town lookin' for Dan, shoots it out, loses, and retires to his hotel room, only to find a Gideon's bible. A highly amusing piece of nonsense, especially given the twangy aside of Rocky, "gonna get that boy!''

The album rolls on, through pure blues ("Yer blues''), through Donovan Leitch imagism ("Savory Truffle''), through middle Beatles rock ("Birthday'' and "Helter Skelter''), through radical revolutionary songs like the incomparable "Piggies'' ("What they need's a damn good whacking''). There is a calypso ("Ob-La-Di, Ob-La-Di''), a piece of wildly experimental electronic music ("Revolution 9''), even one of those dreamy choral reveries that always closed 1930's film musical extravanganzes. There is art and there is anti-art, most prominently "Why Don't We Do It In the Road," Lennon-McCartney's parody of thousands of invitations to love (from "Birds do it, bees do it,/Even educated fleas do it" right on up to their own "If I Fell In Love With You"). In its totality it runs like this:

Why don't we do it in the road?
No one will be watching us
Why don't we do it in the road?

Many of these lyrics reward careful attention, and most are better than the Beatles' early work. On the other hand, what has been gained in smooth professionalism has been lost in raw enthusiasm. Ultimately the album is not on a par with *Magical Mystery Tour* because the Beatles—individually and collectively—are simply attempting too much for everything to come off. Nor are these songs equal in quality to those of *Sgt. Pepper*—but what else in rock music really is? Probably the album is under-rated: had it appeared before *Sgt. Pepper* it would have been hailed as a fine album; had it been less pretentious (and less expensive) it might have been better received; had we not been set for something psychedelic it might have proven less startling. But the Beatles had already committed themselves to the plentitude of rock, and the *Pepper-Mystery Tour* albums represented only a stage at which they could not or would not rest. Curiously, people who do not much like this album also do not much like rock music of the late sixties: less and less cohesion, less good old rock-n-roll, constantly proliferating genres and subgenres.

One last thing ought to be said in defense of the white album: while it evidences none of the linear movement of *Sgt. Pepper* or the thematic focus of many other concept albums, its lyrics do interrelate. Whatever political reading is given "Back in the U.S.S.R." is to a great extent validated by songs like "Piggies" and "Revolution 1." "Dear Prudence" appears a clarified "Lucy In the Sky" partially because it immediately precedes "Glass Onion," with its complex allusions to Beatles' music of the "Lucy In the Sky" era. It draws for its gentility partly on "Julia," partly from contrast to something like "Helter Skelter" and "Sexy Sadie." The death-resurrection pattern in "Blackbird" looks forward to "Yer Blues" and back to "While My Guitar Gently Weeps". "Why Don't We Do It In the Road?" needs "Helter Skelter" and perhaps even "Honey Pie" and "Dear Prudence" for its own anti-metaphoric aesthetic to make any sense. The joke of following that particular cut with "I Will" speaks for itself. The Beatles are obviously fragmenting on this album, musically and personally, and it is not what we might have hoped for. Nevertheless, there is much more here than meets the eye, much more than appears on subsequent albums of the whole or dissociated Beatles, and the album deserves more attention that it has received.

After the white album, the disintegration of the Beatles accelerated, prompted partially by the death of Brian Epstein and tensions between Allen Klein and John Eastman over management of Beatles' affairs, partially by tensions between Linda Eastman (Paul's second wife) and Yoko Ono (John's second wife), partly by tension between McCartney and Lennon themselves, partly by economic difficulties or confusions, partly by the rifts which inevitably develop between four human beings growing up and apart. The entire story has been told from every conceivable point of view and with every imaginable degree of bitterness and sympathy in the many interviews given by all parties involved ever since the break-up. Their stories are often contradictory; the collected fragments never make much sense. Perhaps the real key lies in the Beatles' music itself, which became increasingly fragmentary, incoherent, diffuse. *Abbey Road* and *Let It Be* exhibit extremely proficient musicianship and flashes of genius, but they simply aren't "together" albums.

"Something slick to preserve the myth," John said of *Abbey Road.* Slick it was—subtle, proficient, filled with haunting imagery and very lovely melodies. It is in some respects an album-long version of "I Am the Walrus," or "Strawberry Fields," nearly an hour of surrealistic poem. If anything in rock comes close to the collage form, it is *Abbey Road,* especially the second side which spins melodies and echoes of melodies across the entire twenty-five minutes, working one image off against another, populating the scenario with figures right out of *Yellow Submarine:* Mean Mr. Mustard, Polythene Pam, the Sun King. In this respect side one does well enough for itself: "Old Flat Top" in "Come to Gether", Maxwell with his silver hammer, the magnificent woman who inspired "Something."

Now there can be no denying that this album has its moments: "Something" is probably one of the most beautiful, mature, easy love songs in all of rock, although its lyrics are more prose than poetry. "Octopus's Garden" can be a cute kid's song if you ignore its vague insistence on something, anything heavier. The melodies of side two are beautiful, the whole "experience" of side two quite pleasant. The problem with *Abbey Road,* however, is that generally it defies meaning and thus analysis. It is a consummate work of high pop art (as distinct from, say, low pop or strictly proletarian art the likes of Lennon's later "Working Class Hero" or good old rock-n-roll). It is an experience, a thing, an impression, a rarified happening, but it defies rational discussion. There is much fine art of this sort abroad these days, and you should see the art critics talking *around* it. The same might be done for *Abbey Road.*

On the other hand, this sort of art walks a thin line: having no apparent conceptual core (a necessary adjunct to its denial of meaning), it tends to fly apart. And when you see things flying apart, disintegrating into Donovan Leitch image-mongering, or filling whole minutes with chant, you begin to question just how much is there. The more you look, the less you see. Ultimately you quit looking, because you just can't make sense out of "Come Together," "Mean Mr. Mustard," "Sun King" or "She Came in Through the Bathroom Window." Of this last, Paul remarked, "This forms part of a medley of songs which is about fifteen minutes long on *Abbey Road*. We did it this way because both John and I had a number of songs which were great as they were but which we'd never finished."

That, boys and girls, says it all: the Beatles' heads had so exploded that things could not get finished. Where the white album was an album of amplitudes and dispersion, we now get individual songs of amplitudes and dispersion. And fragmentation. This fragmentation of form and meaning continued in *Let It Be*. The title cut proved successful because it turned its infinities into a suitable ambiguous central figure ("Mother Mary") and settled on a chant as a form which, having no real form, needed no real finishing. In fact, the developing use of the chant, traceable from "I Am the Walrus" through "Strawberry Fields" to "I Want You" (*Abbey Road*), "Let It Be" and the incomparable "Hey Jude" may be one mark of the Beatles' disintegration. The other being, of course, simple nonsense, continued on *Let It Be* in a song like "Across the Universe." Both the movement toward nonsense and the tendency toward fragmentation reached a peak in "Uncle Albert/Admiral Halsey," which—wonder of wonders—managed AM popularity!

After *Let It Be* the Beatles released one more album: *Hey Jude*, a collection of heretofore unreleased singles reaching all the way back to "Paperback Writer." As a group the Beatles were finished.

Individually the Beatles have been disappointing, although no more disappointing I suppose than Bob Dylan in the early seventies or the dissociated Simon and Garfunkel. Lennon and McCartney both turned quickly to their own excesses, one to radical politics and Yoko Ono, the other to sentimental silliness. Ringo Starr turned to country and western and pre-rock pop standards. Harrison's head flew eastward to a soft religiosity and produced *All Things Must Pass*, its major claim to fame being "My Sweet Lord," a competent but scarcely a remarkable song and a musical plagiarism. No single Beatle has dominated pop music as the group did collectively, mainly because their material is simply no better than run-of-the-mill seventies rock.

CHAPTER IV
THE ROLLING STONES

Beatles and Stones: the cream of the British Invasion, revered gods of rock's Pantheon whose names tumble together from the lips with no more thought than goes into saying Tweedledee and Tweedledum, rhythm-and-blues, rock-and-roll. How alike we have made them here at a decade's distance: both British, both rockers of the sixties, both super-heavies.

In fact, however, the Beatles and the Stones offer an almost classic study in contrasts, two very different styles of rock. Some of the contrasts are obvious: one was largely domestic and almost pretty, the other untamed and seamy; one was polished, the other deliberately flaunted its rough edges; one celebrated life's wholesomeness while the other threatened satanism, perversion, and destruction; one group turned quickly reticent and retired to privacy while the other remained public and accessible; one easily assimilated virtually any and all forms of pop music, the other settled early on rhythm-and-blues style rock-n-roll and never really strayed too far from home base; one changed rapidly and flamboyantly until it burnt itself out, the other remains with us after a decade of gradual evolution. Of course you can find exceptions to these kinds of generalizations—the Beatles, Lennon has revealed, were in some respects pretty nasty people; "I Am the Walrus" certainly does not sound like a celebration of life; the Stones were pretty much out of sight between 1966 and their Hyde Park appearance of 1969; songs other than those of their *Satanic Majesties Request* show a variety of musical influences on the Stones ("Keith has always been country," Jagger told Jonathan Cott)—but by in large they represent accurate if overly pat generalizations about the Beatles' and Stones' art.

The easy contrasts conceal more fundamental and therefore more important differences. In recent years especially the Stones appear to have taken seriously their role as prophets and priests of high pop, living as it were a life of Felliniesque debauchery and indulgence. On the other hand, the Beatles, because of either their reticence, their hip denial of any commitment (even to pop), or nothing more than fundamentally different perspective on things, neither managed a committment of similar strength and duration, nor inspired the sociological interest and commentary which follows the Stones wherever they go. The Stones are a way of life, a walking talking mythic vision, a legitimate sociological and political threat which fuses art and life. You get artistic and paraliterary criticism of Beatles' lyrics, but psychological and social criticism of the Stones' "experience." Terry Southern is fascinated; so is Truman Capote. What interests them is not so much the Stones' poetry or music, but their life style: "Mick Jagger and the Rolling Stones: Surreal or Super-Real?" asks Southern in *Saturday Review*. What you have here is a real life piece of pop rebellion, virulent and dangerous and extremely interesting. Alan Beckett and Richard Merton's essays in the *New Left Review* are early manifestations of this social criticism, and Michael Parson's objection to both is in one sense well taken: their evaluations are based on external, non-musical standards. In the wider perspective, however, Jagger and the Stones have chosen to exist in a sociological/psychological context and really insist on evaluation in those, rather than literary or musical terms. In *Rock from the Beginning*, Nik Cohn wrote, "More than anyone, more even than Bob Dylan, they became their time." Their musical impact is subservient to their social impact . . . and their poetic impact subservient to both. The Stones, I suspect, have made music do what John Lennon appears to want his art to do: function in the world outside of art.

The Stones' poetry, then, makes concessions to concerns beyond art, and has done so from its very beginnings, partly because rhythm-and-blues makes those same commitments, partly because of the Stones' on involvement in the world of pop. Significantly the Stones managed to fuse art and real life without hurting either music or poetry. It's a different kind of poetry, of course, a poetry of statement akin to blues: art involves no pretense, no refraction of life; it grows directly out of life experiences unpurged by tinted glasses or the indirections of sophisticated imagery and metaphor; lyrics are direct and to the point, and music reinforces lyrics. Suffering, neurosis, aggression are not so much sublimated into art as mitigated by singing about the world as it actually is. The genius of the Stones is that they could take this sincerity of rhythm-and-blues and maintain it in treating another culture, another time, another place. Rock-n-roll managed some of this same honesty in dealing with emergent urban youth culture during the middle fifties but quickly lost itself in the falsifications of metaphor and the sublimity of angels, junior proms, and chapel bells. The folk music movement never really managed it until singers stopped trying to sing about things they'd never seen nor experienced and turned their attention to the world of the sixties. Most British rhythm-and-blues lacked legitimacy because it tried consciously to ape mannerisms, verbal idiosyncrasies, and the personal styles of Howlin' Wolf, Muddy Waters, Bo Diddley, and other black

Americans, with the British singers from an entirely different culture. The Stones never transcribed, they translated, both in their performances of American rhythm-and-blues artists, and in their adaptation of blues to their own culture. More important, as their culture changed, so did their music and life style, turning surreal as the world became surreal, always maintaining an integration of art and life.

Early Stones albums are filled with translations: songs of other artists—both rockabilly and rhythm-and-blues—not so much covered as interpreted by the Stones. Their first, released in May of 1964, contained only one Jagger-Richard original: "Tell Me," a rather plaintive if hoarse cry of lost love closer to C&W than blues. The album led off with Buddy Holly's "Not Fade Away," rolled through a few blues numbers ("Honest I Do," "Little By Little," "I'm a King Bee"), hit Chuck Berry for "Carol," and wound up with the American rock-n-roll hit "Walkin' the Dog." The album is so eclectic as to give scant indication of the shape of things to come; most noteworthy, in retrospect, is the rather overt sexuality of many songs (like "I Just Want to Make Love To You"), and the preponderance of blues material. "I'm a King Bee," resurrected more recently by Elvis Presley as "I'm a Steamroller," is representative: "I'm a king bee, buzzin' around your hive; Well I'm a king bee, baby, buzzin' around your hive. Yeh I can make honey, baby, let me come inside." It was good, nasty, aggressive, sexual music, complete with asides: "sting you babe," "buzz when your man is gone."

The Stones' second album (*12X5*) led off with Chuck Berry's "Around and Around" and followed it with "Confessin' the Blues": heavy rock-n-roll, then heavy blues. Album three (*The Rolling Stones, Now!*) led off with a very black rhythm-and-blues "Everybody Needs Somebody to Love," then followed it with the half blues, half country "Down Home Girl," and then ripped off Chuck Berry for "You Can't Catch Me." As late as their fifth album (*December's Children*), the Stones hit Chuck Berry again for "Talkin' About You" and the very country and western Hank Snow for "I'm Moving On." Now what all this suggests is that while a Stones social and musical style was unmistakable from 1964 on, the group remained eclectic in selection of material. That such variety could all sound pure Stones indicates the extent to which source material was transmuted in performance.

Scattered among these albums were Keith Richard and Mick Jagger's early originals: "Good Times, Bad Times," "The Last Time," "Heart of Stone," "Satisfaction," "Play With Fire," "Get Off My Cloud." Most of their early work shows a heavy rhythm-and-blues influence, both in themes (sex, faithless lovers, money problems) and in the straight-forward prosy language and simple metaphors of its poetry. The same influence can be seen in their early big hits. "Satisfaction," called by some the greatest rock song ever, is pretty pure blues: direct statement repeated and repeated again, no metaphor at all, a strong sense of rhythm, a stronger sense of the voice as instrument, an almost surface sexual inuendo, a loose form. It makes an important universal statement, but the effect is outside of the song's poetry even its music: "I can't get no satisfaction." That says it all—but there's not much you can say about it.

"The Last Time" is classic rock-n-roll: meter, rhyme, and explicit male sex: "You don't try very hard to please me; With what you know it should be easy. Well, this could be the last time . . . ." "Heart of Stone" took one very simple metaphor (perhaps from an earlier rock-n-roll hit "Hearts Made of Stone"), added the Stones' own brand of rhythm-and-blues, and produced a simple but compelling lyric. "Play with Fire" and "The Spider and the Fly" also use simply blues-like metaphors, the kind that literature teachers wave in front of students to demonstrate the prevalence of metaphor in everyday life, the kind that have in fact become so commonplace as to have no real metaphorical significance. Even "Get Off Of My Cloud," which appears at first complex and surreal, reduces to three very real-life scenes: the door-to-door promotion man, the wet blanket who calls the cops to kill a good party, and tickets for parking a car overnight. Nothing here like what goes on in some of Dylan's nightmares—or a couple of later Stones lyrics. On these early albums the Stones were singing to everyday (white) modern (urban) experiences with the techniques and strength of rhythm-and-blues. The art is in expression, not in transformation of external reality to aesthetic construct or in complexities of imagery and metaphor.

One thing these and other lyrics of the pre-*Satanic Majesties* period do allow: psychological and sociological probing of a nature not found heretofore in white music. One of the Stones' favorite subjects was the proud, powerful, sexually aggressive, vain, potentially dangerous, mean-as-hell male whose masochistic violence covers an extremely vulnerable, defensive ego. It's the sort of thing Paul Simon does less well in "I Am a Rock": strong, almost aggressive isolationism on the one hand, weak sentimentalism on the other. The Stones have it another way: defensiveness manifests itself not in sullenness but in anger and aggression. Jagger once owned movie rights to Burgess' *Clockwork Orange,* and in these songs you can see what he had in mind: "Heart of Stone," "Play With Fire," "Get Off Of My Cloud," "The Last Time." A more poignant and less characteristic presentation of the persona comes in "I'm Free": "I'm free to do what I want any old time. So love me, hold me, love me, hold me." "Cheap punk sexuality" runs the standard tag, although that is oversimplification.

The counterpart to this aggressive male is the strung-out, well-bred and usually rich, pain-in-the-ass bitch of "Play With Fire," "Gotta Get Away," "19th Nervous Breakdown," "Miss Amanda Jones" and some later lyrics. She resembles closely some of Dylan's women ("Leopard-skin Pillbox Hat" or "Like a Rollin' Stone") and appears in slightly different guise in the Stones' own later songs: "Up and up she goes, the honorable Miss Amanda Jones."

A few early lyrics break these stereotypes, this insistence on hard-headed realism, this denial of imagistic and metaphoric complexities; a couple require special comment, not because they invalidate earlier generalizations, but because they point toward later Stones' work. Very early, for example, the Stones showed a genius for satire, a bitter satire closer to Bob Dylan than the Beatles of "Nowhere Man," "Eleanor Rigby," or even *Sgt. Pepper*. "The Under-Assistant West Coast Promotion Man" sits waiting for a bus in L.A., thinking "just how sharp how I am/I'm a necessary talent behind ev'ry rock-n-roll band." In "Flight 505" some King of Kool realizes he's unhappy with life, hops the first place outta here, then crashes (literally and figuratively) in the sea: "Well, I sat right there in my seat, feeling like a king/With the whole world right at my feet of course I'll have a drink." There's no sympathy and less sentiment in these lyrics, nor will there be in later satires like "2,000 Man," "You Can't Always Get What You Want," "Parachute Woman," and "Brown Sugar."

In one or two early songs the Stones did show a softer side: "Tears Go By," "Some Things Just Stick In Your Mind," "Lady Jane," "Ruby Tuesday." These are lyrics we sometimes forget belong to the Stones, they are so uncharacteristic of Jagger's sneering pose. They represent a soft belly to the sexual punk, and make him more psychologically complex and compelling than we think of his as being. "Some Things" is imagistic in a Donovan Leitch sort of way, and foreshadows lyrics like "Paint It Black" and songs of *Their Satanic Majesties Request*. Also imagistic, but much softer, is "Ruby Tuesday":

"There's no time to lose," I heard her say;
"Cash your dreams before they slip away.
Dying all the time.
Lose your dreams and you
Will lose your mind.
Ain't life unkind?

Rarely do early Stones—or even later Stones, for that matter—get this romantic, but the imagery of "Paint It Black" and "Some Things Just Stick In Your Mind," and the sentimentalism of "Ruby Tuesday" suggest another side of the Stones, and imply that even without the influence of the Beatles' *Sgt. Pepper* the Stones might have moved in the direction of traditional metaphoric/imagistic poetry.

"*Their Satanic Majesties Request,* as everyone soon recognized, was an abortive experiment with the Stones, a showcase for some of their most obtrusive weaknesses. At its worst it sounded like a bad parody of *Sgt. Pepper,* borrowing themes, techniques, even images and philosophical revelations. The notion of a concept album is pure *Pepper,* as is the psychedelic jacket and even the 3-D cover. "She's a Rainbow" sounds like "Lucy In the Sky" filtered through *The Secret of the Golden Flower,* a Tao classic that Mick Jagger had been reading when many of these songs were composed. It's hard to tell whether the album's pseudo-mysticism owes more to the Tao book or George Harrison; I suspect the latter, and I further suspect it was the Beatles who first put Jagger's nose into eastern religion. Either way, this performance is not the Stones. Likewise "Sing This Song Together," while it may show Taoist influences, also sounds suspiciously like the opening cut of *Sgt. Pepper.* The Stones use the song to open and close side one of *Satanic Majesties* as the Beatles used "Sergeant Pepper" as a reprise near the close of their album. The electronic music and over-dubbed bits and snatches of "On With the Show" are copped straight from the Beatles, and the song itself sounds suspiciously like "Sergeant Pepper": "Good evening one and all, We're glad to see you here. We'll play your favorite songs While you soak up the atmosphere." But the Stones were not comfortable with these experiments, nor were they flexible enough to assimilate musical styles the way the Beatles gobbled them down. They also lacked a producer of George Martin's capabilities: heretofore Andrew Loog Oldham had handled production, but with *Satanic Majesties* the group was on its own. Finally, the Stones' strength had up to this point been what David Dalton called "the mother lode of rock"—blues, country and western, and rhythm-and-blues, conservative music in form and theme—the exact artistic antithesis to that gaudy psychedelic rock *Satanic Majesties* attempts. The Stones' failure on this album is less surprising than the fact they attempted it at all . . . at least at first glance.

Thematically *Satanic Majesties* presents two contrasting views of human existence: the beatific vision of the elect, the nightmare of the damned. The dichotomy is eclectic, incorporating elements from eastern-western, rationališt-mystic, hippie-straight dualisms as well as more conventional disjunctures like the generation gap. This diffuseness does little for the album's coherence; neither does the Stones' mixture of metaphors: the carnival of side 2, lead cut, on the one hand; a journey *to* and *into* (shades of *Magical Mystery Tour*) on the other. The journey in time and culture predominates, and in a scene very much out of *2001 A Space Odessy* the Stones open the album with the suggestion, "Why don't we sing this song all together?'' ''Let the pictures come,'' we are urged. The pictures do indeed come, bringing first the surrealist horror of contemporary civilization: flags flying dollar bills so thick you can't see the concrete hills on which they wave. This is the hard, commercial world of the damned. It is, in turn, is followed by the obverse view, the beatific vision of sand and ·sea and sky, castles blue, and love, and love, and love in ''Another Land.'' Variations on a theme are played through ''She's a Rainbow'' and ''Gomper''; new and old visions come together in the generation gap satire of ''2000 Man.'' The Stones return to their journey motif in ''200 Light Years From Home,'' the album's second to last cut, and finally to the show motif in a grand finale: ''On With the Show.''

Conceptually the album is loose; this much we might expect, since the Stones had previously attempted nothing coherent—indeed, nothing conceptually weighty. More impressive is the album's imagism, which colors Stones lyrics of the post-*Satanic Majesties* period and provides continuity between earlier albums and this one. The conceptual heaviness we find surprising and objectionable; the imagery proves the ultimate development of earlier singles like ''Ruby Tuesday'' and ''Paint It Black.'' Most striking in their surrealism are ''The Citadel,'' quoted above, and ''2000 Man.'' ''She's a Rainbow'' presents both an unusually fresh and striking metaphor and an array of color far broader than the earlier ''Paint It Black.'' It is a delicate lyric, with a richness of rhyme that colors the lyric's sound as the woman colors the air. ''The Lantern'' is nearly overripe with symbol, imagery, metaphor, and a stark allegorical landscape reminiscent of middle Dylan; so too is ''Gomper.'' A surprisingly untogether performance,'' comes off better as an imagistic poem, like something out of the Arthurian cycles.

After the uncomfortably disoriented music and mediocre jamming is forgotten, the lacy imagery and lush surrealism of *Satanic Majesties Request* remains. While the Stones retreated quickly from this psychedelic disaster and seemed to return to pure rhythm-and-blues (''Love in Vain,'' ''Prodigal Son,'' ''Midnight Rambler''), their best later work presses earlier psychological probings, formal tightness, and their peculiar brand of sociological analysis, and adds to it a surrealism and an imagism borne of *Satanic Majesties*. The resultant fusion produces an art as fine as anything the Beatles did.

Beggars Banquet was widely hailed as the Stones' return to their senses, a comeback, ''the final end of all the pretentious, nonmusical, boring, insignificant, self-conscious and worthless stuff that's been tolerated during the past year,'' as Jan Wenner, editor of *Rolling Stone* magazine, put it. All this it both was and was not. Certainly it *was* a backing off from over-produced, arty, studio experimentation in the *Sgt. Pepper* mold. But the return to rhythm-and-blues was only partial; there's a fair amount of country-and-western on this album, and in many respects *Beggars Banquet* is as art-conscious as *Satanic Majesties.* Just proves again the old rule: you never really go back, because no matter how hard you try, you can't ignore where you've just been. The album is eclectic: new and old, art and rock-n-roll. And it's great.

"Stray Cat Blues" is right out or urban rhythm and blues: sex on the sly with a fifteen-year old piece of young blood, teen-aged jailbate. One simple metaphor, the old Jagger aggression, and dirty as hell: you got a friend, wilder than you? Bring her upstairs too! It ain't no hanging matter, even if you are just 13. "Bet your mama don't know you bite like that." You might make the mistake of taking it all seriously if you didn't have something like "Parachute Woman" on the same album. "Parachute Woman" is pop-blues with a pop image and pop sexuality that shows all the art-consciousness of *Satanic Majesties* (or the Who), and undercuts any pretentious "Stray Cat blues" might have to serious, gutty, dangerous porno-violence: "Parachute woman, land on me tonight; Well, I'll break big in New Orleans and overspill in Caroline."

"Dear Doctor" is a country-and-western satire in the tradition of "Under-Assistant West Coast Promotion Man": boy on wedding day "soaking up drink like a sponge" is saved when his honey leaves a note that she's down in Virginia with his cousin Lou "and there'll be no wedding today." Nothing heavy, and as a light, almost comic narrative it's rather un-Stonish.

Like "Salt of the Earth," which gets pretty sentimental: let's drink to the hard working people, the lowly of birth, the salt of the earth! Or like the very C&W "Factory Girl," which is also sentimental: her knees are fat, she wears a scarf instead of a hat, her zipper's broken down the back. Or "No Expectations," which is not only sentimental but imagistic as well. "No Expectations" is a song without aggression—only a quiet understatement quite in keeping with the situation but not at all in keeping with standard Rolling Stones' image. It's very unbluesish, in its form and the regularity of its rhythm and rhyme, in its metamorphic content (water splashing on a stone is beautiful, almost oriental, almost—gasp!—poetic), in its subject matter. It is a song that will stand up very well on paper, printed as a poem. It's arty in an un-self-conscious way, and offers clear evidence that the Stones were far from finished with *Satanic Majesties Request.*

Even further evidence is to be found in the two great songs of *Beggars Banquet,* "Sympathy for the Devil" and "Street Fighting Man." "Sympathy for the Devil" is a curious song to come from Mick Jagger—curious in the devil it presents, its request for sympathy, its allusiveness. This devil is a very civil, urbane, gentlemanly chap, polite as a U.N. diplomat, a man of wealth and taste, one who's been around: "I was there when Christ had his moment of doubt and when Pilate washed his hands, when the tzar was killed in St. Petersburg, during the religious wars and Kennedy's assasination, in the blitzkrieg. Pleased to meet you." What he wants is "courtesy, sympathy, taste." You wonder just what his game is; certainly this is not the devil Jagger's presented us in the past: violent, nasty, uncouth. And just as certainly this sprightly little theatrical tidbit undercuts Jagger's satanism the same way the pop of "Parachute Woman" undercuts the sex of "Stray Cat Blues." You can have either the sophistication of "Sympathy for the Devil" and "Parachute Woman," or the simple strength of devil-Jagger and "Stray Cat Blues," but mix them together and you get very heavy, very arty ironies.

Finally there's "Street-Fighting Man," a great song, the Stones' best ever, better even than "Satisfaction," better than "No Expectations" and "Brown Sugar" and "Honkey Tonk Women." It's good, howlin', hell-raisin' rock-n-roll on the one hand. On the other, it's a statement on the *nature* of rock-n-roll, on the Stones, on musical as social revolution. The Birchers have this great fear that rock somehow perverts American youth, peddling sex and drugs and revolution in its lyrics. Periodically they mount a concerted effort to take the revolution and sex and drug songs off the air and play "clean rock-n-roll." But there just ain't no clean rock, something they sense but never really articulate: as a form of music, rock is revolutionary, far more revolutionary, in fact, than all the political movements of the sixties. If you want to know just who changed the consciousness of American (and British) youth during the decade of the sixties, forget Abbie Hoffman and Bobby Seal. It was the Stones and Dylan and the Beatles and Chuck Berry. And they did it as much with music as with words (although there is a lot of sex, drugs, and revolution in their lyrics). Like the devil, standing in the shadows at St. Petersburg as the czar was killed. Don't matter what the song's about—you got good rock-n-roll, you got a revolution.

The Stones know all this better than anyone else except, perhaps, Bob Dylan, and in this song they let you know they know: "What can a poor boy do, 'cept to sing for a rock-n-roll band?" No matter whether the song is about *fighting* in the streets or *dancing* in the streets (the allusion is to Martha and the Vandellas' "Dancing in the Streets"); you got the singing, you got the social revolution . . . and social revolutions are always so much more permanent than political revolutions.

After *Beggars Banquet* the Stones produced a number of important songs: "Midnight Rambler," "Honky Tonk Women," "Wild Horses," "Dead Flowers," "Brown Sugar." They've also copped a great single

The Poetry of Rock

from Chuck Berry—"Little Queenie," all of these songs are more or less standard rhythm-and-blues style rock-n-roll. There's a string of drug songs through here—"Sister Morphine," most prominent among them—and some good basic blues. But for the most part turn-of-the-decade Stones continued the guarded experimentation and innovation that marked *Beggars Banquet,* coupled with a new nightmare vision of hate, brutality, violence and death.

Take "Dead Flowers." It's the old rich girl-poor boy story with a touch of drugs and a magnificent juxtaposition of images: dead flowers and roses. The ragged singer and queen of the underground may owe something to the Dylan of *Blonde on Blonde,* but what's most impressive about this lyric is pure Stones: the ambiguity of life and death emblemized in dead flowers for the living, roses for the dead. "Midnight Rambler," another recent Stones hit, takes the sexual slippin' and slidin' of rhythm-and-blues and combines it with some pure Stones pornoviolence to produce something both old and new. Neither song is at all pleasant. You notice this about later Stones: the further they go, the more violent they get, mirroring the degenerating western culture of the late sixties and early seventies, reflecting the fascination so evident in our tastes in films with the grotesque, the violent, the horrorific. Like "Let It Bleed": "you knifed me in my filthy, dirty basement, with that jaded, faded junky nurse." Like "You Can't Always Get What You Want": "In her glass was a bleeding man." Like "Wild Horses": "Let's do some living after we die." This dark vision is neither rhythm-and-blues nor rock (which was basically affirmative, beautiful, exciting music). It is late sixties, after-the-Lincoln-Park-massacre, post-Altamont nightmare surrealism. In setting themselves up as embodiments of sociological movements, the Stones forced themselves to reflect the nightmare that was the late sixties-early seventies, a grotesque reality reflected in movies like *Clockwork Orange* and *The Exorcist.*

All this comes to a head in "Brown Sugar." If "Street Fighting Man" is not the Stones' greatest song for the reasons I mentioned, then "Brown Sugar" has to be. For one, it's just a great rocker: good beat, you can dance up a hurricane to it. For another, it brings the Stones' earlier sexuality up to date. For a third, it manages a delicate tonal balance between satire and straight-forward nasties. Finally, it has that one great image: brown sugar. All that Eldridge Cleaver had to say about racism and sexuality in *Soul on Ice,* all the perversion of Victorian underground pornography, all the suppressed desires and sexual hangups of a very sexually hung-up age, all the youth-adult attractions of *The Graduate,* all in one image: brown sugar. "How cum you taste so good?"

72

As the seventies set in in earnest, the Stones seemed confused, uncertain, perplexed, and—most of all—tamed. The mindless, overwhelming, violent aggression of the earlier sixties, the decadent perversion of *Let It Bleed* and *Sticky Fingers* began to fail. What appeared on earlier albums to be parody of country proved a legitimate serious C&W side to the Stones. Elements of big band music cropped up on certain singles. The quality of lyrics declined: "Angie," a much-promoted single from *Goat's Head Soup* is as far from "Brown Sugar" as *Soup* is from *Fingers*. Things like "Star Star" (with its chorus of "star, fuckin' star, fuckin' star") and "Turd On the Run" sound like bad parodies of bad John Lennon or worse Jefferson Airplane. The albums are there: *Goats Head Soup, Exile on Main Street, Hot Rocks* and *More Hot Rocks;* the singles are not.

In a 1971 review of *Sticky Fingers,* Griel Marcus wrote, "when these options of smack and a sexual sneer are closed off the Stones will no longer be singing about them, because true to their name, they are not much for nostalgia, and they don't look back." With 1972, 1973, 1974 it was obvious that smack and the sexual sneer were as gone as flower power, political revolution, and sexual decadence. Nothing was in—a bland, frightened, frightening nothing. The Stones toured in 1972. Robert Christgau wrote:

> But the Stones who are touring the country right now are—almost—good guys. They are less arrogant, less gleefully greedy, and more clearly concerned that their tiny portion of utopia—concerts for their still-expanding audience—be achieved as fairly and efficiently as possible.

Demythologized Stones, it seems, were no Stones at all. What *It's Only Rock'n Roll* indicates remains to be seen; in one sense the album is a frank admission of what Bob Dylan learned a decade earlier: deified rockers can't no way live up to the expectations such beatification raises. It's only rock-n-roll, after all. In another sense the album seems to recognize the passing of one Stage of Stones: "Time waits for no one, and he won't wait for me," sings Jagger in an eerily mellow lyric. Where the Stones go after time has passed, where rock goes after time has passed, remains to be seen.

CHAPTER V
THE DOORS

In his brief but colorful career, Jim Morrison provoked a wide variety of critical responses. Jon Landau didn't much like him, and didn't much mind saying so: "Take the Doors. To me they sum up what a completely dead end this side of popular music is. Their lyrics are invariably pretense. They are cast in the mold of poetry, but what they really are is posturing and attitudinizing." Albert Goldman *did* like the group and also didn't mind saying so: "The finest of these West Coast groups is the Doors . . . They produce a purifying catharsis that leaves their audiences shaken but surer in themselves." Other comments ranged from "Jim Morrison: poet and musician" to "the American Mick Jagger" to "pure pretentious bullshit." Few people ever agreed on the Doors. Harvey Perr, writing in the *L.A. Free Press,* stated most clearly the cause of their variety of opinion: "The art of the Doors is, more and more, removed from those standards of art by which rock music is measured. It is, therefore, understandable that the Doors keep getting the worst imaginable reviews."

And when you get right down to it, Morrison was not the average rock-n-roller. In reviewing the Doors' first post-Morrison album, Alec Dubro went so far as to say, "Morrison never struck me as an authentic rock and roller. There was not enough joy to his music, and too much a sense of its being a strenuous way out of a set of problems, or, for all his genuine unhappiness, a defiant pose." Little was clear about either the man or his music or his commitment. Goldman, for one, praised it as total, but the variety of Morrison's interests—film, stage, music, poetry—bespeaks a certain shallowness or at least a dispersal of energies. Indications are that he was at the moment of his death tired of his old image as psychopath and exhibitionist and searching frantically and perhaps desperately for a new self. Morrison died not on the California shore, but in Paris, France, where, according to his manager, "he'd found some peace and happiness and worked L.A. out of his system. It may be heard to understand, but it was hard to live here in Los Angeles and live what everybody thought he was." The love-hate relationship of

The Poetry of Rock

his "L.A. Woman" was very much autobiographical. Apparently his commitment to the role of aggressive, exhibitionist, sexual rock star, while at first undeniably whole-hearted, degenerated as his twenties wore on into an act he found confining. "Jim just couldn't get away from the part he was acting," a friend said after his death.

Then there was the confusion surrounding his assorted arrests for molesting a stewardess (not convicted), or exhibitionism in Miami (guilty and appealed) and in New Haven, Connecticut (acquitted). According to one story, the New Haven bust, his first, was police retaliation for Morrison's on-stage behavior, which was his own retaliation for some back-stage hassling. What was real, what was stage? In later years even his off-stage public behavior became increasingly mechanical: "It got to a point of his having a technique . . . It was all so conscious." Many pieces of the later Doors play like formulaic reruns of the psycho-mythic theatrical pastiches of the early albums, and on later albums you find a turn to blues and to non-Freudian, non-mythic imagistic poetry. My own feeling is that James Morrison was about to flower at the moment of his death . . . but that his flowering would have been theatrical or poetic, not musical. In fact, when you come right down to it, the music of a Doors piece is just not that important: it's the poetry and the theater that make most of them run.

In any event, whatever Morrison meant to the Doors, his death left the group suspended and enervated, nerveless in a sea of formulaic passion and coolwhip music. The best work of the Doors is on those early albums—the earlier the better.

The group took its name from Huxley's title *The Doors of Perception,* with perhaps a passing reference to Blake's remark that "there are things that are unknown, and things that are unknown; in between are doors." As a group, these Doors opened to us those areas of our personality—the libido, the id—which civilization has sealed off from our conscious examination. As such they were well within the mainstream of rock traditions: the Rolling Stones in their psychological character analyses, Dylan in his own nightmare visions, the Beatles, the Grateful Dead, the Procol Harum all dealt at times with that terrible psychological reality which surfaces only in our dreams and tabloid crime. But the Doors focused steadily on these themes and elevated libidinous patterns of behavior to mythic drama. Morrison's own background was in poetry and the classics at UCLA, and he kept in constant touch with contemporary theater, and he thought of rock in dramatic terms:

> In its origin the Greek Theater was a band of worshipers, dancing and singing on a threshing floor at the crucial agricultural, seasons. Then, one day, a possessed person leaped out of the

crowd and started imitating a god. At first it was pure song and movement. As cities developed, more people became dedicated to making money, but they had to keep contact with Nature somehow. So they had actors do it for them. I think rock serves the same function and may become a kind of theater.

Certainly rock has in some respects become theater: *Tommy; Jesus Christ, Superstar; Hair,* the *Rocky Horror Picture Show;* Alice Cooper. Not the type of theater Morrison envisioned, but definitely a form of theater akin in many respects to what Morrison had done. Albert Goldman recognized this element of performance in the Doors and commented upon it early:

> The Doors need to be heard in their own milieu. They really do belong to the misty littoral of Southern California, facing the setting sun and leading a hippie tribe in their shamanistic rites. One can see Jim Morrison in the centre of the circle, his finely chiseled features framed in flowing Dionysian hair, his hands clutching, his mouth almost devouring the mike, as he chants with closed eyes the hallucinatory verses of "The End."

Central to the Doors' brand of rock was performance—performance which served to reveal new realities, performance which set them apart from the standards by which most rock was evaluated, performance to which they sometimes sacrificed both music and poetry. Performance which threatened to and perhaps actually did devour Morrison whole.

The songs of the Doors, then, are frequently adjuncts to performances of a kind of msycho-mythic drama; their poetry is often little more than a script. At least this is true of their most familiar, most often analysed, most memorable work: "The End," "Moonlight Drive," "When the Music's Over," "The Soft Parade," "Celebration of the Lizard," "Riders On the Storm," perhaps in a certain light even "Light My Fire" and "L.A. Woman." Invariably these lyrics run a course of more or less explicit Freudian porno-violence, allude with more or less subtlety to Oedipal and Electral complexes, then end in perversion distilled to a very few primitive and highly suggestive images.

"The End," earliest of such songs, is in many respects the most superficial, its Freudianism so overt, its sexuality most surface. Not inexplicably, Morrison's performance of this particular drama at the Whiskey-A-Go-Go led to the group's expulsion. Its title is vaguely apocalyptic, but you're never quite sure just what's ending: life itself? a drug trip? a sexual encounter? innocence? all of these? none of these? Each is hinted at by different elements of the lyric: two by Morrison's chant of "kill, kill, kill, kill, fuck, fuck, fuck, fuck"; one by the Oedipal conversation recorded toward its conclusion; the last in the psychological depths reached by snakes and lakes, killers and the ancient gallery. Sophomoric, perhaps, but in person Morrison carried it off quite well. "Come on, baby, take a chance with us," Morrison urged, a busride to the subconscious and to oblivion, to self-knowledge and mythic terrors, to fucking and killing brothers and sisters and fathers and mothers. Probably "the End" is better music than poetry, better theater than music, an amorphous form from which Morrison could build as the whims of a particular performance moved him, a script to be interpreted and reinterpreted, with much room for adlibbing.

"Moonlight Drive" is a shorter piece in the same vein, but a better poem. Here the invitation is to "swim to the Moon," to "climb through the tide," both sexual images with just a hint of death by suicidal drowning. The combination of sex and death is, of course, nothing new to either rock or poetry, although Morrison touched a very deep-seated nerve in all of our psyches, and it works well. The second-to-last stanza was especially vivid:

> It's easy to love you
> As I watch you glide
> We're falling through wet forests
> On our moonlight drive.

The forests of the sea, made more unworldly and strange in the eerie moonlight, suggest the surrealism of a drug trip (which the song is certainly not about) and the strange ecstacies of sex. The image combines Lucy floating downstream with Alice falling down her rabbit hole with water as a common sexual image. It takes the couple, parked beside the ocean for a late night bit of uh huh, deep into their subconscious selves. There is just a hint of death, and one is reminded vaguely of those last lines of Eliot's "Prufrock":

> We have lingered in the chambers of the sea
> By sea-girls wreathed with seaweed red and brown
> Till human voices wake us, and we drown.

The final lines are a poetic as well as a sexual come-down, with their insistence on a couple literally parked by the shore and a realistic, vulgar lay: "going down, down, down." That sort of nonsense ruins a song, as it wrecks a poem—but it need not necessarily have destroyed Morrison's on-stage performance.

The best of the Doors' efforts in this psycho-mythic drama was a long piece titled "Celebration of the Lizard," and subtitled "lyrics to a theatre composition by the Doors" on the album jacket of *Waiting for the Sun,* produced by the group in 1968. The lyrics trace the flight of Lizard King out of the city's heart and south across the border to Mexico, where he resurrects himself (sexual implications fully intended) in those recesses of the human mind so often explored by the Doors. Snakes, rain, minister's daughters, highways and shores—they are all there in proper Morrison-Doors stage positions. Mr. Mojo was risin! Thinking back in 1972, Harvey Peer wrote, "not that he [Morrison] wasn't capable of the old theatrical excitement, as he proved in one electrifying moment when he disappeared from the stage for a few minutes, then showed up, suddenly in a blue flame (all right, so it was only a blue light shining on him!), above the audience's head (on the scaffold left over from the HAIR set), growling out 'The Celebration of the Lizard.' For me it was the personal pleasure of seeing what Morrison could really do . . . .''

But the psycho-mythic narrative was prone to unraveling: "the Soft Parade" (1969), from the album by the same title, became so diffuse and subtle as to lose its focus. Morrison begins as a seminary student denying that the Lord can be petitioned with prayer, and in general revolt against his calling. In desperation he runs seeking sanctuary/asylum, and ends up with mini skirts, candy, and a girl named Sandy. How to get himself straight? He sleeps, travels, heads for the hills, loves his neighbor "till his wife gets home." Perversion follows perversion as the heretic seminarian progresses through catacombs, nursery bones, women carrying babies to the river, cobra and leopard people hunting deer women in silk dresses who love it. The scene is very L.A., very *La Dulce Vita,* very decadent, although it's been done better in any one of half a dozen films. And Morrison's pun on *god* and *dogs* (who are called upon to rescue this damned crowd) does not enhance the lyric's sophistication appreciably.

"The Soft Parade" ends in typical Doors fashion:

When all else fails, we can whip the horses' eyes
And make them sleep and cry.

But nothing here connects with anything else. The long montage will not make it, even in a free-association sense, and the lyric is unjustifiably prosey. In the last analysis, "the Soft Parade" offers less insight into the magic of Doors' theater, than a key to its failure: the drama is ultimately a dead-end process, for one soon runs out of myths and characters, and loses himself easily in loose connections.

The obvious solution to this dead end was to try something less grandiose, bite off smaller pieces of the grand theme and examine them more closely in smaller, tighter lyrics. Or you might apply the technique of theater to non-mythic plots, to themes other than those from Jung or Freud. The first is precisely what Morrison does in his shorter myth pieces; the second is attempted in longer lyrics like "L.A. Woman."

The Poetry of Rock

The most striking aspect of the Doors' short lyrics is the frequency with which a few key images reoccur: water, masks, strangers, crystal, night, highways, horses, snakes, fire, eyes, earth, forests, wind, all those images of boundaries -- doorways, shorelines, the edge of town, the outskirts of the city. Some are sexual: fire, water, snakes, and the whole host of phallic symbols. Some appear simply because they have a primeval quality that takes us back to those days of worshippers dancing and singing on a threshing floor. Others are images for the demonic, the subconscious, unexplored realities to which the Doors are trying to take us: strangers and strangeness, doorways and shores, masks and highways. Some come from classical theater, some from standard psychology. They weave their way in and out of the Doors' best short lyrics creating complex webs of meaning. In this sense every Doors lyric comments on every other Doors lyric. In the context of several lyrics, one image takes on a variety of connotative meanings. Water, for example, means many things to Morrison. Of course it is sexual, constantly sexual, overwhelmingly sexual, as in "Moonlight Drive." But because water is sexual, and sexual experience is primeval and mythic and forbidden, and the Doors are initiating us into the world of the primeval and mythic and forbidden, water also becomes a symbol for the new and the unexperienced. "The rainman's comin' to town," sing the Doors in "L'America", "He'll change your weather, change your luck, he'll even teach you how to find yourself." "Outlaws live by the side of a lake," sing the Doors in "Not to Touch the Earth." And in "Yes the River Knows" come these lines, combining the drunkeness of water with the drunkeness of wine: "I promised I would drown myself in mystic heated wine." "Follow me across the sea," sings Morrison in "Tell All the People." But this new world is also dangerous; insofar as a new awareness destroys old preconceptions, it threatens death and destruction. "Breathe under water until the end, free fall flow river, on and on it goes," sings Morrison in "Yes the River Knows." The ladies "Soft Parade" are carrying babies down to the river . . . for baptism or for death? or for both? And the rain of "Riders on the Storm" is as apocalyptic as the howling wind of Dylan's "All Along the Watch Tower." Death, rebirth, sexuality—water means a great many things in Doors lyrics.

So also do other images. Earth usually symbolizes the common, the ordinary; wind usually connotes passion or apocalypse; forests are sexual. Night and day carry their usual symbolic significations, although Morrison and his crew clearly prefer the night. Snakes are phallic, and horses usually carry their Freudian connotation of raw, masculine, sexual power. Eyes and masks: the face of the seer and the see-er, the cold, penetrating, emotionless gaze of the prophet. And blue, Mary's blue, the blue of water and the sky. Blue is an amorphous image in the Doors' songs, sometimes carrying its traditional connotations of faith and potentiality, often alligned with water to connote death, and/or sexuality, sometimes used in the old sense of "feelin' blue." "Wishful crystal water covers everything in blue," sings Morrison in a Robbie Krieger lyric, "Wishful Sunful." "Can't fight the runnin' blues," sings Morrison in "Runnin' Blues," a lament for Otis Redding. "Wintertime winds—blue and freezin'," sings Morrison in "Wintertime Love." And round and round the albums swirl in an imagistic kaleidoscope of meanings and submeanings.

Three lyrics present themselves as the quintessence of early Doors' technique: "Horse Latitudes," "Twentieth Century Fox," and "Crystal Ship." The first is a free verse poem, read to an atonal cacophony which builds gradually to a deafening crescendo, approximately the terror of the horse . . . and poet and audience. It is a free verse poem; in fact, the Doors' songbook offers no music at all for it. It records with almost photographic detail that awkward instant when ships caught in the dead of the doldrums jettison their cargo of horses to take advantage of the very minimal breezes available. So visual is it that it reminds one of that graphic description of "Pharoah's horses" popular half a century ago. The first three lines are all one clause, long and uninterrupted by the pauses of rhyme. They conclude with the rhythmically static line, "True sailing is dead." Then there's the description of the horse's death, a description of an instant which seems an hour, a description made more vivid by breaking one line into four, and by the imagery of a line like "stiff green gallop." A fine miniature on its own, the piece related in many respects to the Doors' other themes and songs. For one thing, it focuses on the perverse: "sullen and aborted," "tiny monsters," "mute nostril agony." For another, its images of horses and water are found throughout other Doors' lyrics. And finally there is the insight into human nature: the sea may breed its own monsters, but man has a nasty one or two in his own self. The sea kills sailing; man kills the horse. Insofar as the horse represents a part of man's own nature, his sexual self perhaps, the poem becomes even more poignant: ourselves we kill, our selves we "carefully refine and seal over."

"Twentieth Century Fox" is more a song than "Horse Latitudes": it has a melody and rhythm and rhyme. But it is also very much an imagistic poem. There is more overt satire in this song than one finds in most Doors' lyrics, and the fox is not so overtly Freudian as snakes and horses. Nevertheless, D. H. Lawrence found the fox an appropriate symbol for sexual longings, and certainly the Doors work off the fox as predator in this song. It's a brilliant image, carrying a variety of associtions: sexual appetite, woman the huntress, the tinsel glamor of Twentieth Century Fox films. And there's the pun here on *fox* and *fucks* (listen to Morrison sing the song). Then, in addition to the fox, come clocks, plastic, and box, with their connotations of artificial, wind-up, *Playboy* sex. Added to all this is the sarcasm of *fashionably* lean and *fashionably* late and "she's no drag." And on top of that is the rhyme of "No tears, no fears,/No ruined years," accentuating Morrison's sarcasm. And on top of that there's the jaunty, sassy, rhythmic music of the chorus. A fine piece, this, and while it's not really in the mainstream of Doors' psycho-mythic theater, it may be one of the best things the group ever did.

Late in his career with the Doors, Jim Morrison seemed to be working away from the psycho-mythic theater of his earlier work and into imagistic poetry. The two are not utterly divorced, as I've suggested: the grand themes of his longer mythic dramas can be broken to pieces easily manageable in imagistic poetry. And the dramatic pieces were imagistic, and something like "Twentieth Century Fox" and "Horse Latitudes," early Doors lyrics, suggest a poetic talent even during the group's early years. Not every cut on those first albums runs to eleven minutes! As the sexuality necessary to psycho-mythic drama became increasingly formulaic and more and more of a drag, Morrison reached in two directions: toward the short poem and toward longer pieces that were not archetypal or Jungian or Freudian. *Morrison Hotel* represents Morrison's lyric comments on a variety of topics. "Peace Frog" treats the "blood in the streets" as a new nation appeared to be emerging in the late sixties. In a statement more characteristic of W. B. Yeats or Phil Ochs than James Morrison, he commented "Blood will be born in the birth of a nation, blood is the rose of mysterious union." That's a political statement, no mistake about it.

But "Miss Magic M'Gill" is a character sketch, pure and simple. "Ship of Fools" is partly political, mostly a put-down of folks who, tired of "hangin' out, hangin' up and hangin' down, hangin' in and holdin' fast," climb aboard a new ship in hopes of keeping themselves together. "You Make Me Real" is a love song, much softer and very different from older Doors lyrics in its implication that simple, romantic, honest-to-goodness basic human love is what makes one free and happy. "Land Ho!" is the old tale of the sea and man's need to escape every now and again—mythic in the old romantic business about freedom and the sea and "ports unread," but not in the way we're accustomed to the Doors using myth. "Queen of the Highway" concerns the way highway queens and blind tigers of the road get married, settle down, and begin the cycle all over by producing the new American Boy and the All American Girl. And so on.

Obviously this is a different breed of Doors album: the old psycho-mythic themes are softened in some cases, absent from many lyrics, altered or replaced in still others. The Doors are overtly political. And there are other lyrics as well, each one short, concise, focused. In a couple of cases the lyric has been distilled to a slogan to almost nothing: "I love you the best, better than the rest." You'd almost think the Doors had grown old.

L. A. Woman, the Doors last album with Jim Morrison, is a real mixed bag. On the one hand it contains "Riders on the Storm," a toned-down piece of mythic theater based on the story of "the Demon Lover," about a girl who deserts husband and children to run off with her former lover—only to discover that he's a demon and she's damned. It combines old Doors images and a real sense of apocalypse with the traditional myth of the unfaithful woman. Also reminiscent of older Doors styles are things like "Love Her Madly" with its horses and deep blue dreams, and "Hyacinth House" with its brand new friends and lions. Neither measures up to earlier work. A song like "L'America" is something of an application of older techniques to political narrative, producing a mythic narrative about the regeneration of a country by "friendly strangers" come to town. Most noteworthy, however, are the songs in the blues form, and "L.A. Woman," an application of older Doors techniques to social commentary.

This is a heavy blues album. "Been Down So Long," despite the by-line crediting the Doors and Morrison with composition, is standard, very conventional blues:

Well I been down so goddam long that it looks like up to me.
Well I been down so goddam long that it looks like up to me.
Yeah, why don't one of you people come on and set me free.

The confinement in prison and the later plea for sex are compatible with Doors style, but basically they're blues. So too is both the image and form of "Crawling King Snake":

Well, I'm a crawling king snake in the room I've been.
Well, I'm a crawling king snake in the room I've been.
Well, no messin' with my mate, goin' to use her for myself.

"Cars Hiss By My Window" also uses the blues form, although theme and imagery are closer to earlier Doors style. Here is a music not much explored by the Doors on earlier albums, although it is certainly compatible with their psycho-mythic sexuality, and it may well have been that had Morrison remained alive the group would have turned in a blues direction.

Or it might have continued its development into social-political themes. "L.A. Woman" is a song in just such a vein, and it's the finest on this album. One thinks immediately of Morrison's own love-hate relationship with Los Angeles, which has found its way into this lyric: Los Angeles is this L.A. woman. The anthropomorphizing of the city is a stroke of genius on the Doors' part: it allows them to infuse the song with typical sexuality while maintaining an essentially sociological theme: "cops in cars, topless bars, never saw a woman so alone." The light/night dichotomy, long a Doors' staple, is perfectly appropriate to Los Angeles, as is the vaguely mythical sexuality of "Mister Mojo risin'." "The world began in Eden, but it ended in Los Angeles," wrote Phil Ochs, one also familiar with the southern California scene. "L.A. is a great big freeway, put $100 down and buy a car," sang Dionne Warwick. For the Doors the area becomes a city of night inhabited by lonely, lost angels (pun intended) with the blues. Nevertheless, the Doors love it. Poetically the lyric exhibits a genuine facility with rhythm (as in the opening two lines), alliteration ("lucky little lady in the city of light" or "motel money murder madness"), and rhyme ("cops in cars, topless bars"). It's a fine song, clearly Doors in style and conception, yet not tied specifically to the psycho-mythic theater which could wear so thin.

James Morrison died on July 3, 1971. The Doors' next album was titled *Other Voices,* although the featured voice was that of Robby Krieger, guitarist, who had in fact produced some earlier Doors lyrics. Despite its title, the album was a collection of reruns: not old songs, but new songs in the old style. With none of the reverse, the bite, or the variety toward which the group—under Morrison's direction or, at the very least, with Morrison's presence—had been working toward. The lyrics are vaguely sentimental and tend to rework tired themes in tired ways. The philosophies sound second hand and very banal . . . like the images. The vocals were bad. Trends which continued, I might add, on the group's next album, *Full Circle.* The group was on its way to becoming a rock group, just another rock group with poetical aspirations which could not be realized and made their music all the thinner. One gets little sense of myth of theater. In short, since Morrison's death the group has not sustained itself, has fallen into the mire of soft romanticism which has claimed so many of rock's best heads in the early seventies. Whether Morrison would have sustained the group or not is a mood question; the Doors are now dead. R.I.P.

CHAPTER VI
THE WHO

"A group that was nurtured in gimmickry," wrote Alfred Aronowitz of the Who in a *Rolling Stone* review headlined, incidentally, "*Tommy* Does Not Vindicate Them." Well, yes and no. On the one hand, Mod's flamboyant consumerism and preoccupation with kiddie kulture seem at a decade's distance vacuous, bogus, adolescent; it undermines the deliberately Mod stance of the early Who. On the other hand, *Tommy* did in fact vindicate the group. Say what you want about Keith Moon's disintegrating drums and Pete Townshend's smashed guitars, about contrived aggression on stage, about narcissism and showmanship, about 150 a week on clothes—this group has played the Kennedy Center for the Performing Arts. There is more here than meets the eye.

And that more has been precisely *Tommy*—and, more recently, *Quadrophenia,* perhaps the most important album of the 1970s.

"Happy Jack," "My Generation," "I Can See for Miles." *The Who Sell Out,* an album complete with Radio London spots and Who commercials for baked beans and underarm deodorant. This was the early Who, the Who of the sixties, the Mod Who, all gilt and flash, musical embodiment of that great rebellion of working class youth from which England has not yet recovered. Leisure, youth, speed, consumption, multiplicity, throw away: these were the values of Mod and the values of the Who. Not much in the way of hard work, deliberation, conservation. Instruments deliberately destroyed after each performance; clothes bought to be worn once, twice and tossed away; underplayed sexuality; Entwistel's passivity, Daltrey's aggression; all tied the Who to a social revolution of which the group became as much a part as a reflection. More than consumer fads, the French fashions, Italian motor bikes, pills and music were the quintessence of Mod, the Who the quintessence of Mod music. So the smashed guitars and flamboyant kineticism can be explained as more than gimmickry; they were a commitment to a social revolution quite as significant as the Free Speech Movement or the Civil Rights Movement across the Atlantic. "Talkin' about my generation, hope I die before I get old."

The Who were important for reasons other than their embodiment of social values, however. "My Generation" is musically interesting in the way it builds a rock song without benefit of a lyric guitar. Theatrically the Who were even then in a league of their own, unmatched by the Stones then or Alice Cooper since. Poetically they managed some middle weight material in "Substitute," and "Pictures of Lily." As much social and sexual commentary as legitimate poetry, such lyrics point the way to *Tommy* and *Quadrophenia* in a way that "Happy Jack" and "My Generation" do not. And, although they will certainly not rank the Who with the Beatles or Stones, they are competent rock poems.

What gained Pete Townshend his status among the rock poets was his "rock opera," *Tommy*. Let it be said, first off, that *Tommy* has its defects: its mythology is thin, its perceptions are frequently shallow, its music is exhausting but uneven and at times repetitious (many of *Tommy's* best riffs had appeared earlier in Who songs). *Tommy* will not compare with *Sgt. Peppers, The Messiah, I Pagliacci,* or *Iolanthe.* Yet it's important in rock history because it solves some purely technical problems raised by album-length work, and because it stands largely alone in its achievement. You can't ignore a dinosaur, especially if it's the first and finest of a very few dinosaurs.

For although this work made the idea of a "rock opera" quite popular, most extended works since *Tommy* have been closer to musicals than whatever *Tommy* is (in form it seems closer to an oratorio than an opera). *Hair* lacks *Tommy's* coherence, and *Jesus Christ, Superstar* lacks its predecessor's insight and sophistication, although it has a superior mythic center. (For all the complaints about *Tommy's* fuzzy edges, you never do know just what "Jesus Christ Superstar,/Who are you, what have you sacrificed?" is supposed to mean.) Jethro Tull's *Passion Play* never achieved much popularity. *The Rocky Horror Picture Show* is a cabaret piece. Shorter efforts—the suite technique used by Stephen Stills, Elton John, Cat Stevens, Carole King—have proven more popular and, I think, more aesthetically pleasing, but they lack *Tommy's* scope.

And so there remains the Who's *Tommy*.

The oratorio is not without ancestors, however, both in the Who's repertoire and elsewhere in rock. *Pepper's* and its progeny had already developed the album as a more or less linear progression of songs, and by 1969 the idea of the concept album was well established. Dramatic monologues have always been popular as songs (the Who had done several themselves), and dialogue within a lyric—rock or otherwise—is not uncommon. The Doors had for some time been toying with the theatrical potentialities of rock. Out of these beginnings came the form of *Tommy*.

Gradually. The oratorio did not emerge full blown from the head of Pete Townshend; we can trace its development and growth back to the early Who. On the *My Generation* album the Who did a short lyric titled

"La-La-La-Lies," which concerns itself with an apparently abortive attempt at seduction recounted in first person by the husband/boy friend of the seducee as he puts down the unsuccessful seducor. "How can I be lost," he crows, "when I've still got my woman?" There is not much here to suggest the complexities of *Tommy,* but here are (1) a dramatic situation, (2) dialogue, and (3) the triangle so important to Tommy's catatonia. From "La-La-La-Lies," the Who progressed to "A Quick One While He's Away" on their next album (*A Quick One* in England, *Happy Jack* in the U.S.). In her *Rock Encyclopedia,* Lillian Roxon called this lyric "a very complicated twelve-minute rock opera," although it may be slightly shorter and less complicated than she suggested. It is the story of a lonely wife, Ivor the engine driver, an illicit child, and a quick one while he's gone. All is forgiven (in fact forgiveness rolls like a baroque seven-fold *Amen* through the lyric's last minute and a half), as the wronged husband accepts human frailty and transcends his instincts. The song divides musically and lyrically into distinct segments, each with its own tempo, combination of voices and solos, and instrumentation. The dramatic situation is more complex than that of "La-La-La-Lies," a variety of characters has been introduced, and the segmentation of an oratorio has set in.

From "A Quick One" to *Tommy* is merely a matter of scale, and if there is one thing evolution teaches, it is that scale is more easily changed than form. Given the oratorio form, in miniature, Townshend's fertile genius easily moved from twelve minutes to two discs, 4 sides. The result is a legitimate tour-de-force: classically formal archetectonics (an overture, for example, to state most of the major musical motifs); elaborate and delicate orchestration of individual performers; incorporation of a variety of themes, ranging from the teachings of Meher Baba to Townshend's personal belief that music can effect the boy independent of the normal auditory mechanisms. The whole is flavored by Mod in general, and more particularly by the relationship between Mod audience and Mod rock group. In content if not in form, *Tommy* is a monument to the social scene of sixties' England.

Tommy concerns itself, as almost anyone who has seen the movie or bought one of two separate performances on record can tell you, with the childhood experiences and resultant personal aberrations of Tommy Walker. As a veritable child Tommy sees his father murder his mother's lover, and is told by his frightened parents, "You didn't hear it/You didn't see it/You won't say nothing to no one." Tommy does not: he withdraws into catatonia, saying nothing to nobody about nothin'. Initially this withdrawal liberates Tommy into a magical world of his own beautiful thoughts and emotions. But quickly he becomes a plaything for nasty cousin Kevin ("I'll put glass in your dinner/ And spikes in your seat"), for the Acid Queen ("I'll tear your soul apart"), and perverse uncle Ernie ("Down with the bedclothes,/ Up with the nightshirt,/ Fiddle about, fiddle about"). Tommy's dad worries about him at Christmas: all he does is pick his nose, smile, and play poxy pinball. How can a deaf, dumb, and blind kid ever know Jesus? And if he doesn't know Jesus, how will he be saved? The child's plea to be seen, felt, healed falls on deaf ears, and his retreat into himself is re-enforced by the mistreatment he receives from those around him.

Tommy does, however, develop a facility for playing pinball—here, in fact, is salvation of sorts. Pinball machines do not mistreat Tommy, and they respond to his touch. His withdrawal allows him single-minded concentration and a deft wrist more normal kids lack. Tommy's father, meanwhile, visits an eminent doctor, hopeful of a miracle cure, but is told that the source of Tommy's problems is his "inner block" which no doctor can reach. The block is broken ultimately by the shattering of a mirror into which Tommy has been gazing narcissisticly. Cured, Tommy becomes something of an evangelist pinball wizard, preaching to masses restrained by the same police lines used to restrain rock fans at Who concerts. One disciple, Sally Simpson (one of the Stones' spoiled rich-bitch types), sneaks off from home, rushes the stage to touch her idol (an irony here), is thrown back by the police lines, and receives sixteen stitches and a permanent scar to remind her of the concert. Tommy, oblivious to reality, carries smugly on. Obviously something has happened to the child: he shows as little love for others as Kevin, Ernie, and the Acid Queen showed him. In "Tommy's Holiday Camp" he and Ernie brutalize his legions: "So put in your ear plugs, put on your shades, and you know where to put the cork." Finally Tommy's fans leave him ("We forsake you, gonna rape you") and he retreats to his former withdrawal, pleading once more for feeling, touching, healing, rejoicing in his self, his music, his opinions, his story.

The central concern of *Tommy* is the development of the individual in modern society, although subthemes radiate from its core in myriad and at times contradictory directions. In the one sense, for example, Tommy is Everyman, and the narrative an allegory of any sensitive child confronting the perverse, hostile, brutal world in which we all live. Tommy's discovery of salvation in his own mirrored image emblematizes nicely the turning inward of modern youth, their neo-romantic individualism; that he should at the same instant reach out to others so pathetically reflects youth's perhaps naive demand for love and attention. Tommy is the paradoxically jaded and innocent child of a paradoxical age. On the other hand, Tommy also represents those rock deities fabricated almost daily by record companies, the press, radio and television, but most of all youth itself; in this respect Tommy is scarcely an Everyman. The relationship between Sally Simpson and Tommy, for example, is that between adoring teeny-bopper and remote superstar. She and Tommy are "worlds apart," and significantly they do not touch—despite the heavy irony that Tommy's text is "come unto me, love will find a way." What we have here is a failure to communicate, the failure of rock musician to meet rock fan.

The motif of the rock performance surfaces once again in the album, just before its ambiguous conclusion. Turned off by the demands imposed upon them by their mortal god, Tommy's fans turn on him, forsaking him, raping him, consigning him ultimately to the worst death of all, oblivion: "Let's forget you better still!" In *Revolt into Style,* George Melly has written of the pop hero:

> My feeling then is that the love and fury is not resentment as such, but something more primitive; a religious impulse; the need to sacrifice the Godhead in order to elevate it above temporal considerations. And just because the overt emphasis is sexual rather than spiritual in no way invalidates this argument. Throughout history religious enthusiasm at this level is frequently indistinguishable from sexual hysteria.

> Equally mysterious is the sudden extinction of this dangerous divinity in any one artist or group. Quite suddenly, often in a matter of weeks, the screaming stops, the crowd dissolves, and the artist or artists, often with a certain regret, find it possible to walk unmolested in public places.

The Who turn Tommy into a religious cult hero for obvious reasons: the similarity between rock star and primitive deity works to explain the almost canabalistic ritual in which his followers devour him, destroy him, relegate him to oblivion.

Other themes permeate the oratorio. When Townshend outlines his developing conception of this album to Jann Wenner in *Rolling Stone,* his emphasis was on music as a preconceptual mode of communication:

> But what it's really all about is the fact that because the boy is "DD&B," he's seeing things basically as vibrations which we translate as music. That's really what we want to do: create this feeling that when you listen to the music you can actually become aware of the boy, and aware of what he is all about, because we are creating him as we play.

In "Amazing Journey" Tommy pictures himself as lost in a pleasant world of quiet vibrations and musical dreams, each sensation a note in his symphony. In "Sensation" Tommy sings, "You feel me coming, a new vibration; from afar you'll see me, I'm a sensation." And in "Go to the Mirror," in some of the most well known lines from *Tommy,* his father sings, "Listening to you I get the music, gazing at you I get the heat . . ." "Pinball Wizard" implies a kind of extrasensory perception, a playing-by-vibrations consonant with Townshend's theories. Even after his cure, Tommy communicates more with vibrations than words: what he says to young Sally and his assembled followers is far less important than the vibrations radiating from his person.

The central problem of the oratorio, however, is that this non-verbal communication fails (between Tommy and his father, between Tommy and his audience), either because of its own inherent inadequacies or because of alterations in the character of Tommy himself. In this last respect we are back to the issue of rock star and fan: music functions initially as a bond between the two, as a language that bodies speak and understand. But deification of the performer strains and ultimately destroys that bond: the Beatles claimed, "There are only perhaps a hundred people in the world who know what our music is about." Tommy finds himself estranged from his fans. Even with the strange and supernatural language of music, communication proves impossible.

Another interesting, if minor, theme of Tommy is the peculiar commonality of two generations' experience. Constantly at the back of the Mod mind was the threat of age: inevitably one must grow old, and age did not appear in any way desirable. In at least one respect (his voluntary return to catatonia at the end of his youth and the close of the oratorio) Tommy can be said to treat this issue of age. But the gap between generations, between the old and the young, is not really so great as has been made out. Their experiences are remarkably similar. "The Hawker" posits physical love as a form of salvation, healing, and health: "Every time she starts to lovin' she brings eyesight to the blind . . . She's got the power to heal you, never fear." The entire relationship between Tommy's mother, her husband, and her lover hinges upon the need for love. Both father and mother (and probably lover as well) are reaching out for the same personal relationship Tommy seeks; their attempts are as pathetic and perverse and self-centered as his become; they visit anxiety and stress upon Tommy, as he will offer little more than a gash across the cheek and palpable mistreatment to his followers. Tommy denies reality by retreating into himself; his parents deny reality as well. In fact, the parents' denial is cause of the child's denial. Tommy is in too many respects his parents' progeny for us to escape the obvious implications: perversion is life's inevitable destination, as all attempts to establish healthful, sane, loving relationships end in sickness, insanity, death, and hate. Ultimately you cannot blame the assailants, since ultimately we are all assailants and all victims. The proposition can be extended logically even to Ernie, Kevin, and the Acid Queen, for in each case their brutality grows out of frustrated need for love and companionship: "I've got no one to play with today," Kevin tells Tommy; "Your mind must learn to roam just as the Gypsy Queen must do," the Acid Queen tells Tommy; "Do you think it's alright to leave the boy with Uncle Ernie?" Tommy's mother asks his dad before they leave. The problem is in finding a victim who is not also an assailant. Nobody's pure: *Tommy* is as disturbing in this respect as *A Clockwork Orange.*

Tommy's primary thematic concern is religion: from the father's formalistic Christianity to Tommy's own fundamentalist preaching, religion permeates the libretto. What is significant, however, is the desperate predicament into which religion has fallen: pietistic superstition on the one hand, pop-shlock on the other. Tommy's claim to messianic power is predicated on his ability to play pinball machines: no love here, merely reification of man into machine, mechanical manipulation of bumpers and digit counters. Like the religions of pop and Mod, religion of the pinball machine does not speak to the basic human condition: it offers nothing permanent, nothing living, nothing significant. There is glitter and action, the trappings of significance, but at the core only a vacuum. For all Tommy's teachings about love finding a way, we discover in Tommy neither real love nor "the way" in any sense of the word. The apotheosis of Tommy ("The few I touched are now disciples, love as one, I am the Light") involves a deification of the mechanical, the amoral, the inconsequential, the narcissistic. Tommy has learned only self-love in his catatonic state (it was the mirror that first disenchanted him), and he has not transcended the human condition except to turn himself into machine. He has learned to play pinball, and ultimately the pinball machine will not satisfy his followers. The ear plugs, shades, cork, and Uncle Ernie Tommy offers to his holiday campers are not Tommy's benevolent attempt to bring his followers through his own experiences to his peculiar brand of salvation; rather they are Tommy's abuse of others, Tommy playing Cousin Kevin and Acid Queen. His followers react precisely as he reacted, learning hate and violence, not love and communication. The religious salvation of *Tommy* is that offered by a mere mortal to desperate followers.

Tommy's conclusion is, it seems to me, ambiguous: a retrospective glimpse of Tommy at the height of his powers at the very moment of his return to isolation and anonymity: "Following you I climb the mountain, I get excitement at your feet!" Is this ironic? Does it imply Tommy will rediscover the amazing journey in his new loneliness and regain thereby some of his power? Does it admit the bankruptcy of that power and heat? I don't know. One thing is clear: the beatific vision and the strength Tommy derived from it have not enabled him to communicate the vision to others. Retreat to anonymity, assume the role of victim, and you glimpse salvation; achieve the power and fame prerequisite to spreading the message, and you lose it. The paradox is insoluble, and even if Tommy were to regain his own vision in a new catatonic withdrawal, we can be certain that he will never effectively share it with anyone else. This is the mortal predicament.

Thematically, then, the oratorio is complex and relatively sophisticated in its assessment of modern man and its integration of disparate but related motifs. Thematic subtlety will, in fact, justify the work. Lyrically Townshend's talents are less in evidence. "Cousin Kevin," "The Acid Queen," and especially "Uncle Ernie" are pretty thin as dramatic monologues, failing generally to explore their character as fully as we might wish; they are certainly inferior to Townshend's psychological explorations of *Quadrophenia*. "Christmas" does so much more in this respect, embodying the paradox of faith in love coupled with the inability to love, and hinting at Tommy's father's literalistic Christianity, genuine fear of Judgment Day, and equally genuine fondness for children and Tommy. The dialogue between Tommy's parents and doctor is as thin as "Uncle Ernie," and "Welcome" takes too long to do whatever it tries to do . . . which, as nearly as I can determine, is little more than to offer Tommy's version of "Go ye therefore and teach all nations." Finally there is the problem of the mythic substructure of *Tommy*. *Jesus Christ Superstar* had its myth ready made, and the myth was an important one. That is why, for all its contrivance, theological oversimplification, and general hokeyness, it is in one sense superior to *Tommy*. The myth of *Tommy* makes obvious concessions to pop—the pinball wizard as new messiah—and because pop denies its own significance, the commitment to pop undercuts consistently what thematic pretensions *Tommy* does have. At best you get the self-conscious art-about-art which has marked too much modern poetry and graphics; you get a classy piece of throw-away.

And that, fans, was the one problem the Who failed to solve in *Tommy*: the problem of themselves, their Mod origins, their relationship to pop. At the time, it probably never occurred to Townshend to question pop, the Mod ethic, or himself; after all, it was quite enough that the Who should produce the great pop rock "opera." In the sober seventies, however, both Mod and the Who demanded examination. The Who had moved beyond gimmickry to a technical proficiency with their post-*Tommy* album *Who's Next;* Mod had all but faded into oblivion with the advent of the new decade; *The Who Sell Out* appeared more silly than revolutionary. With Mod dead and the Who without a movement, with the world gone to musical and theatrical (also social, political, and economic) hell, charged with "mere technical proficiency" (at least the "gimmickry" rap was gone), the Who were forced to confront themselves honestly and squarely. They did so in their next great oratorio, *Quadrophenia*.

Quadrophenia lacks *Tommy's* easy narrative lines, opting instead for a psychological examination that both presupposes and reveals by bits and pieces the patient's biography in the best James Joyce tradition. Structurally, the work is more complex and infinitely more sophisticated than its predecessor. Moreover, Jimmy (the youth in whom no less than four separate personalities are embodied) is an aging Mod and a long time fan of the Who. This device allows the Who to examine both Mod as an ethic and their own role as high priests of the mid-sixties movement. It's a brilliant structural device, and it works: the Who criticize the Who. It's a great album.

The road from *Tommy* to *Quadrophenia* runs right through *Who's Next,* an album consistently praised for its studio technique and musicianship (as well it should be), the content consistently taken for granted (as it should not be). Thematically this is a new brand of Who: lyrics are not defiantly celebrative the way "My Generation" was, nor are they particularly Mod. The album is heavily country, both thematically ("Baba O'Riley," "Goin' Mobile," "Song Is Over") and musically ("Love Ain't for Keeping"). There is little rebellion (except that of a wimpy husband who lives in the proverbial fear and trepidation of his domineering wife catching him out boozing). One key lyric, in fact, actually talks about "gettin' in tune to the straight and narrow." There's a lot of love, the sexual love so underplayed by Mods. There's a lot of uncertainty and a real sense of wasted time. "It's only teen-aged wasteland," we hear in "Baba O'Riley"; "The song is over, it's all behind me," we hear in "Song Is Over." There is a profound sense of growing older gracelessly: "But my dreams they are as empty as my conscience seems to be" sings the persona of "Behind Blue Eyes," a romantic ballad about seeing things through the eyes of the bad guys. Most of all, because it looks in many directions at once, *Who's Next* is thematically a very mixed album. Schizophrenic. Transitional, we'd call it.

In retrospect, some thematic explorations become especially important in that they prefigure *Quadrophenia:* emphasis on the regenerative power of love (only a minor theme in *Tommy*), occasional accommodation of societal norms, a pervasive sense of wasting time (or, more correctly, dissatisfaction with wasting time), conscious alienation and self-examination. Some explorations are less important, since they're discarded in *Quadrophenia:* all the trappings of country and the pastoral tradition, for example. Of crucial importance is the Who's new willingness to explore multiple alternatives to the social bankruptcy of modern life, and a realization implicit in songs like "Baba O'Riley" and "Won't Get Fooled Again" that the generation of the sixties was had: "The parting on the left is now a parting on the right, And the beards have all grown longer over night." Here's the Who, ready to fight just like before, playin' guitar just like before, but very conscious of the fact that nothing's changed and they've been taken . . . and very circumspect lest they be taken again. "Meet the new boss," the song concludes, "same as the old boss." And pray we don't get fooled again.

Implicit in *Who's Next* is an uncertainty that hints at self-consciousness and self-examination. Explicit self-examination was two years in the making: the great *Quadrophenia.* As *Tommy* traced the search of deaf, dumb, and blind Tommy for touching and healing and feeling, *Quadrophenia* traces the search of Jimmy, a young Mod, for self-understanding. Tommy's problems were largely imposed from without: mistreated, he was very much a product of his environment. Character was a function of internal reactions to external forces. Jimmy's problems are more internal: he's confused, dissatisfied with both his straight parents and Mod friends, unable to cope with divergent elements of his own personality. Behavior is an external manifestation of internal conflicts. This makes for a far more interesting character. In addition, there is little of *Tommy's* narrative in *Quadrophenia:* while Jimmy certainly has a life history (which emerges by bits and snatches in the best James Joyce fashion), the two-record album is more a psycho-analysis of his assorted personalities than a linear biography. This makes for a far more complex, subtle art. Add to these differences of form and content the Who's injection of their old Mod selves into the album, an increased psychological subtlety, a willingness to question Mod presuppositions and attitudes, and a persistent suggestion that Jimmy's psychological problems are those of his entire age . . . and you get a remarkably sophisticated album.

Jimmy's biography may, with a minimum of effort, be abstracted from the pictures, songs, and album jacket monologue which comprise the whole album package of *Quadrophenia.* Jimmy sort of gets on with his parents and sort of doesn't. On the one hand he can sympathize with and tolerate them, on the other hand he finds himself bummed out by eels, fried eggs and booze. His parents object to his pills ("Each to his own sewage," Jimmy philosophizes) and to his involvement with the Mods, particularly when they wreck the Grand Hotel at Brighton in pursuit of a couple of rockers (a BBC radio report of the event is included on the album at the end of "Cut My Hair"). Jimmy takes a job for a while . . . two whole days as a dustman (garbage collector). Sore at his girl (now interested in Dave, his best friend), angered at his job, and weary from two nights' sleep under the Hammersmith overpass, Jimmy wrecks his motor scooter, gulps about twenty pills, and escapes to Brighton for some reminiscing. Brighton, though, is even more of a bring-down as Jimmy realizes that mod is dying, unsatisfying, an inadequate response to his problems. The bellboy at the Grand Hotel turns out to be the very character who led him and a couple of hundred other mods in that glorious wrecking operation in 1963. "Me folks had let me down, Rock had let me down, women had let me down, work wasn't worth the effort, school isn't even worth mentioning. But I never thought I'd feel let down by being a mod," Jimmy tells us. He steals a boat, does some gin on top of his pills, and turns out to sea toward a rock in the ocean. Freaked out entirely, he tries suicide. Unsuccessfully. As the opera takes place he's under psychiatric care.

That's Jimmy's story, the story of one bundle of contradictions: a boy who both needs and rejects his parents, a rebel and a conformist, a worker and a loafer, a dedicated but self-conscious mod, a joiner and a loner, a very sensitive kid. On the surface of things his behavior is inexplicable; in actuality it results from four different forces within Jimmy. He's not schizophrenic, he's "bleeding quadrophenic."

Each of Jimmy's four selves is embodied in one member of the Who, examined in detail in a specific song of the oratorio, represented throughout the album by a single identifiable musical motif. These motifs are presented early: a two-minute introductory collage, "I Am the Sea," gives us a line from each while "Quadrophenia," the third cut of the album, presents each in its entirety. They reappear as bits and snatches woven into other songs throughout the entire album. Separately and in their entirety, however, the four characters are not presented until very late in the oratorio.

The first to appear is Jimmy's suicidal self, the "Helpless Dancer," presented ironically by Roger Daltrey (in earlier days the epitomy of Mod's anger and aggression): they have all the trump cards, this song implies; the bosses will get you in the end. If you complain, you disappear "just like the lesbians and queers." All you can do is "stop dancing." Throughout *Quadrophenia* Jimmy asks himself "Why should I care?"—about his parents, about mod, about work and girls, about life itself. In the end he tries suicide, the ultimate resignation, the ultimate refusal to dance. "Helpless Dancer" explains much of Jimmy's behavior.

So too does "Bell Boy," Keith Moon's theme. In the narrative of *Quadrophenia,* "Bell Boy" represents Jimmy's conversation with the aging mod now working at the Grand Hotel in Brighton. Psychologically it represents that part of Jimmy which can accommodate the straight world of working middle class Britons, which can bury dreams of escape and rebellion and spend the day licking boots: "Bell Boy! I got to get running now . . . Always running at someone's heel."

The third persona presented is "Dr. Jimmy," the Dr. Jeckyl of Jimmy's Mr. Hyde. Portrayed again ironically by John Entwistel (who sat passively through early Who concerts with a dead-pan face that betrayed no emotion at all), "Dr. Jimmy" represents the aggressive, destructive, violent, and mod aspect of Jimmy's character:

What is it? I'll take it.
Who is she? I'll rape it.
Got a bet there? I'll meet it.
Getting high? You can't beat it.

Clearly no passivity here, only the aggression, sexual violence, street fighting, clothes-consciousness of high mod.

The fourth aspect of Jimmy's character is finally presented in full in the album's last cut: "Love Reign O'er Me," Peter Townshend's theme. It is Jimmy the romantic, the transcendent, the mystic. The song is richly affirmative in its insistence on love as healing (echoes of *Tommy,* although it gives *Quadrophenia* a far more positive ending than *Tommy's*): "Only love can make it rain the way the beach is kissed by the sea . . . Love, reign o'er me." The pun may be bad, the "dry and dusty road" something of a convention, but the potentiality of water is used here as effectively as in Eliot's "Waste Land," from which the Who's lyric just may derive. Jimmy's attempted suicide by water and the thunderstorms that fill *Quadrophenia* from initial cut to final line both make this use of water to represent potentiality and rebirth all the more effective. The Who aren't quite saying "All you need is love," but certainly they have come a long way from "the group with built-in hate."

The suicide, the worker, the Mod revolutionary, the mystical transcendent: these are the four elements of Jimmy's personality . . . and, I suspect, of the Who's collective personality. You can find elements of each in *Tommy,* in *Who's Next,* in pre-*Tommy* Who. But in *Quadrophenia* the group, through Jimmy, experiences a major reordering of component parts comparable to Dylan's reordering of his own self in *John Wesley Harding,* or the Band's coming to terms with itself and society in *Cahoots.* Mod is now dead, both historically and—as far as the Who are concerned—as a viable resolution to the neuroses of modern life.

This reordering, among other things, is the job of *Quadrophenia's* other lyrics, which serve one or more of three functions:

1) explore the tensions created between two or more elements of Jimmy's personality.
2) examine the Who's earlier relationship to Mod and to Jimmy, their fan.
3) universalize Jimmy's problems and neuroses.

A typical example of the first sort of lyric is "Cut My Hair," the fourth cut on the album. It explores the tensions between Jimmy the worker and Jimmy the Mod rebel, embodying the worker in each stanza, the rebel in each refrain. On the one hand Jimmy is a reluctant, self-conscious lad who gets along well enough with his parents and could chuck the whole Mod business; on the other he knows living at home won't last and wants nothing so much as a zoot suit, pills, a motor scooter, and a beachfight. Behind both worker and and rebel stands the suicide with his dark question, "Why should I care?" So what if I have to cut my hair just to please the old man? He's really okay, except what I really want to be is mod, but other kids get on with their parents, but mine just found my dope and are gonna kick me out, and a fried egg first thing in the morning just bums me out!

In other songs Jimmy expresses self-consciousness over his dress ("So how come the other tickets look much better?" he asks in "Sea and Sand"), confronts himself honestly on his own unimportance, and claims to have had enough of both girls and fighting. His anxiety reaches its ultimate heights in "I'm One (At Least)": "I blend in the crowd, fingers so clumsy, voice too loud." A really reluctant Mod, this kid. By the same token, he frequently expresses disgust at his parents and regularly leaves home. The paradoxes of "Cut My Hair," like those of other songs, pervade the entire album because they are constantly part of Jimmy's personality.

Other lyrics explore other tensions. "I'm One" combines suicide ("I'm a loser—no chance to win") with Mod ("But I'm one, I am one"). "The Dirty Jobs" combines worker with Mod rebel with just a touch of the transcendent ("Just like a child, I've been seeing only dreams, I'm all mixed up but I know what's right"). "I've Had Enough" mixes all four elements of Jimmy's personality in one of the key songs on the album. In this particular case the suicide is dominant: bored with fashions and acting tough (the mod rebel), weary of bosses' surveillance at work (the worker), and filled to the lid with attempts at love (the transcendent), Jimmy decides to quit dancing.

But Jimmy's problems are not entirely his own; they are those of the Who and of modern British (and modern western) culture. Jimmy, as we've said, is a fan of the Who. In his informal psycho-biography on the album jacket he recounts his relationship with the group:

I saw the posters going up outside the Odeon for a Who concert. I'd seen them down at Brighton. They were a mod group. Well, mods like them. They weren't exactly mods but mods did like them. They had a drummer who used to play with his arms waving about in the air like a lunatic. The singer was a tough looking bloke with really good clothes. If I hadn't have seen him near home I would have said his hair was gold. Real gold I mean, like gold paint. The guitar player was a skinny geezer with a big nose who twirled his arm like a windmill. He wrote

some good songs about mods, but he didn't quite look like one.
The bass player was a laugh. He never did anything. Nothing.
He used to smile sometimes, but the smile would only last half
a second then it would switch off again.

Two things are interesting in this description: first, the whole thing is
past tense. This is the way it was. And as we see members of the Who
portraying different aspects of Jimmy, Daltrey the suicide and Entwistel
the rebel, as we arrive at Jimmy's final invitation "love reign o'er me,"
we realize just how past tense the Who's Mod selves are. Second, we note
that the Who's commitment—like Jimmy's—was only half-hearted to
begin with. They don't quite fit the part. They're not quite Mods,
although the Mods like them. A harsh judgment this which tends to
validate Aronowitz' charge of gimmickry, but probably true. Like Jimmy, the Who contained other elements of personality, which conflicted
with the spirit of mod.

In one sense, then, the Who measure their earlier commitment to mod
by examining Jimmy's relationship to their former selves. In another
sense Jimmy becomes a surrogate for the New Who confronting the Old
Who. "The Punk Meets the Godfather," for example, is subtitled "A
mini opera with real characters and a plot." The epigraph is at first puz-
zling, since there doesn't seem to be a real plot to the piece, and neither
the punk nor the godfather appears any more substantial than Jimmy,
Bell Boy, or Dr. Jim. The godfather's first speech, however, reveals that
he is an embodiment of the Old, Mod Who, brought forward here to face
the charges of a New Who (the punk), and confess, as it were, his sins:
"I'm the guy in the sky, flying high Flashing eyes, no surprise, I told lies,
I'm the punk in the gutter." and later in the song, "I'm the punk with
the stutter." The Who refer, of course, to their early mod hit "My
Generation," done with a stutter by punks from the gutter. "You only
became what we made you," charges the punk; "I can't pretend that I
can teach" admits the godfather. A very clear expression, this, of the
Who's disenchantment with their earlier selves. (But we won't get fooled
again.)

The problems of *Quadrophenia* are those not only of Jimmy and the
Who, but of a generation, of Britain, of western culture. *Quadrophenia*,
recognizing both the bankruptcy of Mod and the neuroses from which it
sprung, seeks to confront those neuroses in terms that relate to all
elements of society. Townshend is not the first to explore the racking an-
tipathy between mindless, monotonous, soul-stifling work and man's
need for important, meaningful labor. Both are literary and sociological
commonplaces. But the appearance of such themes throughout
Quadrophenia expands the album's focus to encompass virtually all contemporary society. *Tommy's* problems were to some extent universalized

in that we all suffer from hate and isolation, but the Everyman role of Tommy was very much underplayed. Jimmy's role as modern Everyman is much more explicit. "I've Had Enough" vibrates between the first person "I" and the generalizing "you" in a rather obvious attempt to universalize Jimmy's dilemma. But the most explicit universalizing of Jimmy comes in "Is It In My Head": "I see a man without a problem, I see a country always starved." Jimmy asks, "Is it in my head?" No, obviously it is not in Jimmy's head, nor is it in the heads of only the Mods or only the young. It's in all our heads as the decade whirls on toward 1984 and the millennium.

Lyrically, thematically, structurally *Quadrophenia* is a plenty sophisticated album, and musically it is absolutely superb studio rock, the likes of which virtually no major rock group was producing in the 1970's rush toward country simplicity, live performances, and the rock-n-roll revival. *Quadrophenia* is, in fact, rock out of time, rock of the late sixties long after the late sixties ended. Having the benefit of two years' reflection; the experimentation of *Sgt. Pepper, After Bathing at Baxters, Their Satanic Majesties Request, Tommy,* and countless other concept and studio albums; and the remarkable ironic distancing permitted by using rock as a vehicle to examine rock and a Mod group to examine Mod, *Quadrophenia* is a very remarkable album, almost flawless in conception and execution. It's the best thing the Who have done—and, given the tentative resolution of "Love, Reign O'er Me," probably the best thing they ever will do. I would go so far as to say it's the most significant rock album of the early seventies.

CHAPTER VII
THE JEFFERSON AIRPLANE

The Who were far more important in England than America, mainly because their mod style never really happened in the States the way it happened in England. What transpired over here was San Francisco, then Lincoln Park, then Richard Nixon. What was important over here was the Jefferson Airplane, later to become the Jefferson Starship.

As mod interposes itself between the Who and any serious attempt to deal with their work, so San Francisco, then Lincoln Park, then Richard Nixon interpose themselves between us and the Airplane. In fact, it is only in terms of what was happening to American society during the sixties and early seventies that the Airplane makes any sense at all.

The group's random, for example. Always a loosely defined organization, the Airplane consisted of a core of important musicians (Grace Slick, Paul Kantner, Jorma Kaukonen, Jack Cassidy, Marty Balin)—some of them culled from the defunct Great Society, some of them lost between *Jefferson Airplane Takes Off* (1966) and *Long John Silver* (1972)—and a loosely defined peripheral cast that could at times grow to dozens of musicians, including at various moments the likes of Jerry Garcia, David Crosby, Graham Nash, Papa John Creach, and John Barbata. At times people associated with the Airplane produced work on their own (e.g., Papa John Creach, or Slick and Kantner) or formed splinter groups: Hot Tuna, for example. Rock music itself has developed in this direction, and indeed, American society now consists structurally of a never ending series of "adhocracies," organizations like NASA or the Watergate Committee, set up to tackle a specific problem, funded for an interim, then allowed to dissociate into component persons and parts, which can then be rearranged into new adhocracies for a new project. That's America, and that's the Airplane.

Or take the thematic focuses of their albums. In the mid-sixties, the Airplane freaked out with Tim Leary in his pharmaceutical revolution. In the late sixties it followed Abbie Hoffman and Jerry Rubin down the road to social and political revolution for the hell of it. Like the rest of America—and rock—the Airplane next ducked underground, and spent the early seventies waiting for RMN to go away, escaping into rock-n-roll revivals or wild voyages into the future-past.

101

The Poetry of Rock

Or take the Airplane's curious ambivalence about their own work. Like San Francisco, like America of the sixties, the Airplane is nothing so much as kinetic: it's an act, a performance, a scene. At its best, it's Disneyland; at its worst, it's throw-away trash. "I like 'It Doesn't Mean Shit to a Tree', Ben Fong Torres, managing editor of *Rolling Stone,* once told Grace Slick in an interview. "It doesn't. Don't get serious about it at all. 'Cause it's not serious," Paul Kantner retorted. And he continued, referring both to the interview and his song, "We didn't even know what we were doing when we started doing it. Looking back, all we were saying was, 'Look, we're having a good time.' And nothing else. Just sitting around having a good time with all this shit going on around us." Of course the Beatles used to engage in this sort of self-depricating banter in their own interviews, and Dylan has done the same thing. So did Robert Frost, and so does Norman Mailer. But press them on the subject of their writing, and they all turn suddenly serious, defensively aggressive. One thing the Beatles and Dylan took seriously was their own art: that fact more than anything else strikes you as you read through their put-on interviews and listen to their songs.

But the kind of nonsense that characterizes an Airplane interview is different in that you sense immediately an ambivalence toward their art, just as you sense pop's self-denial in the Who's stance. I have heard the new *Tommy* defended (or explained) because it was the company's idea, not Townshend's; but it was certainly Townshend's idea to "sell out" on *The Who Sells Out*—and the idea of a London Symphony *Tommy* and pop Who commercial advertisements are not that far apart, really. For their part, of course, the Airplane has produced commercials for Levi's: "I like Levi's and I'll do an ad for anything I like," says Paul. "We'd love to do a toilet paper ad." One might make several unkind remarks about that, but the point is that an Airplane toilet paper ad would obviously be a pop put-on. What is to suggest that their albums are not also pop put-on?

Mostly the music itself. For example, there can be little doubt that "White Rabbit" and "Somebody to Love" and "Comin' Back to Me" and "Lather" and "Crown of Creation" and "We can Be Together" are very serious songs that know precisely what they're about and do not expect to be taken lightly. The same can be said of "Rejoyce" and the two Pooneil pieces, although they are obviously less focused than some of the others. You can be less sure of something like "My Best Friend" or "Wild Tyme," but these are not important, and everybody is allowed his failures in an unguarded moment.

For that is precisely what all this nonsense is: an unguarded moment, or a peculiar way of looking at art, or at a peculiar form of art. You *can* be too serious about art, and it's good that the Airplane and other contemporary artists guard themselves against such dead earnestness. On the other hand, art can be or probably should be fun, so that saying "we are just having a good time" does not necessarily exclude the secretion of fine art. And finally there *is* a kind of art which is throw-away art, just fooling around, just having fun. I doubt that Eliot would defend *The Old Possum's Book of Practical Cats* as containing much high seriousness, and I don't think he should have to. Similarly, a nothing lyric like "Watch Her Ride" or a nothing instrumental like "Spare Chaynge" (both from the pretentious *After Bathing at Baxter's* album) really need no apology. They also need little comment.

The Airplane's lyrics, like their art, are a mixed bag. Grace Slick brought several with her when she left the Great Society to join the Airplane; subsequent lyrics have been provided by both Paul Kantner and Grace Slick, and—with decreasing frequency—by Marty Balin. Several came from outside the group. Musically the Airplane drew on jazz, blues, rock, various Mid-Eastern and Far Eastern musics, and electronic gadgetry, to tick off only the more pronounced influences. Clearly there is no such thing as a typical Airplane lyric, although there is an identifiable Airplane production and a more or less identifiable set of standard Airplane themes. Although some of their best singles are highly structured, the group tended toward an expressionist free-form which lends itself to the kind of words-and-music-and-good vibrations-and-light show productions popularized by San Francisco groups of the post 1967 era. Musically the group worked best when Grace Slick and Marty Balin spun their separate voices into filagrees of vocal lace ("Spare Chaynge" is an instrumental equivalent), or when Grace's strong solos dueled with Balin or the rest of the group, instrumental and vocal each threatening to destroy each other, both building together a wall of kinetic energy.

Thematically the Airplane passed with the sixties through stages: from good-time, drugs-love-and-peace music of the San Francisco period they moved to political and social protest (sometimes in the form of satire) to escape into fantasy or the musical past, always with just an undercurrent of wistful nostalgis. Their best work is to be found on the middle albums; *The Jefferson Airplane Takes Off* never quite did, and *Bark* (1971, after a two-year rest) was one of the worst air disasters of the decade. Those middle albums, however—*Surrealistic Pillow, After Bathing at Baxter's, Crown of Creation,* and *Volunteers* (add the live *Bless Its Pointed Little Head* if you wish)—were as fine a music as rock has yet produced.

Oddly the Airplane's two greatest singles both arrived with Grace Slick from the Great Society: her own "White Rabbit" and Darby Slick's "Somebody to Love." Their genesis may explain their atypical tightness a four-stanza pattern of the first, a couplet-chorus arrangement of the

The Poetry of Rock

second. Thematically the lyrics reflect the Airplane's interest in drugs and, of course, love in its sundry forms; musically they reflect one mode of performance with which the group had considerable success: the bluesy, brassy voice of Grace with occasional harmonies from Marty, backed up by a wall of sound cooked up by Paul, Jorma, Jack, Spencer, and Marty. "Somebody to Love" also provides a good example of rock's ability to standardize lines of different lengths ("Your mind is so full of lead" and "But in you head I'm afraid you don't know where it is" are both second halves of couplets), of the voice used as an instrument, of effective use of incremental repetition, similar to the choruses of the popular ballad "Lord Randall." The song procedes through an assortment of emotional crises (truth discovered to be lies, estranged friends, a head that don't know where it's at), and asserts among all this the primacy of love. "Love is all there is." "I just need someone to love." "Love, reign o'er me." We are on the streets of Haight-Asbury, summer of '67.

"White Rabbit" is a drug song—there ain't no two ways about it, and if you think it should be banned from the airways and the Airplane taken out and shot, then so be it. "One pill makes you larger, and one pill makes you small." It also happened to be a first rate lyric, building on *Alice in Wonderland* and *Through the Looking Glass* in a fashion reminiscent of "Lucy In the Sky" and, I believe, for similar purposes. Probably Alice and her adventures are more central to the success of this lyric, however, since it would make no sense at all without an understanding of Lewis Carroll's fiction. While Slick never bothers to explain Alice to the uninitiated (let alone the men on the chessboard, or the mushroom, or the hookah-smoking caterpillar), she makes certain we do not miss the point of her allusions: "Feed your head." This last, though, is curious. The Dormouse gave no advice to Alice, although one chapter of *Alice in Wonderland* is titled "Advice from a Caterpillar." Mostly the mouse slept, awakening only to tell a very short tale of three sisters living in the bottom of a treacle well. Never did he suggest that we "feed our heads." That advice comes from Grace Slick.

Several other songs on *Surrealistic Pillow* relate to the drug-fantasy theme: "3/5 of a Mile in 10 Seconds" ("sometimes the price is $65") "She Has Funny Cars" ("Your mind's guaranteed, it's all you need"), "How Do You Feel?" ("Just look into her eyes"), "DCBA--25 ("Too many days are left unstoned"), perhaps even "Plastic Fantastic Lover." We've seen images like these before in the work of Jim Morrison, although the Doors used them without suggesting drugs. Some of these songs are good second-line poems, drawing on a standard comparison between women and drugs (like so many other rock poems—"Along

104

Comes Mary," "Lucy In the Sky," "Norwegian Wood", or acid or speed, but the surrealistic world into which all of these drugs introduce us. Like "I'd love to turn you on," "Feed your head" suggests much more than drugs. They are important only insofar as they alter perception of reality and life style. In retrospect, you can be jaded about the validity of a rebirth of wonder predicated on drug usage, but at the time the world needed such a rebirth even more than it needs it now (and we are in desperate situations), and drugs were then more innocent than they are today.

"Comin Back to Me," by Marty Balin, was the other unquestionable gem of *Surrealistic Pillow*. Evocative, unashamedly romantic, delicate in its imagery, it captures that mood in which we have all found ourselves at one moment or another: something happens to remind us of a time or a person or an event long gone, and for an instant we relive the pain and pleasure of that lost moment: "I saw you. I saw you comin' back to me." The song draws, I suppose, on "Tragedy" ("Oh come back, be sincere . . ."), but clearly the girl of this lyric is purely metaphorical, a symbol for all things past that return through the hazes of our mind when it wanders between the lines of a book or out open windows. The lacy delicacy of Balin's imagery and assonances is re-enforced by his own delicate vocals, and an astringent arrangement which is precisely the opposite of "White Rabbit." And no drugs here, either—just floating, dreaming memory. The pair of lyrics makes a fine set piece of contrasting styles.

Like *Sgt. Pepper* and *Their Satanic Majesties Request,* with which it invites comparison, *After Bathing at Baxter's* was experimental—so experimental that it alienated many of the Airplane's new-found fans (again parallels with *Pepper's* and *Satanic Majesties*). Paul Williams thought this their best album at the time, although its successor retreats from its extremism and produces what is on the whole a better piece of music (more parallels with the Stones). Structurally the album subdivides itself into suites (one of them titled "How Suite It Is"), although the relationships among songs within a suite are frequently unclear, and as a structural concept the technique does not come off. One cut—"A Small Package of Value Will Come To You, Shortly," is an experimental sound collage in the mold of the Stones' "On With the Show" or the Beatles' "Revolution Number 9." It contains everything from "Joy to the World" to "No Man is an Island" (with the Joycean retort, "he's a peninsula"). It is also an artistic failure because it lacks focus. Imagistic poems and good collages are difficult to do, partly because they seem so easy: you throw together a bunch of interesting tidbits, some related to each other, some in there just for fun, and there you are. Only there you

105

are not, because you don't have a thematic center, and you don't have a structure. Similarly unsuccessful are "Wild Tyme" (a collage of phrases from other lyrics on *Baxter's*); "Won't You Try" (Balin and Slick counterpointing on "Won't you try?" and "Saturday afternoon" in a loose, vague, jazzy piece); "Martha" (a Doors-like enigma: "Martha she keeps her heart in a broken clock"); "The Last Wall of the Castle," words and point of which escape me; and perhaps "Watch Her Ride," which can offer only sun and moon and golden beaches of the mind (mediocre) and "You're so fine in my mind" (very bad). Other defects are the general and sometimes pointless formlessness of many of the album's lyrics and some nonsense puns in the tradition of John Lennon and debased James Joyce.

The album also has its strengths: some fine jamming in "Spare Chaynge," real vocal and instrumental fireworks on most cuts, and a series of excellent lyrics: "The Ballad of You and Me and Pooneil," "Young Girl Sunday Blues," "Rejoyce," and "Two Heads."

"Pooneil" builds on A.A. Milne's books in a manner different from what "White Rabbit" did to Carroll's fiction. Pooh Bear and Chris Robin are not bodily present in the lyric, but their spirit pervades both it and—to a lesser extend—its successor on *Crown of Creation,* "The House at Pooneil Corners." Its final stanza alludes glancingly to Pooh's plan to disguise himself as a black cloud floating beneath a blue sky so as not to arouse the suspicions of the bees on whose honey he is intent. Pooh sings,

> How sweet to be a Cloud
> Floating in the blue!
> It makes him very proud
> To be a little cloud.

Kantner writes,

> You were a cloud and you sailed up there
> See me here in the fields and say
> "Doesn't the sky look green today."

But basically the song is a tone piece, capturing the nothing/important/to/do/today/so/let's/go/out/and/find/an/adventure spirit of a scene like this:

> Edward Bear, known to his friends as Winnie-the-Pooh, or Pooh for short, was walking through the forest one day, humming proudly to himself. He had made up the little hum that very morning, as he was doing his Stoutness Exercises in front of the glass: Tra-la-la, tra-la-la, as he stretched up as high as he could go, and then Tra-la-la, tra-la--oh, help!--la, as he tried to reach his toes. After breakfast he had said it over and over

to himself until he had learnt it off by heart, and now he was
humming it right through, properly . . .

Well, he was humming this hum to himself, and walking
along gaily, wondering what everybody else was doing, and
what it felt like, being somebody else, when suddenly he came
to a sandy bank, and in the bank was a large hole.

"I have a house where I can go, when there are too many people around
me," writes Paul, and again, "I'll come out in springtime flashing
through ribbons on my mind." The wind takes him away, and wherever
he goes, that's where he wanted to be today. A drug song, yes, and the
wind may be anything from pot to acid. You can, if you wish, read this
as a specific reference to that great house in California—the one the
Beatles and Stones rented for awhile—in which the Airplane sat for a
summer and watched the surreal world go by. But the song is more than
that. It's a vision of life after that non-violent revolution: the minds and
bodies of a generation are free to go where they will and do what they
want. Certainly the tone here, careless and without any sense of urgency,
is very close to the spirit of Pooh.

"Two Heads," Slick's second contribution to the album, was
criticized by Paul Williams as "less obvious than the rest of the group,"
but if anything this song has a clearer conception of what it wants to do
and how it intends to do it than most of *Baxter's* lyrics. It's difficult to
mistake lines like "Keep a lock on her belly at night," or "Your women
are tired of dying alive, if you've had any women at that." What we have
here is an early women's lib piece urging male chauvinist pigs to take a
dual perspective on the dual standard and break out of the town in their
heads, the jails of their private rooms.

But it is in "Rejoyce," that Slick really gets herself together to produce
a first rate piece of pop art. The lyrics are built on and around Molly
Bloom's last, chapter-long monologue from *Ulysses,* feature Molly and
Stephen and Blazes and Bloom, manage one of the album's few clever
and intelligent puns. Joyce's characters actually appear in the song,
along with the very Joycean worldplay ("Molly's gone to Blazes,
Boylen's progenezes") and some of the actual details of the *Ulysses*
story: "Anyone whose husband sleeps with his head all buried down at
the foot of the bed." Molly, though, is secondary; mostly Slick creates
her own counterpart for that long last soliloquy of Molly's. "There are
so many of you," Slick-'n-Molly-'n-mother reflects, suggesting the
sexual escapades of Joyce's heroine, Slick's own adventures, and the
curious social relationships of a song like "Triad." Arms and legs permeate her thoughts (echos of Joyce), mingling with political concerns:
"Stephen won't give his arm to no gold-star mother's farm. War's good

business, so invest your son; I'd rather have my country die for me.'' And here we begin to see divergences between Slick's Molly and Joyce's; the patriotism of Grace Slick breaks from that of James Joyce, the alienation of the American differs from that of the Irishmen. 1968 is a distance from 1921. Joyce fills Molly's head ultimately with affirmation: yes and yes and yes and all yes, strung together as he drives her off to sleep. Slick's song ends with the more cynical and hard-headed "But somehow it all falls apart.'' The unity of subconscious experience so important to Joyce is here denied, along with the affirmation he managed half a century before our time. The song exhibits, then, little rejoicing, merely Re-joycing. And the strange linear unity of the song's music (it contains repeated musical motifs, but nothing stanzaic), which procedes with variation but no real sense of direction to that closing line, is illusory. Never before has so much been destroyed by a final line.

Like *Pepper's, Baxter's* was more than a simple collection of random songs, even of random suites. The album is a celebration of the social, gentle, pharmaceutical revolution that took place in California in the middle to later sixties. It is an album of sex and love and drugs, but more than that it is an album that alternatively celebrates the new order and eulogizes the dead order. So on the one hand you get Kantner's enthusiastic "It's a wild tyme!'' On the other hand, you get "things falling apart'' in Slick's "Rejoyce.'' After *Bathing at Baxter's* closes with an invitation to join the greening of America, you return to the album's cover to study a multi-colored, rickety biplane trailing marijuana and love down over a black and white, litter-strewn America below. Ah, the America of the middle sixties!

Crown of Creation, which followed *Baxter's,* may well be the Airplane's finest album, combining the solid old Airplane sounds with some of the experimentation of its predecessor. It is literarily allusive, what with Kantner's reference to Lonesco's *Rhinocerous* in "The House at Pooneil Corners'' and Jorma Kaukonen's "Ice Cream Phoenix.'' It contains a poetic variety ranging from Slick's narrative "Lather'' to Crosby's dramatic monologue "Triad'' to the strangely beautiful lyric grace of Balin and Blackman's "If You Feel.'' It stretches thematically from politics to love, and from the sublime ("Crown of Creation'') to the ridiculous ("Share a Little Joke''). Musically it is superb.

The thematic center of the album is its little title lyric: "You are the crown of creation, and you have no place to go.'' In the paradox between potentiality and bankruptcy, modern man confronts the myth of his original sin, the fact of his incapacity and inadequacies. From that paradox the Airplane develops another statement on revolution, more precise and harsher than *Baxter's.* Man strives for a stability granted only among "the fossils of our time." The loyal right cannot tolerate young minds; young leftist minds bent on the transformation of society cannot, in loyalty to kind, tolerate obstruction. The issue is partly political: to change or to remain fixed? Kennedy or Goldwater? And it biological: are you alive or dead? A growing organism, a dead fossil? The Airplane answers obliquely its own question: "Life is change, how different from the rocks." Man is both an organism and a fossil, a life on its way to becoming rock. His obligation to himself, to others, to "kind," is to stay alive as long as possible, to gain new worlds, "to survive." Paul did a fine job with this poem, compressing political, religious, sociological, even biological considerations into a poem which, for all of its overt certainties, totters on the ironic edge of self-doubt long enough to give it the tension that marks good poetry: "Soon you'll attain the stability you strive for," he tells us. We all strive for it, even revolutionaries, and we all attain it.

From "Crown of Creation," the album expands to variations on "our minds" and "their kind," and tensions between the two. Slick's "Lather" describes a thirty-year old man-child who must remain true to his visions of the world, even though it means confrontation with his friends (a banker and a tank commander in the success of their young maturity) and his mother. Lather would rather draw pictures in the sand and drum hot licks on his nose (a drug reference). "But that's all over," Slick informs us; Lather too has grown up—or freaked out, or fossilized, which is what growing up in this song amounts to. The narrator can only thinkk, "I should have told him, 'No, you're not too old—and I should have let him go on smiling baby wide'." Of course there is a great deal of that romantic longing for lost childhood in much of rock, but put in context of "Crown of Creation," the lyric also implies those tensions between stability (the banker's chair) and spontaneity (lying about nude in the sand) with which the album concerns itself.

"In Time" is a love poem by Balin and Kantner, but one which poses alternative life styles and other worlds, mutation by the organism: "Soon we'll be in another country." The same theme is developed in David Crosby's "Triad," where "me and him and you and me" all live together in a crazy love relationship, unbothered by mother's ghost or rules learned in school: "I don't really see why we can't go on as three," sings Slick. "Star Track" treats the process of opening minds and "Share a Little Joke" treats the opened minds . . . the new consciousness, the forces of life against the fossils. But side two of the album focuses with growing intensity on the forces of the fossils, the realization that "it all falls apart." "Tell me why if you think you know why people love if there's no tomorrow?" asks Jorma in "Ice Cream Phoenix." Images fade in his magic vanishing memory machine, and ultimately people have to go. In "Greasy Heart," Grace confronts a variety of disillusionments: faded suntans, automatic men, greasy women with paper dresses, falling empires, cracked walls. It's a very unpleasant song.

Finally Balin and Kantner destroy the magic of Pooneil in "The House at Pooneil Corners": "You and me we keep walking around and we see all the bullshit around us," the song begins. It looks beyond the apocalypse, to a world grown quiet again, the rains washing away the ashes of mankind's violence. "There will be no survivors, my friend," we are warned. The album titled *Crown of Creation* closes with a dark epitaph:

> The cows are almost cooing,
> The turtle doves are mooing
> Which is why a poo is pooing
> In the sun
> Sun.

This is the way the world ends, this is the way the world ends: cows transformed to doves by nuclear catastrophy and genetics gone awry, doves become cows, and images of poop and shit. Lo, the end of man's potentiality. The album cover imposes a double exposure of the Airplane over a nuclear fireball.

If *Crown of Creation* suggested a growing awareness of the deficiencies of San Francisco flowers, love, drugs, and grooving, that they were not saving and, in fact, were probably incapable of saving the world, *Volunteers* does little to change that impression. In fact, this is an album of increased politicism and cynicism. Against an ironic presentation of the traditional "Oh, Good Shepherd" (feed my sheep), and another equally cynical view of a retreat to the country ("The Farm"), we are urged to become blood-stained bandits, long-tongued liars, and shotgun devils in the key thematic song of the album, "We Can Be Together": "We are all outlaws in the eyes of America." The response here (as should be obvious) is to "Crown of Creation," with its sense of responsibility to kind and to other people. This lyric, however, casts responsibility into bloody, violent outlawism absent from the previous album but historically and theoretically the only viable solution to the problems of flower-power impotence. How else does one deal with the new Nixon? "Up against the wall, mother fucker!"

"We Can Be Together" is an important lyric, important for *Volunteers,* important for the development of the Airplane's thinking, important in the way it reflects social and political developments in America, 1969. The times were angry—none of the docile silent majority you found in the early seventies, sitting back and applauding while 1984 was ushered in a decade ahead of schedule. The radical movement had reached a critical point. "Either go away or go all the way," sang Slick in "Hey, Fredrick," and that's the way it was. "If the government won't shut down its war machine, then we're going to shut down the government," claimed the leaders of the radical left. They were not fooling around, and neither was the Airplane, which in reflecting radical political thought had worked itself into the same corner. *Volunteers,* is a radical political album, full of radical thought, radical music, radical poetry.

"Wooden Ships" packs the activists safely on board while predicting the death of those poor bastards who remain on shore; "Song for all Seasons" satirically berates those who retreat into cars and music and record albums instead of confronting the revolution. Then there's the title song, the last lyric of side two: "Look what's happening out in the streets (Got a revolution Got to revolution) . . ."

Well, the revolution never came off, and Abbie Hoffman chats amiably with Dick Cavett and Rennie David has got religion, and Tom Hayden lobbies with Jane Fonda down in Washington when he's not running for Congress. Perhaps it serves the Airplane right for deserting the high art of *Baxter's* and *Crown of Creation* for "mere politics," for the insipid, prosey rhetoric of *Volunteers,* for musical formlessness and stupid "radical" punctuation games (like dropping all the apostrophes from contractions on the printed insert, when they print *fred* instead of *fuck*—now how radical is that?). No sir, the revolution never came off, and *Volunteers,* being little more than revolutionary rhetoric, looks pretty silly right now. The walls are higher than ever these days, and still building. All that's torn down are trade walls with Russia and China—a clear indication that those countries no longer offer any legitimate alternative to the social and political and economic institutions of the west.

And the Airplane? From *Volunteers,* it went into a two-year period of hiding, from which it emerged with three bad albums: *Bark,* which was awful, *Long John Silver* and *30 Seconds Over Winterland,* which were no better. Then, with *Sunfighter,* it began the imaginary journey (aboard the hijacked intergalactic spaceship) which would take them right out of this here decadent planet and off to a beautiful new birth somewhere, some time. The art of these albums—the graphic art, that is—was interesting; the music weak, the poetry weaker yet. The Airplane laments the mess that man has made of mother earth, apologizes to Diana, and in *Blows Against the Empire* (more interesting graphics) splits:

Hi Jack the starship
Carry 7000 people past the sun
And our babies wander naked through the cities of the universe

Comon—
Free minds   free bodies   free dope   free music
The day is on its way, the day is ours.

Thus the Airplane became the Jefferson Starship (and Hot Tuna, and Papa John Creach, and Paul and Grace), and disintegrated into nothing.

Perhaps it was the final disintegration, from which the Airplane/Starship has yet to recover, in which the group most reflected the state of American pop music. For, as has been so often observed, the music scene was by 1973 in a stage of advanced putrification: Dylan gone soft, Morrison and so many others dead, Paul Simon a little goofy, nothing ut nothing vital appearing on the horizon, everyone in a desperate search for the next messiah. Where else was left but the underground and the far side of space? What else was left but resignation and farewells?

CHAPTER VIII
BOB DYLAN

1973 was a rough year: inflation running wild, shortages of gasoline and beef, Watergate investigations revealing ever-widening circles of political corruption in Washington, rising unemployment, international uncertainty . . . and yet another year of mediocre television, movies, and music. Hard times and nothing to take your mind off them. *Rolling Stone,* the six-year-old (and, therefore, venerable) chronicle of rock and dope, turned more and more to political and social journalism, unimpressed with Alice Cooper, Bette Midler, David Bowie, and the Osmonds. If you had asked *Stone's* editor Jann Wenner for a candid appraisal, he'd have probably told you "a bummer all around." If you'd have asked just what he thought might get the country goin', he'd probably have suggested—in ascending order of desirability and descending order of probability—a presidential resignation, a reunion of the Beatles, and a resurrection of Bob Dylan. And in August of 1973, believe me, you'd have thought Nixon would be dead and in his grave before Lennon saw McCartney or Bob Dylan saw anybody.

And then, who woulda thunk, Bob Dylan—*the* Bob Dylan—announced plans for a good-old-fashioned all-across-the-country-concert-a-day-sometimes-two tour for January and February, 1974. *Rolling Stone,* the press in general, rock fans everywhere, and nearly a million chosen few who actually got tickets all went prudently insane. Dick Nixon had not resigned, Lennon was being kicked out of the country, but Bob Dylan was back, and for a moment everything seemed right. As the tour rolled across America, it was received with a combination of reverence and enthusiasm you just don't never find in a rock concert. Everyone knew and said openly that the tour was mythic, as historically significant as Woodstock, something you'd tell your kids about twenty years later. As each concert burned to a close, each darkened stadium glowed with the lights of thousands of matches and cigarette lighters—votive candles to Bob Dylan, god with us. It was, indeed, a mighty moment.

The honest truth is that nobody—not even the Beatles, not even the Stones—inspires the awe, the adulation, the respect that Dylan inspires. He is absolutely and unequivocally the king. Individuals, whole groups still spring fully grown from his head, and his influence on pop music remains inestimable . . . despite nearly six years of musical mediocrity between *John Wesley Harding* and *Blood on the Tracks*. Not that he was entirely original: early albums reveal very clearly just how much he stole and from whom he stole it. Not that he never slipped; some of the early, late, even some of the middle material is too personal, too loose, too obscure, and at times just plain lousy. Not that his melodies aren't at times repetitious, his rhymes jangling, his images banal. Not that he was always kind, humble, likeable, unassuming. But what he's got, he's got, and nobody else has it: incredible proficiency in a variety of styles and forms, an absolutely first rate intelligence, a poet's facility with words, and that *sine qua non* of true genius, insight. The man's an artist. And in 1974, with rock in the hands of promoters and gimmick-propelled mediocrity, his artistry was never more needed or apparent than on his epic tour.

A non-stop run-through of Dylan's collected works—either on record or in his *Writings and Drawings* (Knopf, 1973)—impresses a body with both the unevenness of his work and its diversity. Lennon and McCarthney and Harrison may have achieved something to rival Dylan's eclecticism on that white album, but nobody else has even come close. Jazz, blues, rock-n-roll, rock, folk, country-and-western, ballads, talkin' blues, dream visions, allegories, narratives, monologues, lyrics of all kinds and descriptions, protest songs, biographical lyrics, a benediction, even what Craig MacGregor called a psalm—he wrote 'em all, and wrote 'em well.

Some aspects of Dylan's art, however, seem more important than others. For example, his early talkin' blues lyrics are interesting and amusing, show a lighter side to an otherwise earnest young man, and foreshadow in some respects his protest lyrics—but they are hardly the stuff of which greatness is made. The same might be said, perhaps unkindly, about Dylan's early performances of blues shamelessly copped from real blues singers (Leadbelly, Cisco Houston, Blind Lemmon Jefferson) and from New York-Boston imitation folk-blues singers. More important are Dylan's many love songs, some of them delicate and fragile ("The Girl from the North Country"), some of them hard-nosed and cold ("Don't Think Twice"), some of them bursting with scorn and emotion ("It Ain't Me, Babe," "Just Like a Woman"). Also more important are Dylan's country pieces, most prominent in *John Wesley Harding* and later albums, but detectable as early as his first album in a song like "Pretty Peggy-O." Most important to Dylan's musical and poetical monument, however, are the protest lyrics of his early period, the surrealistic, frequently self-projective allegories of his middle period, and the coherent thematic statement of *John Wesley Harding*. These lyrics are our primary concern here.

114

Bob Dylan

It was Dylan's protest songs that first attracted national attention; indeed before he began writing protest Dylan was just another folk-blues singer in the Village coffeehouse scene. It was protest songs that *Sing Out* most frequently printed: "Masters of War," "Hattie Carroll," "Blowin' In the Wind." It was protest music that first attracted Joanie Baez to Dylan (and, if I read "to Bobby" on *Come From the Shadows* correctly, still does). It was protest music that first got Dylan played, that defined almost exclusively his public self. Given "Girl from the North Country" and Dylan's romantic devotion to the Woody Guthrie folk myth, there should have been less surprise than Albert Goldman registered when "That angry kid went all over romantic" in later albums; given the rock-n-roll of his high school days, *Highway 61* and *Bringin' It All Back Home* should have proven no real shock. But protest had so defined Dylan's image that people saw little else. In actuality, they saw very little of Dylan's protest music, for in the early 1960's people read what they thought into those songs, ignoring what Dylan had put there.

His own attitude, almost from the beginning, was ambivalent. There was genuine white hate and simplistic good guy-bad guy divisions in some of his early protest, but very quickly Bob saw behind the black/white distinctions most protest writers drew, just as he was one day to see that (1) people misunderstood him, (2) the adulation heaped on him because of his protest music threatened to make him "one of them rather than one of us," and (3) there were roads to revolution other than marching in the streets. "Oxford Town", written in 1963, indicates quite clearly Dylan's ambivalence: "I don't even know why we come, goin' back where we come from." People didn't hear that song; they didn't really hear the others either. "Blowin' In the Wind" is a very ambiguous phrase; it suggests, I think, that there are no answers, and that talkin' and talkin' and talkin' about answers is a lot of gas. But most people heard the line as "blown in the wind" and were unperturbed. What *did* bother folk was Dylan's performance in front of the Emergency Civil Liberties Committee:

Inside the balloon, I really got up tight. I began to drink.
I looked down from the platform and saw a bunch of people who had nothing to do with my kind of politics. I looked down and I got scared. They were supposed to be on my side, but I didn't feel any connection with them. Here were these people who'd been all involved with the left in the thirties, and now they were supporting civil-rights drives. That's groovy, but they also had minks and jewels, and it was like they were giving the money out of guilt. I got up to leave, and they followed me and

115

caught me. They told me I had to accept the award. When I got up to make my speech, I couldn't say anything by that time but what was passing through my mind. They's been talking about Kennedy being killed, and Bill Moore and Medgar Evers and the Buddhist monks in Vietnam being killed. I had to say something about Lee Oswald. I told them I'd read a lot of his feelings in the papers and I knew he was up tight. Said I'd been up tight, too, so I'd got a lot of his feelings. I saw a lot of myself in Oswald, I said, and I saw in him a lot of the times we're all living in. And, you know, they started booing. They looked at me like I was an animal. They actually thought I was saying it was a good thing Kennedy had been killed. That's how far out they are.

What did attract attention was Dylan's public disapproval of his protest songs in 1965, his refusal to sing them in public performances for a period of several years, and his departure from protest on *Highway 61* and *Bringin' It All Back Home*. The real irony, of course, is that Dylan was right: in the final analysis the Rolling Stones produced more revolution than "Eve of Destruction," which may have been exactly why arm-chair liberals and retired leftists preferred "protest music" to hard core rock. The electric rock "Subterranean Homesick Blues" and "Like a Rollin' Stone" may well have been the most critical—and the most revolutionary—songs Dylan ever did.

As a genre, most protest songs suffer from the same defect: oversimplification. Certainly on issues one cannot equivocate, but where people are concerned only a fool views some folks as consciously, aggressively evil, only a chicken squawks about falling nuclear skies. Few of Dylan's songs indulge in black and white simplicities or unqualified apocalypse. "With God On Our Side" comes quickly to mind, but this is early and utterly inartistic; even Dylan's harmonica introduction to this song sounds pompous and pretentious. "Masters of War", also 1963, is another example of this sort of black/white simplicity. This song, however, is saved by its minor features: the oxymoron of "build to destroy," a brilliant metaphor ("I see through your eyes and I see through your brain like I see through the water that runs down my drain"), numerous religious allusions, and the purity of its hatred: "I'll stand o'er your grave till I'm sure that you're dead." *Intellectually* we know this is an oversimplification (although at times one would think not overly such): *emotionally* we all have moments when we give ourselves over to such irrational, intense, distilled hatred.

The only other protest lyric which might be accused of black/white dichotomism is "When the Ship Comes In," although in turning this lyric into a surrealist fable-allegory, the poet turns weakness into strength. Instead of oversimplified people, Dylan manages a statement of clearly defined moral (not personal) issues. Like "With God On Our Side," the song is heavily biblical, alluding to Pharoah's hosts and David and Goliath, although here the allusions not only mitigate the song's weaknesses but contribute to its strengths by re-enforcing its strong moral content. Moreover, this song demonstrates Dylan's artistic abilities in a way that "Masters of War" and "With God On Our Side" do not: facility with rhyme and stanzaic patterns, a poet's choice of words ("Will have *busted* in the night", "And they'll *jerk* from their beds"), sensitivity to the rhythms of colloquial English, ("Oh the fishes will laugh as they swim out of the path, and the seagulls they'll be smiling"), and effective use of alliteration and assonance ("Oh the time will come up when the winds will stop and the breeze will cease to be a breathin'"). This is a song of exultation, and it sounds exulted. When dealing with clear-cut allegorized moral issues and those non-descript, unhuman "foes" who make a hobby out of cultivating malice, you can rejoice unequivocally and unabashedly.

Few of Dylan's protest lyrics rejoice this way, because they see things in more human (and hence more ambivalent) terms, and because they concern themselves with struggle rather than victory. Only "The Times They Are A-Changin'," which leads off and titles Dylan's great protest album, comes anywhere close to the affirmation of "When the Ship Comes In," but it rejoices in the certainty of change with only the potentiality for permanent resolution of social and political injustices: "And don't speak too soon for the wheel's still in spin and there's no tellin' who that it's namin'." In being realistic, though, the song also ties itself closely to particulars: writers, critics, parents, senators; and while such particulars may have been desirable in the Kennedy sixties, they ring a bit hollow a decade later. What became of that promise "There's a battle outside and it's ragin', it'll soon shake your windows and rattle your walls"?

All other Dylan protest lyric contains either timelessness or insight which rescue them from the oblivion of dated topical protests and easy moral generalities. "Hollis Brown" and "Hattie Carroll" are both topical songs, tied closely to their respective narratives; they borrow much from the blues and ballad folk traditions, both of which revel in particularized situations and details. "Hollis Brown," however, universalizes in true folk tradition and finds itself sympathizing with a mass murderer. "Hattie Carroll" focuses not so much on the brutal murder itself, which is topical and particular, but on the malfunction of justice—a timeless subject if ever there was one. The song tells us not that one black woman has been abused, but that justice simply does not exist for millions of poor people, black people, minority people. That's a universal truth . . . it was then and still is today.

"Only a Pawn In Their Game" best exemplifies Dylan's ability to transcend the smug self-righteousness of most protest singers. It evidences the same understanding (one hestitates to use the word "sympathy") for Medgar Evers' murderer that Dylan exhibited for Lee Oswald at the Tom Paine Award banquet: "it ain't him to blame, he's only a pawn in their game." Poetically the lyric has both strengths and weaknesses. The chess image, while not unique, works well, as do some of the similes ("to walk in a pack," "like a dog on a chain") and a few of the phrases Dylan coins ("took Medgar Ever's blood"). But too many of Dylan's usages are merely eccentric ("He's taught in his school from the start by the rule"), much of his alliteration is pointless ("A bullet from the back of a bush"), and some of his rhyming sounds like Ray Stevens and John Skelton at their worst.

Of all Dylan's protest lyrics, "Blowin' In the Wind" and "A Hard Rain's A-Gonna Fall" come closest to poetry. Indeed, they are veritable compendia of standard poetic devices: metaphor, symbol, allusion, metonomy, refrain, rhetorical questions, imagery. "Blowin' In the Wind" is unquestionably inferior, not so much because it has been over-sung and over-played, but because its content simply doesn't support more than a few repetitions. Roads, white doves, cannon balls, sky, mountains—all are traditional, simple, and perhaps tired images. Simplicity is a strength when the song is first heard: it's easily grasped, its meaning is immediately clear. But at the tenth or ten hundredth hearing, those images have worn thin. Perhaps Dylan intends old, tired cliched images to provide a sharp contrast to his refrain "Blowin' in the Wind," but that's not the way this song comes off. "A Hard Rain" anticipates the surrealism of Dylan's allegories ("Desolation Row," "Ballad of a Thin Man," "Visions of Johanna," "Mr. Tambourine Man," "Sad-Eyed Lady of the Low Lands" and all the others) in its complex imagery and symbolic narrative. It moves beyond "When the Ship Comes In," which used a simple and, in comparison, easily grasped symbol, to a series of dense and enigmatic lines each of which, as Dylan himself once noted, could have been an entire poem. In a question-answer form borrowed from the traditional ballad, "Lord Randall" ("Oh where have you been, Lord Randall, my son?/Oh where have you been my bonny young man?) Dylan examines his own role as a protest singer. Imagistically the song touches on virtually every conceivable topic of protest music: pollution ("a dozen dead oceans"), the wasteland of contemporary existence ("the mouth of a graveyard"), what *Ramparts* magazine calls public welfare for the rich ("a highway of diamonds with nobody on it"), race ("I saw a white man who walked a black dog"), the lack of communication ("ten thousand talkers whose tongues were all broken"), child abuse ("guns and sharp swords in the hands of young children"), neglected interpersonal relationships ("One person starve, many persons laughing"), denial of art and religion ("the song of a poet who died in the gutter"), the lack of love ("one man who was wounded in love") . . . and on and on. If the song has a fault, it is either this enormous and—given the song's melody—almost monotonous recital of tribulation, or Dylan's own apparent renege on the song's commitment. I do not consider either of these a fault, because it is precisely by amassing this freight of evidence that the lyric justifies its conclusion (a very hard rain indeed has began to fall), and because I don't think Dylan ever really hedged on his commitment.

That is a story best told by the lyrics of *Another Side of Bob Dylan,* for it is in "My Back Pages" of this album that one discovers Dylan's supposed apostasy: "Ah, but I was so much older then, I'm younger than that now." It seems to me, however, that a close examination of that album, coupled with objective view of subsequent work, shows that Dylan did not abdicate social and political criticism, but merely transformed his style. "Subterranean Homesick Blues" is a very political song; the same might be said of the entire *John Wesley Harding* album. What Dylan discovered at this point in his career is the unavoidable tyranny of being a leader. Power corrupts, he realized, and declined the role, much to the discomfort of an army of followers hungry to march. One other thing Bob saw: the ultimate inefficacy, even hypocrisy, of protest which attempts to change others without changing self and proceeds by direct, violent, forceful confrontation. We are all pawns, Dylan had already realized; now he proceeds to the corollary: are we not hypocritical in denying "the foe's" essential humanity, and perhaps a bit stupid in thinking we'll bludgeon him into submission? That attitude permeates this album, from its first cut ("All I Really Want to Do" is be friends with you) to its last: "it ain't me you're lookin' for, babe." This is the album not of Bob Dylan crusader, but of Bob Dylan, friend.

Most of these lyrics make his position perfectly clear. "All I Really Want to Do" tells whoever happens to be listening "I ain't lookin' for you to feel like me, see like me, or be like me." What could be clearer? Maybe the boy-girl cover obscures things a trifle, but Dylan's point should be obvious to a fifth-grader. "Black Crow Blues" shows a similar rejection of role: "Sometimes I'm thinkin' I'm too high to fall, other times I'm thinkin' I'm so low I don't know if I can come up at all." "It Ain't Me" might have been written to the audience at the Tom Paine Award dinner.

It is "Chimes of Freedom" and "I Shall Be Free--No. 10" that really indicate not only Dylan's recognition of the problem confronting him, but his immediate solution. In the former Dylan leaves the mountain and ocean of "A Hard Rain" and ducks inside a doorway, safe from the revolutionary transformations going on around him. He rejoices in change, alright, but remains throughout the song a detached observer. In the latter, a pseudo-nonsense song in the tradition of "Talkin' World War III Blues", he tells us "I'm a poet, I know it, hope I don't blow it." Ambiguous lines, these. And again, "You're probably wonderin' just about now what this song is all about . . . It's nothing'." More enigmatic. But Dylan begins with this: "I'm just average, common too; I'm just like him and the same as you; I'm everybody's brother and son, I ain't different than anyone." No sense talking to me, Bob concludes, it would just be like talking to yourself. These lines are not at all enigmatic, although our first impulse is to disbelieve them: we're being told Bob Dylan is no leader, a man no different from ourselves, to whom we might just as well talk. The rest of the song is nonsense, the self-proclaimed vacuity of which supports the poet's claim to intellectual bankruptcy. Suddenly we find ourselves thrown upon ourselves . . . which is precisely the way Dylan wants it. He didn't blow it, although we might have thought he did. In fact, public disenchantment with Dylan's abdication is precisely the measure of his success. Poets don't tell you, they make you realize things yourself, and they do it with something more subtle than "try to realize it's all within yourself and life goes on within you." Bob Dylan, the protest singer, was retiring; Bob Dylan, the poet was emerging. Involved in the transition was a search for identity—or rather a search for a new identity, a search which led through the nightmare of Dylan's own soul and produced the great rock lyrics of the middle albums.

Problems of self-definition had in fact plagued Bob Dylan most of his artistic career, and very much like the confessional poets (Berryman, Lowell, Plath) he allowed himself to attack those problems in his lyrics and poetry. His work is full of attempts at self-discovery, from the awkward posturing of that first album to the titles and underlying conceptions of *Self-Portrait* and *New Morning*. You see biographical confusion in his early denial of parents and background ("Well, I just don't have any family, I'm all alone," he told one interviewer), in his assumption of a pseudonym (*not* from Dylan Thomas) at a time when he really didn't need one, in the wild and romantic tales he insisted on spinning about a youth spent running away from home, riding the rails, playing piano in a strip joint, listening to Woody Guthrie somewhere out in California. You see his obsession with self on the jacket of each album he ever released: always a picture of Dylan on the front, most likely some of his own poetry or fiction on the back. But most of all you see this concern in the works of his great middle albums—*Bringing It All Back Home, Highway 61 Revisited, Blonde on Blonde* (all produced in about a year and a half), and *John Wesley Harding.* On these albums Dylan's obsession not only provides his themes but dictates the very nature of his art. Developing the dialogue technique used in "A Hard Rain," Dylan addresses himself in one, two, sometimes several alter-egos, holds discussions among several projections of his own self. "Dylan uses masks in his songs," Craig MacGregor has observed in *Bob Dylan: A retrospective.* "In many of them he seems to be writing about himself in the second or third person, as though distancing himself from and then addressing himself; so that the 'you' of the song is really 'I'." According to Tony Scaduto, Dylan once remarked about these lyrics, "I was really talking about no one but me." A mature Dylan himself made the following observation:

> I'll tell you another discovery I've made . . . on a strange level the songs are done for somebody, about somebody, and to somebody. Usually that person is the somebody who is singing that song.

As much as any rock artist, Dylan cultivated ambiguity between singer and subject. Point of view in the middle lyrics presents all the complexities of Marat/Sade or the *Canterbury Tales* as the artist struggles to step outside of himself, rise above himself, achieve an external, objective perspective on himself from which he can objectively define and interpret his own being. This is not a mystical impulse to transcend the finite ego, as Steven Goldberg has suggested; it is rather the rationalist's demand for an objective appraisal of that which cannot really be appraised objectively. The quest after objective perspective leads Dylan to project alter egos, which can then be derided or pitied at arm's length: not only the vague "you" to whom many of his lyrics are addressed, but concrete characters like the blue-eyed son, the juggler and clown, Napoleon in rags, the mystery tramp, even Miss Lonely herself of "Like a Rollin' Stone." And the scorn of a line like "How does it feel to be out on your own?" is as much self-contempt as personal attack on complacent, upper middle class, spoiled society bitches. Dylan is little boy lost in "Visions of Johanna," the Tambourine Man, the lady of "She Belongs to Me." Probably he is, or views himself as, John Wesley Harding, Tom Paine, the fair damsel, Frankie Lee, St. Augustine, the drifter, joker and thief of *John Wesley Harding.* I'm reminded of the fragmented mirror image of Hesse's *Steppenwolf* (a novel which Dylan certainly knows) that becomes chesspieces with which Pablo (also a projection of the Steppenwolf's own self) plays into games of endless varieties and possibilities. Or I'm reminded of the projective autobiographies Joseph Knecht writes in Hesse's *Das Glasperlienspiel.*

Now there's no doubt that most good artists "put a little of themselves into their art," as we like to say, and that twentieth century artists have proven more introspective than most. It is also true that crises of identity confront just about anyone maturing in an age which not only permits, but on the surface of things appears to encourage individuals to define themselves in self-created contexts. Certainly identity is a problem for other Jewish writers and for other rock lyricists (the Who's *Quadrophenia,* Phil Ochs' *Rehearsals for Retirement,* the Bands' *Cahoots,* to name only a few.). But Dylan involves himself more exclusively than anyone else in his search for self; so much so, in fact, that it may well be that none of the allegories of his middle period can be entirely understood in its entirety without an understanding of this quest after self.

Dylan arrived in New York City with no real personality of his own. He had left Bob Zimmerman, son of a Hibbing, Minnesota hardware store owner, behind him in the north country, and was busy playing Woody Guthrie, Cisco Houston, Jack Elliot, Blind Lemon Jefferson, Leadbelly . . . anyone but Bob Dylan. Jack Elliot recalled young Dylan to biographer Scaduto this way:

> Some of the people around were turned off a little bit because Bob was playing the hobo role. I thought he was maybe a little too young to pull it off in the style in which he was doing it. He was trying to sound like an old man who bummed around eighty-five years on a freight train, and you could see this kid didn't even have fuzz on his face yet . . . I thought sometimes he had a lot of nerve trying to get away with that bullshit.

Later Elliot recalls that Bob was experimenting with several different singers and styles, people he'd never heard of, trying on all sorts of different selves. You don't need Elliot's testimony for this, however; that first album reveals Dylan in all his young eclecticism. And not an ounce of it legitimate.

With this protest songs, Dylan quickly found a personality—or had on imposed upon him. He was a leader, a marcher, a civil rights worker, and something of a bardic poet. As we've seen, Bob found the role uncomfortable and deliberately rejected it; but for a while it provided a self which could shoot verbally at the masters of war and emphathize with Lee Oswald or Hollis Brown. The biography on the early albums is pretty straight in songs like "Oxford Town" and "Bob Dylan's Dream" and "Girl from the North Country"; it is painfully, embarrassingly autobiographical in "Ballad in Plain D." Similarly, the poetry printed on these albums is pretty straight stuff. As Dylan himself put it, "Because Dickens and Dostoevski and Woody Guthrie were telling their stories much better than I ever could, I decided to stick to my own mind." His mind, as revealed in his songs and poems, was that of a protest singer-poet, cut off from his past and dissatisfied with himself, searching for a new identity in songs and in people around him.

Another Side is an album of the self independent of others, an album of denial and rejection even of Bob's closest New York friends. It is a mediocre, confused album and flies off in a lot of directions, but it also indicates the direction in which Dylan was heading stylistically and technically. "My Back Pages" is wildly imagistic; "Spanish Harlem Incident" and "Motorpsycho Nightmare" are surrealistic, developing earlier things like "I Shall Be Free," leading us out of folk-protest and into Rimbaud or Brecht. Most important, Dylan has began to view others as actual extensions of himself, rather than merely seeing similarities between other real people and his own self. The distinction is fine, but in terms of technique it's crucial. "To Ramona" contains important ambiguity: Dylan talks to both his girl *and* his earlier self: "From fixtures and forces and friends your sorrow does stem." Is this Dylan to his girl, or Dylan to himself? Or the "Chimes of Freedom," ringing for "every hung up person in the whole wide universe"—is not one of these persons Dylan, imprisoned in his role as high priest of protest? Just who is being convinced that "It ain't me, babe"—us, or some girl, or Bobby Dylan? Or all of these? All of these, I think; many of the people Dylan writes about from here on out will be Dylan himself, either in whole or part. For it was by talking to himself this way that the poet arrived ultimately at what Jon Landau has called "Bob Dylan, moderate man," the self of *John Wesley Harding* and later albums.

In no lyric is the projection of self more skillfully handled, more central to subject as well as technique, than in "Visions of Johanna."

"He gives the same person several names and changes the points of view around over and over, like a rubber ball bouncing down a hill in a wind tunnel—the movement is one way continuously but there are many points of view," Ralph Gleason has said. "In so many songs where Dylan seems to be writing about women, he is really writing about Dylan," Scaduto has stated in a different regard. Both remarks are pertinent to "Visions of Johanna," in which point of view changes constantly and the visions of Johanna that temporarily conquer the poet's mind are nothing more than the debilitating, enervating roles he has allowed himself to play . . . personal illusions and delusions of grandeur. By 1966 Bob Dylan was a prisoner of his own success: "His head was all screwed around from the pressures, the fame, that whole insane thing that was happening to him,'' a friend recalled. Too intelligent to be much impressed with either fame or fortune, and too perceptive to ignore the threat posed to his private self by his public image, the poet had long ago attempted to shed public images and work his way down to psychological bedrock. Only the images had not left hold of Dylan, and they would not until he virtually disappeared from public view for a year and a half following his motorcycle (or automobile) accident. "Ain't it just like the night to play tricks when you're trying to be so quiet?" he asks to begin "Visions of Johanna." "We sit here stranded 'though we're all doin' our best to deny it." Louise and her lover (perhaps Dylan himself), flickering lights, coughing heat pipes, a radio which nobody cares to turn off, and visions of Johanna that conquer the poet's mind: in these images Dylan depicts his own exhausted enervation, his own head screwed around from pressures and fame. The end point of "Visions" is a liberating explosion into Dylan's own art, discovery in song (this song) of that very catharsis the impossibility of which the lyric laments: his harmonica proves to be the key that unlocks his prison, the vehicle of release. The road to this release from the prison of self has led through a series of personae, each offering a new and seemingly objective perspective on a previous self. From the arid room of that first stanza Dylan's point of view opens to the empty lots where the night watchman asks that crucial question, "Is it him or them that's insane?" From there the scene shifts to the hallway where a new Dylan leaves the old Dylan (little boy lost) paralyzed by self-pity. "All we have to get hung up on is hang-ups themselves," Dylan suggests as he prepares to energize himself by the simple act of leaving . . . a symbolic act he has used so often before. Fame is tried and convicted: even Mona Lisa had the highway blues, you can tell by the way she smiles! Dylan, is a favorite guise of a peddler (cf. "Like a Rolling Stone"), confronts an alter ego in the persona of a countess "who's pretending to care for him," denies that self, and breaks free into musical and psychological freedom. Little wonder that the conscience explodes after such a cast of characters, such constantly shifting points of view, such a series of denials. Nor, I suppose, is it surprising that the explosion leaves Dylan with little more than his harmonica and his freedom: a man playing the harmonica is, after all, what he's all about anyway.

"Visions of Johanna" is perhaps too complex: it may attempt one too many twists of point of view, one too many alter egos, one too many visions and revisions. Moreover, for all the apparent affirmation of its conclusion, it's really not a satisfying resolution to Dylan's problem, except insofar as technique frees him from old selves, old philosophical stances. In its technique, however, "Visions of Johanna" is characteristic of several lyrics of *Bringing It All Back Home, Highway 61*

Revisited, and *Blonde on Blonde.* The technique underlies the entire conception of *John Wesley Harding.*

All of those first three albums freely mix three types of lyric: Dylan's nightmare visions of external, objective reality ("Outlaw Blues," "On the Road Again," "Desolation Row," "Gates of Eden," and to a certain extent "Tombstone Blues"); songs in which Dylan offers others advice which he has come to accept personally, thereby making the "you" similar to, although not necessarily an extension of, the "I" ("Like a Rolling Stone," "Ballad of a Thin Man," "Tom Thumb's Blues," "Subterranean Homesick Blues," "Maggie's Farm," "Rainy Day Women No. 12 and 35"); and lyrics in which Dylan addresses himself to what are essentially alter-egos ("Bob Dylan's 115th Dream," "Baby Blue," for all the business above Dave Blue, "She Belongs to Me," "Love Minus Zero/No Limit," "It Takes A Lot to Laugh, It Takes a Train to Cry," "From a Buick 6," "I Want You," "Just Like a Woman," "Sad-Eyed Lady of the Low Lands"). A very few songs appear to be straight satires of individuals or types ("Leopardskin Pillbox Hat," "Sweet Marie"), or traditional departure lyrics ("One Of Us Must Know," "Most Likely You'll Go Your Way"). The first two types have provided most of the popular songs from these albums, perhaps because they are most easily understood, but technically they represent no achievement beyond previous albums. Thematically they fail to move beyond the concerns of his earlier music: protests and put downs. The real visitation of self implied by Dylan in titles like *Highway 61 Revisited* (route 61 runs through his hometown of Hibbing, Minnesota) and *Bringing It All Back Home* takes place in those songs which examine his own problems as they relate peculiarly to himself, and in his obsession with death and resurrection imagery culminating in *John Wesley Harding.*

Bringing It All Back Home, the earliest of these three albums, is filled with transcendence and resolution: Dylan seems to imply that the hang-ups of "Subterranean Homesick Blues" (more external than psychological) or of the personal "Baby Blue" can be easily resolved by transcending reality either in art ("She Belongs to Me," in which Dylan posits himself as artist beyond normal conventions of morality and justice, and the great "Mr. Tambourine Man"), or in an idealized self ("Love Minus Zero/No Limit"), or in paradise ("The Gates of Eden"). Conceptually this is a superficial album, in that the poet has only begun to see the problem confronting him; he still appears to believe in a simple solution of "being yourself" ("Maggie's Farm") . . . whatever that is.

Highway 61 Revisited is philosophically more complex, and its lead cut, "Like a Rolling Stone" (quite probably the greatest rock song ever) makes it clear that being free is not all the fun "Maggie's Farm" implied it is. The contempt of this lyric is partially self-contempt, as has frequently been pointed out: it was written not long after Dylan had been booed off the stage at Newport, and you can't help reading his own person into Miss Lonely and Princess on a steeple. "You never turned around to see the frowns on the jugglers and the clowns when they all come down and did tricks for you . . . How does it feel to be out on your own?"

At this point in his career, if the evidence presented by Anthony Scaduto is anywhere near accurate, Dylan was himself on the verge of exploding (Phil Ochs accused him of being clinically insane, and not without justification); this Dylan seems to have sensed himself, as in "Tombstone Blues" one part of Dylan derides another part of Dylan. The title is not insignificant. "Queen Jane Approximately" and "Desolation Row" both reflect Dylan's personal enervation, are both very personal songs. "It Takes a Lot to Laugh, It Takes a Train to Cry" embodied one aspect of the poet in his baby who will make it if he doesn't, just as "From a Buick 6" projects a part of himself into a "graveyard woman, junkyard angel," projecting escape while focusing on paralysis and sterility.

Blonde on Blonde, from which "Visions of Johanna" comes, takes Dylan into the core of the storm and, apart from producing some of his finest music, contains some of his most complex visions. The poet is dissatisfied with himself, with the world and people around him, and with the direction in which he sees everything heading. The album abounds in lyrics of separation, hate, scorn, departure. "You'll Go Your Way And I'll Go Mine" is a simple lyric of separation and distances: "I just can't do what I've done before . . ., I'm gonna let you pass." "Temporarily Like Achilles" scorns the poet for becoming *temporarily* vulnerable, temporarily like a conventional lover, and ends in rejecting both: "How come you get somebody like him to be your guy?" "So what's with you, Bob?" he seems to be asking himself. "Fourth Time Around" presents a persona who, not unlike Dylan himself in some of his angrier moments, has been used three times and takes his frustrations out by using someone else for a change. "Absolutely Sweet Marie" carries Dylan's invective to its extreme: "Well, anybody can be just like me, obviously but then again, not too many can be like you fortunately."

"Memphis Blues Again," a crucial lyric, describes an insane world in which nobody maintains his balance; it offers, moreover, a key to the rest of the lyrics from this period: "You see, you're just like me, you can't hide." These other characters Dylan has been addressing are virtual alter egos, and in their sickness we see some of Dylan's revulsion toward his own person and the world he has created. His head is shot ("it strangles up my mind"), and all he can wonder is "Oh, mama, can this really be the end?" Like the album as a whole, this lyric implies little hope: "And here I sit so patiently waiting to find out what price you have to pay to get out of going through all of these things twice."

Psychologically Dylan is approaching absolute zero. The hope of "I'm Pledging My Time" is a carrion comfort. "Sad-eyes Lady of the Low Lands", in one sense a projection of Dylan into an ideal self similar to the lady of "Love Minus Zero/No Limit," is at best ambiguous. We are ready for the joker's remark: "There must be *some* way out of here."

Artistically Dylan has created an art which sees himself *in* others and *as* others, and—more frequently—others as himself. *John Wesley Harding* takes this art one step further, orders the metaphysical positions embodied in the personae of successive lyrics, annd in doing so resolves Dylan's identity crisis and allows him to relate himself to others. The album is unquestionably Dylan's great work, product of well over a year's contemplation and introspection, bearing the marks of musical, philosophical, poetic, and psychological maturity. In it Dylan finally achieves the salvation he claimed in that infamous *Playboy* interview was all he had to look forward to: "Close your eyes, close the door, you don't have to worry anymore, I'll be your baby tonight." It would be seven years before Dylan moved beyond this statement. Subsequent work would be mere philosophical, poetical, technical elaboration, what salvation must be like after a while. After affirmation, what?

The affirmation of this album, however, is slow coming; the stark allegories of its first side are as dark, brooding, terrifying as anything Dylan had previously written. To tick them off quickly, one treats the outlaw-hero myth with all its violent overtones; another deals with justice so perverse that you have to apologize for desiring freedom; a third focuses on martyrdom and sin; a fourth portrays human existence in stark, claustrophobic terms; a fifth recounts the death attendant on twentieth century materialism; only in the last does anyone finally escape. The first side is filled with a very Judeo-Christian sense of guilt and the need for atonement, considerable Christian imagery, and a profound realization that despite his best intentions, man is inherently sinful. A depressing statement—but only in terms of such realizations does Dylan's final affirmation of love make any sense. "Love is all there is," Dylan has told us more recently; "All you need is love," sing the Beatles . . . but unless we have traveled with them their own routes to such awareness, that kind of insight came only after an artistic lifetime spent searching, both in person and masked behind various personae on this album and others.

The first cut on the album is its title song, "John Wesley Harding." The name alone is a curious blend of the strict Calvanistic religion of John Wesley and the loose amorality of John Wesley Hardin, Texas outlaw. Tensions between the two are explored further in such juxtaposed phrases as "friend of the poor," "traveled with a gun in every hand," "never known to hurt an honest man." That phrase of Dylan's "to live outside the law you must be honest" runs through our heads here, and increases our uneasiness. We begin to ask questions: why should an honest man hide? How can you help people with guns? Just what sort of a stand is John taking? If he's so helpful and good, what's he charged with? To the extent we ask questions, Michael Gray is correct in saying the song poses more problems that it answers. But answers emerge in the very contradictions of the outlaw's name and the tensions between what is traditionally right and just, and what seems right and just in this case. Obviously we find ourselves in a world in which generosity is criminal, honesty proscribed, and wisdom more characteristic of outlaws than duly constituted authority. This myth underlies any number of cowboy films—Bob has acted in one himself—and Dylan is drawing on them all here (lines like "all across the telegraph" and "track or chain him down" come right out of the wild west mystique). But the motif is also as current and political as Daniel Ellsberg or Phillip Berrigan. Whether Harding is a projection of Dylan's own self, or a recreation of the Texas outlaw, or merely a construct created out of western tradition, it is clear that he represents a starting point for Dylan's movement toward salvation: traditional patterns òf justice and morality have become perverted, the generous man lives outside conventional law and faces its strictures and hostility. Certainly Dylan has come to view himself as an outsider, living in but resisting the demands of American society, and the stance taken in this lyric is personal as well as public and political.

"As I Went Out One Morning" pushes the vision further by reversing point of view: no longer the outlaw-hero, Dylan aligns himself with forces constraining freedom. The tensions of "John Wesley Harding" are again present: "fairest damsel" is juxtaposed against "chains," which in turn conflict with "meant to do me harm." How has one so fair come to be chained? How can one in chains work harm? Her situation is that of a damsel awaiting rescue; the narrator deliberately eschews the role and orders her to depart. What's with this guy? Her request amounts to a plea for liberty (although flight will be south rather than north, an interesting inversion reminiscent of Twain's *Huck Finn*); it is denied first by the narrator and then by the great libertarian Tom Paine himself. In fact, Paine actually apologizes for her actions! But while the inversions and perversions of this lyric are those of "John Wesley Harding," Dylan's view of himself has shifted so as to align himself with slave-master Tom Paine instead of outlaw-hero John Harding. Thematically this lyric turns on Dylan's ability to discover a portion of himself in everyone from Hollis Brown to Lee Oswald, from victim to

aggressor—Tom Paine is like Simon Legree, and Dylan is like both. This
moment of awareness frees Dylan from the self-righteousness of "John
Wesley Harding," allows Dylan to recognize himself as a part of the very
restrictive society he formerly felt himself outside of, and prepares the
way for his subsequent salvation and regeneration.

John Wesley Harding is an album pervaded with sin and redemption,
and associated concerns for the soul, for guilt and the expiation of guilt,
for salvation. "A penitent's album," MacGregor has called it, "ridden
with shame, guilt, and desire for atonement—Dylan's *Ash Wednesday* as
surely as 'Desolation Row' was his *Waste Land*." "As I Went Out One
Morning" introduced a recognition of sin to the album, and implied the
need for forgiveness, although in a very misdirected line: "I'm sorry for
what she's done." Sin and contrition are at the core of the album's third
cut, "I Dreamed I Saw St. Augustine." Like Tom Paine, Dylan's saint is
not an historical personage (neither St. Augustine of Hippo or St.
Augustine of England was martyred), but his name—like those of Harding and Tom Paine—is intended to be suggestive. Augustine tears frantically through this country searching for lost souls, lamenting the death
of prophets and martyrs in this modern wasteland, and offering his own
message of comfort: "know you're not alone." For his troubles, he is
martyred himself, and the narrator of this dream vision finds himself
among the company of those who put him to death: Paul holding the
coats of those who stoned St. Stephen as it were. The myth is clear:
always man kills the prophet, the martyr, the Christ; the human condition is such that no man can rise above his own sin; every man is implicated in every death. Dylan has moved somewhere here, from
recognizing that he is *like* Lee Oswald to realizing he *is* Lee Oswald. It's
the old truth that we are all implicated in all social and political injustice,
even though we do not ourselves perpetrate it. The revelation comes to
Dylan in a dream, but it cannot be dismissed as only a dream because, as
the narrator realizes, it contains a valid truth. The measure of that truth
is to be found in those closing lines: "Oh I awoke in anger, so alone
. . ." St. Augustine died in the dream and it was in the dream that his
presence allowed men to know they were not alone; and yet the
narrator's recognition of loneliness following Augustine's martyrdom
comes outside of the dream context.

Dylan's recognition of what theologians would call "man's inherent
sin" occasions a series of reactions: anger, terror, prayer, and the contrition of tears. The first, I suppose, is a remnant of the rage which
Augustine elicited and which no doubt provoked his death: it is yet
another link between the world of the dream and that of reality. The
second is a reaction to Dylan's recognition of his own capacity for evil
(the same recognition, incidentally, provokes a similar reaction in Phil

Ochs' "Crucifixion"). The third and fourth are important theologically: recognizing himself for the sinner he is, Dylan feels the need of prayer and contrition. "The glass" may be interpreted in two ways, each of similar significance: either it is a looking glass in which Dylan sees his own reflection and his own sin ("Yet I swear I see my reflection somewhere so high above this wall" he sang in "I Shall Be Released," which dates from this same period and treats similar themes), or it is a window through which Dylan can see visions of what ought to be, but through which he cannot pass to realize those visions. In either case, it is the view into or through this glass which occasions his awareness of his own personal need for grace.

In three songs Dylan has come, through a series of personae, a long way from the position of "John Wesley Harding"; yet his journey has just now begun. Aware of his own sin, Dylan at first despairs, then escapes from his own despondency, then expiates his guilt, and finally achieves the salvation and affirmation mentioned earlier.

"All Along the Watchtower" and "The Ballad of Frankie Lee and Judas Priest" are desperate lyrics. The one bangs frantically on walls ("There must be some way out of here"), the other describes mistaken paradises and resultant spiritual death. No exit. Both are riddled with Judeo-Christian theology and imagery. Of the two, I think "All Along the Watchtower" is more effective because it is more concise and much more evocative. "The Watchtower" suggests, of course, the Jehovah's Witness publication, Isaiah's Watchtower, Christ's admonition that we watch and wait for we know neither the time nor the hour, a sentinel outpost designed to provide advanced warning of future developments, and—to me at least—the cross. The wildcat reminds me of Dante's leopard, the approaching riders suggest the horsemen of the apocalypse, the howling wind recalls Good Friday. Fanciful, perhaps, and I would not press my own associations too far or too strongly . . . but obviously something apocalyptic is up. Jon Landau speaks of "experiencing" a poem and of the mood evoked by this particular poem; certainly this is a mood piece, but such vague intangibles don't explain what's happening here. The lyric presents us with an imagined conversation between "the joker and the thief." One clearly represents an extension of the claustrophobic terror at which Dylan himself had arrived in the song previous ("I put my finger against the glass"), but it extends him in a new direction. Businessmen drink his wine, plowmen dig his earth, the joker tells us—lines which would not be utterly inappropriate in the mouth of Christ, although you needn't be so specific. Certainly the joker is a man of importance ("*my* wine, *my* earth"), certainly he finds himself trapped, certainly he has power and knowledge beyond other people. The thief (back to John Wesley Harding) responds with an assurance we might better expect of his deific counterpart: "we've been through that," he assures the joker, "and this is not our fate." The closing lines of that speech, however, suggest a certain uneasiness, as if the thief now suddenly senses not only the urgency of their extremities, but the doubts of his companion: "Let us not talk falsely now. Haven't you told me so yourself? And now you're no longer certain?" The joker does not answer. Dylan turns his attention to externals: princes watching and waiting, imminent disaster in approaching wildcats, riders, storms. The veil of the Temple was rent in twain, darkness covered the earth, dead walked the streets.

"The Ballad of Frankie Lee and Judas Priest" concerns itself with temptation and death, Judas Priest (another interesting and significant juxtaposition of names) playing the role of tempter, Frankie Lee playing his willing victim. We have not seen such a congenial demon since the Stone's "Sympathy For the Devil": "when Frankie Lee needed money one day, Judas quickly pulled out a role of tens." Franklie senses something wrong and requests time to think; Judas, sensing that he just may lose his victim, sends for him . . . and Frankie Lee comes running. This is a fatal mistake, and the former atheist ("I don't call it anything at all") rushes to sell what he has and give it to the poor while the mission bells toll his death. Too late; after sixteen days of raving Frankie Lee bursts into the arms of Judas Priest. "Died of thirst," Dylan tells us, recalling again Christ on the cross. The song ends on a couple of curious notes: the guilty neighbor boy and his cryptic comment that nothing is revealed, and the moral Dylan appends to the tale. The two, I believe, are at odds with each other; the latter is a typically Christian aphorism to the effect that one should help his neighbor; the former suggests that what is offered as a moral is not Dylan's prime concern. In fact, I rather suspect that the guilt of this apparently innocuous child, so peripheral to the story's plot, is more important than it first seems. "We are all guilty," Dylan suggests, simply by virtue of being born—a rather bold statement of the orthodox doctrine of original sin, and a position at which Dylan has already arrived intellectually in "St. Augustine" and "All Along the Watchtower": man hates and kills, and there is no apparent way out of here.

No *apparent* way, that is. For in the last lyric of side one Dylan, in the personage of an old drifter, makes his escape. "The Drifter's Escape" involves a Kafka-esque recognition of man's inherent guilt and his inability to comprehend his own sin ("But I still do not know what it was that I've done wrong"), a very un-Dylan-like recognition of weakness, and a very human plea for help ("Help me in my weakness"). This last is most interesting, since it frankly admits the drifter's inability to help himself and is manifestly answered. We are unclear as to who is addressed, but indications are clear that it is not "that cursed jury" and probably not the judge who has stepped down. The crowd seems bloodthirsty, eager for condemnation in a manner reminiscent of the crowd that dispatched St. Augustine; the judge, like the judges and lawyers of Kafka's *Trial*, largely ignore the drifter. As Kafka discovered, man is guilty and it is just that he die . . . and that is all he needs to know.

But the drifter does not die. In what can only be described as a classic and very symbolic act of divine intervention (a lightning bolt which strikes the courthouse out of shape) the drifter escapes while others pray. "The Drifter's Escape" is nothing more than the dispensing of grace, the only salvation available to a Dylan who has finally recognized his own condition and weakness, and set is pride aside long enough to request grace.

The 1966 *Playboy* interview, for which Tony Scaduto would have us believe Dylan wrote both questions and answers, records the following conversation:

Playboy: You told an interviewer last year, "I've done everything I ever wanted to." If that's true, what do you have to look forward to?

Dylan: Salvation. Just plain salvation.

Playboy: Anything else?

Dylan: Praying.

In discussing *John Wesley Harding*, Craig MacGregor once wrote, "In many ways, in fact, Dylan's metaphysical progress (from rebellion to spiritual confusion to acceptance) has been very similar to that of a poet whom he has read and sometimes derided, T.S. Eliot." MacGregor is on target, although his evaluation is only partially true because it ignores the progress within the album itself, from persona to persona, from isolation to guilt to contrition to penance to grace. Most of Dylan's shame and guilt are concentrated on side one; atonement and an actual state of grace appear on side two.

"Dear Landlord" demonstrates a kind of understanding of self and others absent in most of Dylan's poetry. Someone has suggested Dylan wrote the song to set off "Now each of us has his own special gift"; I suspect the second stanza is more important. This lyric takes us back to Frankie Lee and Judas Priest, to "Like a Rolling Stone," to the hang ups which have plagued Dylan for most of his career. Dylan's beyond all of them now, ready to forgive others and—more important—himself. Most significant, however, is his tone here: understated, quiet, purged of the scorn and bitter anger which marked everything from "Masters of War" to "Positively 4th Street." The poet accepts his subservience to a landlord who is neither humane or understanding. Instead of scorn and bristling hostility, however, Dylan offers sympathy. Three successive pleas in three successive stanzas are remarkable from Bob Dylan, as is the refusal to argue or to judge. The final line takes ua ll the way back, both linguistically and tonally, to the relatively peaceful days of Bob Dylan the protest singer doing "Talkin' World War III Blues": "I'll let you be in my dream if I can be in yours."

Where "Dear Landlord" offered sympathy, "Lonesome Hobo" offers advice. The character, a cross between the drifter and John Wesley Harding, sounds suspiciously like Dylan of "Like a Rolling Stone": Perhaps that last line is the key: this character has been too proud to beg, to submit himself to anyone except himself. His inability to trust his brother, led him to his fatal doom. Now, like a rich man come back from the dead to warn his five brothers, this lonesome hobo returns from his metaphysical death to warn us all: "Stay free from petty jealousies, live by no man's code, and hold your judgments for yourself."

"I Pity the Poor Immigrant" follows. This may well be the finest lyric on _John Wesley Harding,_ and one of the best in all rock poetry. It is exceptionally tight, ordering each of its stanzas in a series of parallel phrases, using rhetorical parallelisms within those phrases. And it reaches back to other lyrics on _John Wesley Harding:_ "St. Augustine" with its concern for man's propensity to do evil and the glass which would not shatter there; Frankie Lee who fell in love with wealth and feared his death; the joker and the thief who could find no way out of their nightmare. The lyric's central image is carefully chosen: the immigrant, the man estranged from his native land, confused and strange in a world he neither understands nor loves. This immigrant is, in the simplest sense, a foreigner who needs Dylan's understanding; in another sense he is Dylan himself, who spent so much of his career searching angrily for himself, hating, fearing, spending his strength in vain; in a third sense the immigrant is every modern man, for we have all lost control of ourselves, fallen in love with wealth, filled our mouths with laughing and our town with blood. The visions of such as one, Dylan suggests, must ultimately shatter as his own visions have shattered, and the process will be painful. But it will be therapeutic as well: it will be our gladness, it will be our salvation as it has been Dylan's salvation.

"The Wicked Messenger" is straight Dylan autobiography, a redefinition of his own role similar to "A Hard Rain's A-Gonna Fall" done so many years ago. This song personalizes the album just after "The Poor Immigrant" has universalized it. If anything Dylan is too hard on his former self: "When questioned who had sent for him, he answered with his thumb, for his tongue it could not speak but only flatter." He has confronted a few people lately, however—Frankie Lee, John Wesley Harding, St. Augustine, his landlord, a certain lonesome hobo—and his heart has been opened up by a few simple words: "If you cannot bring good news, then don't bring any." Dylan has decided to bring good news, both in the remainder of this album and in succeeding albums: the joyful affirmation of "Down Along the Cove" and "I'll Be Your Baby Tonight", of *Nashville Skyline* (the album he regards as his most satisfying), of his hymn "Father of Night," of the great benediction on *Planet Waves,* "Forever Young." The good news of these albums is cast into simple tunes, simple (even trite) lyrics, clean rhymes, and the basic truth that love is all there is. The clean simplicity of this album's last cut, "I'll Be Your Baby Tonight," offers tremendous relief after technical and philosophical complexities of *John Wesley Harding* and earlier albums, after the dark apocalypse of "All Along the Watchtower," after the despair of "St. Augustine." It is easy as country music is easy as country living is easy; in fact, Dylan adopts country music as a metaphor for this new-found peace and tranquility. Certainly he drops personae after this album, just as he drops the restless searching for himself and his paranoid visions of America. You can almost hear him singing to himself, "You don't have to worry anymore."

Oh, boy, did critics not like *Nashville Skyline!* And they like *Self Portrait* even less. And while many pretended to be reassured by *New Morning,* nobody says much about that either these days. *"Self-Portrait* will be one of the most bought and least played records of recent years," wrote Jon Landau, who, let it be admitted, never really did understand Dylan. "It is the wrong album for 1970 America—so wrong that one wonders who will care about what follows it." "Wallows in its own simplicity" he wrote of *Nashville Skyline,* "Very shoddily made," "nothing outstanding" on it. "Muzak" shouted someone. "Redneck music" accused another. "He's lost touch with the distressing reality of our psychotic times" said Carl Oglesby. The *Rolling Stone* review of *Self-Portrait* opened with "What is this shit?" and proceeded from there. In November of 1970 Raply Gleason proclaimed "We've got Dylan back again" in his review of *New Morning,* and the concert for Bangladesh suggested he was right, but the March 1973 issue of *Intellectual Digest* focused on "what Dylan did." Past tense. Mr. Dylan, he dead.

I guess. For a while. What Dylan produced between *John Wesley Harding* (1966) and that mythic tour of January, 1974 was a kind of music so totally different from his previous material as to make one wonder how the same man could have produced both. Dylan's new music was country, and it was conservative . . . artistically, philosophically, politically. I suspect he always harbored reservations about his liberal/radical commitment, and certainly *John Wesley Harding* is conservative to the point of orthodoxy. But his art was not conservative: imagistic poetry, surrealistic landscapes, fireworks of rhyme and alliteration, a rather loose form. Earlier Dylan always avoided cliches to a fault: he tried so consciously to fork new idioms that many appeared awkward and stilted. His new poetry bordered on the embarrassing: "I must have been mad, I never knew what I had until I threw it all away." "If not for you, winter would have no spring, I couldn't hear the robin sing, I just wouldn't have a clue, anyway it wouldn't ring true if not for you." "Love to spend the night with Peggy Day." An almost conscious, deliberate search *for* cliche here . . . and not because, as Michael Gray has suggested in *Song and Dance Man,* no other words will do the job. All the lyrics of this period are short, unambiguous, un-imagistic and un-surrealistic pieces in praise of love and the simple life. There is, quite frankly, nothing for the critic to explicate: "Lay, lady, lay, lay across my big brass bed." Some of this is more romantic than Paul Simon: "His clothes are dirty, but his hands are clean, and you're the best thing that he's ever seen." There is little if any projection of Dylan into alter-egos, except Bob Dylan the simple country boy. This is not interesting.

Musically Dylan had mellowed. Anger and urgency were replaced by transcendance and self-satisfaction with a resultant decline in energy level. Probably such a transition was to be expected in a man who had finally come to terms with himself; perhaps it is even to be desired, lest the man literally burn himself out. But it sure makes for dull music. You can listen to *Nashville Skyline,* but you don't hear it; you don't even listen to *Self-Portrait* (Landau was, history has proven, correct) because even on the old hard rockers ("Like a Rolling Stone, "The Mighty Quinn") Dylan just isn't cooking. Much of that album wasn't his own material, and he did it poorly ("Take Me As I Am," "Blue Moon") or sloppily ("The Boxer"). A couple of the cuts sound like Dylan just throwing away a song in his living room . . . fun, perhaps, and indicative of happiness and salvation, but not the sort of stuff you play very often. So what's up?

It seems to me that *New Morning,* rather than indicating a new beginning for Dylan, attempts to explain what the new morning begun on *John Wesley Harding* was all about. It begins with a song of love, perhaps personal to Sarah; it ends with a hymn of praise to the Lord. In between, the album traces Dylan's flight from the halls of academe ("The Day of the Locust") to the Black Hills of Dakota and a cabin in Utah, where he discovers peace and tranquility. "Day of the Locusts" comes close to being a song in the old tradition: "the man sitting next to me, his head was explodin'." Imagery, surrealism, perhaps the projected self, the uptight Dylan. He cuts out for the mountains where time passes slowly, where a man can fish and relax and live. He's in Minnesota, he's in Dakota, he's in Utah, running free with no more importance than the dogs, guarding his privacy jealously. "That must be what it's all about," he concludes, and he means it. The simple poetry and simple imagery and cliched language, then, is an artistic metaphor for the simple life. Dylan's form grows organically out of his content, and when the one cools, so does the other. The best songs of this period—"Lay, Lady, Lay," "One More Night," "Day of the Locusts," "On a Night Like This," "Forever Young—are tight, clear pieces with tight, clear points, reminiscent of those which conclude *John Wesley Harding*. I must confess I find them dull in comparison to earlier Dylan, but I think I understand what they're about: the redeemed Dylan, Dylan at peace with his woman and his god.

"Inside the museums, Infinity goes up on trial," Dylan wrote prophetically in "Visions of Johanna"; "Voices echo this is what salvation must be like after a while." Nearly a decade later, in "Shelter from the Storm," he was to look back at the redemption of post-*John Wesley Harding* albums in very similar terms. Whatever this meant for Dylan, it was good news to the rest of the country: after rejoicing over the tour of early '74, and convincing themselves (perhaps against their better judgment) that *Planet Waves* represented a Dylan returned to his sense after the disaster of *Pat Garret and Billy the Kid,* critics went right straight out of their nuts over *Blood on the Tracks* (January, 1975). "The best album of the last five years by anybody," sang Paul Williams, one of fifteen (count 'em) elect chosen to review the album in *Rolling Stone.* "Dylan's best since *Blonde on Blonde,"* all agreed. This time we really had Dylan back.

At this writing it's simply too early to know whether developments reflected in *Planet Waves* and *Blood on the Tracks* indicate a new period in the master's development or are merely spinoff from the '74 tour. In either event, they *are* sound albums, and *Blood on the Tracks* especially appears to be the start of something new, something more akin to pre-than post-*JWH* material. All is not well in paradise; salvation is debilitating, memory haunting, Dylan restless. *Planet Waves,* for example, has a terrific sense of uneasiness beneath its apparent tranquility. On the one hand you have "On a Night Like This," Bob kicking off his shoes around the fire, drinking coffee with his gal, and grooving on reminiscences. There's the love of "You Angel You," and the great rock benediction of "Forever Young," a song which grows directly out of Dylan's salvation, a song which completes that cycle of transcendence. That song lifted the roof right off Philadelphia's Spectrum on the tour, it was so warm, so reassuring, so necessary in 1974. On the other hand, there was an uneasiness to all this: people don't stay forever young, memories are by nature unsettling, the tour itself showed restlessness. Other songs flashed sparks of Dylan's old self: "I'm Goin', I'm Goin',

I'm Gone,'' he sang right after rejoicing around the fire. In "Dirge" he confessed "I hate myself for loving you and the weakness that it shows; you were just a painted face on a trip down suicide row." Even "Wedding Song" sounds curiously ambivalent. No doubt about it, something was awry, as early as 1973.

Blood on the Tracks appears to confirm this suspicion. Let it be said at the outset that this album *may* be explained almost entirely in terms of the tour, for it was obviously the experience of offering in an almost museum fashion pieces from a wide variety of earlier styles, of sharpening not himself but his many selves· for public display, that brought Dylan the range, the coherence so evident on this album. Each song is a new style, or a new combination of styles, all polished the way the tour was and *Planet Waves* was not, all from Dylan's earlier periods. You can almost assign each lyric an appropriate earlier album: "Idiot Wind" to *Highway 61 Revisited,* "Lily, Rosemary and the Jack of Hearts" to *Blonde on Blonde,* "If You See Her, Say Hello" to one of the very early folk albums, right beside "Girl from the North Country," "You're Gonna Make Me Lonesome When You Go" to, say, *New Morning* or *Nashville Skyline.* You can even, if you listen closely, catch Dylan copping Dylan, not merely in images and metaphors we've seen before ("The priest wore black on the seventh day," "back in the rain," "down the highway, down the tracks," "in the costume of a monk") but from previous tunes themselves. "Jack of Hearts," for example, cops tune and meter from "Just Like Tom Thumb's Blues" (*Highway 61 Revisited*). "Idiot Wind" borrows from "One of Us Must Know" (*Blonde on Blonde*). There are reasons why people hear earlier albums throughout *Blood on the Tracks;* primarily they relate to what must have been the exhilarating experience of reviewing the entire corpus before the 1974 tour. When all that music is running through your head, some of it is bound to spill over into new material.

Blood on the Tracks might be explained, then in terms of the tour; I prefer the other explanation, which reads Dylan as bored with or betrayed by salvation, haunted as in "Mr. Tambourine Man" by memories, galvanized into action, and ready to hit the road again. This ia a mature album in more than its musical professionalism; it is an album of the past and the claims of the past, of the solace and enervation of reminiscences. Even in a tender ballad of love past like "If You See Her, Say Hello" Dylan can reproach himself: "Either I'm too sensitive or else I'm getting soft." Even in "You're Gonna Make Me Lonesome When You Go" you catch a stoic resignation that's just a bit hard: "Life is sad, life is a bust; all you can do is do what you must." And the "Shelter from the Storm", while appreciated in one sense, is in another as resented as was the temporary comfort of "One of Us Must Know" back in the *Blonde on Blonde* days.

Blood on the Tracks is more ambivalent, though; "Idiot Wind" is as angry, bitter, as scornful as dark as anything that preceded *John Wesley Harding*. The song, morever, self-contempt, as the final refrain makes clear: "We're idiots, babe, it's a wonder we can even feed ourselves." Content, tone, form, music, delivery: almost pure *Blonde on Blonde*. Even "Lily, Rosemary, and the Jack of Hearts," a light piece, has a dark side: the set-up murder of Big Jim. The Jack of Hearts, mastermind behind the song's murder and burglary, of course, is none other than Bobby D. himself, the poet projected into one of his characters. "Jack of Hearts" closes not unlike a lyric discussed at some length earlier in this chapter, a lyric much related to *Blood on the Tracks,* "Visions of Johanna": the cabaret is empty, the characters are killed or hung, the culprit escaped, and Lily sits thinkin' about her father, thinkin' about Rosemary, thinkin' about the law—but most of all thinkin' about the (absent) Jack of Hearts.

So good to have Bob Dylan on the loose again!

CHAPTER IX
PAUL SIMON

Probably no other pop composer, with the possible exception of Van Dyke Parks, is more consciously artistic than Paul Simon. Although he has on more than one occasion emphatically denied that his songs are poems, Simon, with an undergraduate degree in English lit. from Queens College, is certainly aware of the similarities. Typically a Simon song, especially an early Simon songs, relies heavily on traditional poetic devices like irony, paradox, and metaphor. Typically it is allusive, often in a literary way to literary topics. Typically its form is drawn from literature—more likely than not it's a dramatic monologue. Besides, Simon *pictures* himself a poet in lyrics like "Bleeker Street" and "A Hazy Shade of Winter." Besides, Art Garfunkel has *told* him he was a poet and criticized his songs in sophomore lit. critical style on the jacket of *Wednesday Morning, 3 A.M.* Besides, even Paul was aware that, whatever was on the minds of anybody else's groupies, *his* always wanted to sit down and talk about poetry.

"Maybe it's English-major stuff," he admitted about "Dangling Conversations" in an unguarded moment.

But as a poet, Paul Simon has proven an incurable romantic through most of his career. He is sometimes embarrassingly sentimental, he is extremely self-conscious even when he's being unself-conscious, he can be pretentious, he often poses, he is almost always "too poetic." What seem at first glance "purely poetic images" (the phrase is Garfunkel's in many of his songs often prove uninspired on close examination, just as what may appear hopelessly unpoetic in Dylan usually turns out to be true genius. While the judgment may be harsh, I don't think it's inaccurate to say that Simon's pretentiousness lifts him out of the realm of folk music and pop, but his poetic self-consciousness prevents him from achieving status as a first rate artist. *Bookends,* it seems to me, comes closest to greatness in clean, natural lyrics like "America," "Fakin' It," and "At the Zoo." What came before is tainted to varying degrees by Romanticism; what followed fails to fulfill the promise of *Bookends.* Bob Dylan, the Beatles, other rock poets have suffered similar problems of menopause or premature ejaculation, but they have reached heights higher than Simon. In the final analysis, Simon can neither be dismissed entirely, as *Rolling Stone* tries desperately to do, nor ranked right up there with the Beatles, the Stones, and Bobby Dylan.

To overschematize the early albums a little—but not much—*Wednesday Morning 3 A.M.* suffers from a vague but palpable sentimentalism, *Sounds of Silence* suffers from an excessive concern for the ego, and *Parsley, Sage, Rosemary and Thyme* suffers from a residue of poetic self-consciousness. Each defect is not, of course, confined to the album on which it's most prominent, and each is but one manifestation of Simon's general Romanticism. And each album has its moments. But by in large that's a just assessment of those first three efforts.

Wednesday Morning, 3 A.M. is, in fact, a more or less standard first album for an early sixties folk singer: a bit of protest (including Dylan's "The Times They Are A-Changin'," made to sound like a Doris Day lullaby) a bit of traditional ballad folk ("Peggy-O," also recorded by Dylan on *his* first album), a bit of religious folk music ("Go Tell It On the Mountain" and "You Can Tell All the World"). It was going nowhere, as Paul himself had to admit, until Columbia overdubbed "Sounds of Silence" with drums, bass and electric guitar, and released it as a single. Hitsville. The rest, as they say, is history. But very little on that first album, including "Sounds of Silence," justifies Simon and Garfunkel's later success. Protest colors most of the Simon originals on this album, but his work is largely derivative, frequently sentimental, and sometimes simplistic. "Last Night I Had the Strangest Dream," I grant, is only a dream and thereby admits its oversimplification . . . but only to a point. On the surface the song says "Look, this is only a dream, things don't happen like this." But it goes on to suggest "Wouldn't it be nice if things *did* work out this way?" or maybe even "Don't you think it might, given a try?" Dylan, even in his youth, was less naive: "And I'll stand on your grave 'til I'm sure that you're dead" ("Masters of War").

Or take "He Was My Brother," a topical protest piece "cast in the early Dylan mold" (as Garfunkel gratuitously points out on the album notes). Simon's song works off the clean-cut, simplistic black/white dichotomy drawn by so much 1960's protest: he was my brother, the good guy; *they* shot my brother dead, the dirty rats. The song ends on the affirmative of "He died so his brothers could be free"—all very emotional and heroic, but all very bogus. Or take "Who Will Love a Little Sparrow," the title of which virtually speaks for itself. Or take "The Sun Is Burning," a song about nuclear annihilation that might just as well be about a Sunday School picnic to hear Simon and Garfunkel sing it. By 1964 folk and protest both had moved beyond this Kingston Trio/Brothers Four style, and clearly Simon and Garfunkel would never have amounted to much of anything had they produced nothing but this sort of song in this particular style.

But the *Wednesday Morning 3 A.M.* ablum contained one real gem and another semiprecious stone: "Bleecker Street" and "Sounds of Silence" respectively. "Bleecker Street," written in 1963 and explicated for all us dummies in the album notes by math major Garfunkel, is obviously flawed, but just as obviously an indication of genius. The religious allusions may be pretentious, the first couple of stanzas may be sentimental, the images (fog, a sad cafe, shadows, shepherd and sheep, church bells) may be conventional, but "Bleecker Street" has a certain understatement which redeems it, and leaves holes between stanzas that give people with more than a high school education some room for imaginative speculation. The poem moves from alley to shadows to poets to Canaan, and the mind must step lively to keep pace. The combination of poet and priest is fortuitious: poet becomes modern priest whose failure has produced the sterility of contemporary life. In other words, this song recognizes ambiguous responsibilities, instead of pointing fingers or making black/white comparisons between *them* and *him*. The juxtaposition of poet's sacrament and thirty bucks to pay his rent is startling and effective, an example of moral ambiguity and the kind of gap this song leaves for listeners to fill. And finally, it's a rather tight little piece, working comfortably if a trifle pretentiously within a conventional thematic and imagistic tradition.

"Sounds of Silence" is, I think, not quite up to "Bleecker Street" because it paints the poet in more self-righteous terms. Again the religious allusions ("halo of a street lamp," gods and prophets, those who have ears to hear but do not hear), again sentimentalism in the figure of the lonely poet turning his collar to the cold and damp, again rather conventional imagery (darkness, lonely streets, rain, even neon signs). This time, however, some demonstrably clumsy writing ("the vision that was planted in my brain" for example), and this time a poet who sees his potential audience only as fools who will not listen. Score three more points for the rather crachy oxymoron in Simon's title, a well chosen metaphor in "wells of silence," and Simon's rather early realization that the graffiti on subway walls and tenement halls may be more than irritating eye sores to be erased at the public's earliest convenience. Score a minus for one weak metaphor (silence growing like a cancer). Admit the pseudo-literary nature of subject and treatment, and . . . well, there's been worse done, and there's been better done too. What bothers me most about this lyric, however, is the nagging suspicion that its communication problems stem less from the benighted ten thousand who can't speak and won't listen, than from the egocentric, self-pitying, self-righteous poet-singer himself. A good song, but not up to "Bleecker Street."

141

The over-dubbed version of "Sounds of Silence" was strong enough to draw national attention to Simon and Garfunkel, to title their second album, to warrant its rerelease as the album's first cut. In one way the song works perfectly here, what with its ego-centricity and all, because *Sounds of Silence* is an album of the self. You see this most clearly in its final song, Simon and Garfunkel's next big hit, "I Am a Rock." Here we have a poet (again) in splendid isolation (again) hiding out from love and friendship and the pain they cause. Simon's images—winter, December, snow, sleeping memories—are again more or less standard, as are his metaphors: a shroud of snow, a rock, an island, a fortress deep and mighty, a coat of armor, a room which is a womb. But pure convention doesn't *have* to work against a song, especially when the song itself belongs to a conventional genre. "Bye Bye, Love," a much earlier lyric in this same farewell-to-love genre, is pure convention but makes convention work for it. The failure of Simon's lyric stems from its emphasis on the uniqueness of the individual (he does take himself very seriously, and I think Simon takes him very seriously) when we all know good and well that everybody goes through this, and we all swear off love, and we all run out and love again, so who does this cat think he's kidding? And who does Simon think he's kidding in taking him so seriously? What the song needs is a sense of irony, an awareness that the persona's literary pretentiousness, his self-pity, his high seriousness are not the composer's. This we don't get, and this ruins the song allowing it to degenerate into self-indulgence.

This same self-indulgent ego-centricity pervades the rest of the album: *I* and *my* and *me* echo and re-echo throughout its lyrics, and even such extrapersonal songs as "Richard Cory" and "A Most Peculiar Man" reflect a Romantic's curiosity for strange, lonely, mis-understood individuals. "Leaves That Are Green," for example, is a poem of young love turned cold, with all the self-pity of "I Am a Rock." (In addition to being self-indulgent, the song is probably derivative. "I was twenty-one years when I wrote this song," begins Simon; began A. E. Housman in a poem on a similar theme, "When I was one-and-twenty. . . .") "Kathy's Song" has very little to do with Kathy, really; it focuses on the singer himself, for whom the only valid truth has become his girl and the love they share: "I stand alone with beliefs/The only truth I know is you." A kind of imitation "Dover Beach," right down to looking beyond rain-drenched streets (for Arnold's beach) to England (for Arnold's French coast). "Blessed" carries this egocentric self-indulgence to its logical extension when Simon turns himself into a Christ figure with the painfully obvious and exceptionally pretentious—even for Simon—question, "Oh, Lord, why have you forsaken me?" "Richard Cory" is a Paul Simon rewrite of the E. A. Robinson poem;

"Somewhere They Can't Find Me" is a dramatic monologue from some poor slob who's "held up and robbed"—pardon the redundancy—a liquor store and has to leave his girl (he's not so stupid he can't manage a literary allusion, though—"A scene badly written in which I must play"). "A Most Peculiar Man" records suspicious, gossipy reaction to the suicide of this most unusual person. Each of these three songs looks outside Simon's self, all right, but betrays a Romantic's fascination with characters, with individuals, with unique individuals that reflects more the poet's self-image than his attitude toward others. The ultimate irony of the album, however, is that something so filled with Simon's concern for his own and others' individuality should be so derivative of other poets (Arnold, Housman, Robinson), and that the selves should come out looking so much like everybody else.

Given these first two albums you can see both the truth and the over-statement of Ralph Gleason's observation on the back side of Simon and Garfunkel's third album, *Parsley, Sage, Rosemary and Thyme:*

The New Youth of the Rock Generation has done something in American popular song that has begged to be done for genera-tions. It has taken the creation of the lyrics and the music out of the hands of the hacks and given it over to the poets.

Gleason refers specifically to Dylan, Ochs, John Sebastian, Marty Balin, Tim Hardin, Mick Jagger, Lennon and McCartney and a couple others, but it's obvious that he has Paul Simon most in mind. It's just as ob-vious, though, that heretofore Simon both has and has not been a poet: he *has* in the selfconscious, derivative, bad sense of the word, but he *has not* in any meaningful way produced great rock poetry. This particular album however, marks a turning point in Paul Simon's development: while it contains its fair share of pretentious, self-consciously poetic numbers, it also contains a couple of songs in which he breaks free of the high seriousness so characteristic of all Romantics, and has a little fun. In fact, even the pretentious songs are less clumsy, less overt than "I Am a Rock" and "Sounds of Silence." "The Dangling Conversation" is a dramatic monologue spoken by one half of a pair of cold lovers. It's a literate song (references to Emily Dickinson, Robert Frost, the theater; metaphors like "We are verses out of rhythm, couplets out of rhyme"), a song decorated with art and poetry. Given the ocean's roar, the shells on the shore, the man speaking to his love, it may very well be that this lyric, like "Kathy's Song" before it, is built on Arnold's "Dover Beach." That would be cute, since it *sounds* like Kathy's lover about ten years after. The important thing, though, is that all this artsy-craftsy stuff con-tributes to the song by characterizing the lovers as upper-middle class sophisticates who are smart enough to be analytical enough to produce a

143

monologue like this. They are the kind of people Simon was talking about to the *New Yorker* back in September of 1967:

> I write about the things I know and observe. I can look into people and see scars in them. These are the people I grew up with. For the most part, older people. These people are sensitive, and there's a desperate quality to them—everything is beating them down, and they become more aware of it as they become older. I get a sense they're thirty-three, with an awareness that "Here I am thirty-three!" and they probably spend a lot of afternoons wondering how they got there so fast. They're educated, but they're losing, very gradually. Not realizing, except for just an occasional glimpse. They're successful, but not happy, and I feel that pain. They've got me hooked because they are people in pain. I'm drawn to these people, and driven to write about them. In this country, it's painful for people to grow old. When sexual attractiveness is focused on a seventeen-year-old girl, you must feel it slipping away if you're a thirty-three-year-old woman. So you say, "I'm going to stop smoking. I'm going to get a suntan. I'm going on a diet. I'm going to play tennis." What's intriguing is that they are just not *quite* in control of their destiny. Nobody is paying any attention to these people, because they're not crying very loud.

I don't think, then, that "The Dangling Conversation" is merely the apotheosis of pretentious academic verse, as Ellen Willis charged; on the contrary it represents a giant step forward on Simon's part because it evidences genuine psychological depth in a constructed character of some maturity. It isn't Paul Young Werther Simon feeling sorry for himself. The same may be said of "Patterns," a less successful attempt to look at the world through the eyes of an aging black man, trapped in the maze of life, slave to patterns he can scarcely control. Both songs may be self-consciously academic verse, but they aren't ego-centric.

"Homeward Bound" *is* ego-centric, self-pitying, and self-consciously poetic ("every stop is neatly planned for a poet and a one-man band"), but it's also a genre piece, and after John Denver's "Leavin' On a Jet Plane" and "American Band" and a whole slew of other "singer-on-the-road" lyrics, "Homeward Bound" sounds less self-centered than I suspect it is. And I suppose that in its frank admission of a romantic fascination with lush imagery, "For Emily, Whenever I May Find Her" is poetically self-conscious. But it's self-conscious in a way that makes the Romanticism and imagery work for rather than against the lyric.

The most important songs on *Parsley, Sage, Rosemary and Thyme*, though, are those in which Simon cuts loose from the serious long enough to do something satiric or just plain silly. "The Big Bright Green Pasture Machine" is one of his satiric songs, promoting a big bright green answer to whatever is troublin' you, Bunkey. In its ability to turn *Life* magazine and Crest toothpaste ads into pop art, and in its use of the vernacular ("shoot you down," "is life . . . a drag?" "find a more productive bag," "chuck it all" and that classic first line, "Do people have a tendency to dump on you?") the song prefigures some of Simon's finest later lyrics. In its bright satire it's a welcome relief from the high, pretentious seriousness that has marked everything Simon's done up to now. You can almost hear him reaching back to the old rock-n-roll days (his first songs were, after all, rock-n-rollers) in a line like "Do your cheeks bounce higher than a rubber ball?" and the general light tone of the song. And in the other satire on this album, "A Simple Desultory Philippic (Or How I Was Robert McNamara'd Into Submission)," Simon quits writing protest songs "in the Dylan mold" and begins to satirize the man whose work influenced him and others so strongly. There are specific verbal references to Dylan himself and to "Rainy Day Woman No. 12 & 35" and "It's All Right, Ma," not to mention Simon's Dylanesque composition and delivery. He also pokes a bit of fun at his own pretentious, poetry-loving self—certainly a very good sign.

Then there's "Cloudy" and "The 59th Street Bridge Song." These are pure impression songs, throw-aways, bad-times and good-times pieces respectively. They're cute, fun, absolutely unserious. "They don't know where they're going, and, my friend, neither do I," Simon sings in "Cloudy." "Doot-in' doo-doo, feelin' groovy," he sings in "59th Street Bridge Song." Some of the lines don't even make any sense, as he himself happily admitted: "Of course, sometimes I make a song purely an impression, like 'Feelin' Groovy.' I think: Yellow . . . pink . . . blue . . . bubbles . . . gurgle . . . happy. The line 'I'm dappled and drowsy'—it doesn't make sense. I just *felt* dappled. Sleepy, contented." We are a long way from the protest and gospel-folk of Simon's early days, and a long way too from the lush romanticism of his earlier work.

To hear Simon tell it, he's been through three periods: the "early" songs of *Wednesday Morning, 3 A.M.,* songs written while he was in England ("Homeward Bound" and "April Come She Will"), and songs of "a dry spell" he hit in late 1966 and early 1967. "In fact," Simon said in the introduction to his *Songbook,* "I don't think I regained my stride until about the time of *Bookends* in 1968." Right or wrong about the three periods (I don't find them particularly useful), right or wrong about the dry spell (I think songs like "A Hazy Shade of Winter," "The Big Bright Green Pleasure Machine" and "The Dangling Conversation" good to excellent), Simon is certainly right about one thing: he got his stride with *Bookends.* In fact, *Bookends* contains the best work he's done to date: no pretention, little ego, even a minimum of the old Simon Romanticism. And it is, after a fashion, a concept album, concerning itself tangentially with traditional Simon themes—loneliness, lack of communication, love, social protest—but most of all with the related problems of growing up and growing old in America. *Bookends* is an album about time, the way it passes, and what it does to people as it passes them by: it is a direct result of Paul looking around and seeing these sensitive people, older people, desperate people, and writing about the things he knows.

Side one of the album comes sandwiched between the "Bookends" theme, which sets the album's subject (time, aging) and tone (sympathetic). You don't get much of the theme, however, before you're blasted right into "Save the Life of My Child," a frantic song about a would-be suicide and the crowd he attracts on the streets of New York. Well, perhaps he's a suicide . . . at least that's what everybody seems to think. All we really know about him is that he was looking for a place to be alone, a place to hide, and in New York 1968 you just don't find that sort of thing. But the boy isn't the focus of the song, really; what's more interesting is public reaction: "Good God, Don't jump!" somebody screams in four stressed monosyllables (a magnificent opening line for a poem, incidentally). A man faints; mother freaks out; one woman runs to call the cops; another decides he's high; the police complain about today's youth; the *Daily News,* New York City sensationalist tabloid, gets right on the story. Things build to a melo-dramatic climax (featuring appropriate echoes of "Sounds of Silence," a very good indication that Simon recognizes the self-indulgence of his earlier work) as the scene gets crazier and crazier. Finally, as the police spotlight hits the boy, he flies away! The perfect capper to a madhouse scene full of madhouse people. "He flew away!" Cute, light, mildly sarcastic. You'd get the impression that Simon was down on that crowd of Big Apple morons, and I suppose you'd be half right. They certainly look silly enough here (and elsewhere). But they're only people, Simon will come to realize, and what the hell . . ..

The album's second song, "America," is one of Simon's finest. We're in another world, the world of the anti-culture, the world of hip youth, off looking for a hiding place somewhere in America. It doesn't work, of course; after the jokes, the young love, the adventure, the cigarettes, the adolescent yearning and searching, after all this there's really nothing: counting the cars on the New Jersey Turnpike, all come to look for America. And what they all see is each other, counting cars and out looking for America.

In addition to making an important statement on the nation and the generation, "America" demonstrates a perfect understanding of rock as a pop art, turning Greyhound buses, Mrs. Wagner's pies, Saginaw Michigan, Pittsburgh Pennsylvania, even the New Jersey Turnpike into art objects. It contains some first rate poetic lines (consider the rhythm, imagery, and alliteration of "Counting the cars on the New Jersey Turnpike," for example), and it captures like no other song I know the incredible, epic, surreal tedium of a Greyhound bus ride. Counting the cars on the New Jersey Turnpike.

Bookends is filled with people, each a failure, each a grotesque, each hung up. The mother is hung up on her child, the young lovers of "America" are hung up on each other (or themselves, really), the old folks are hung up on memories. The couple in "Overs" is hung up on habit, Punky is hung up on the draft, Mr. Leitch is hung up on being hung up, and Mrs. Robinson—well, we all know her hang-ups. It's quite a collection. And it's quite a collection of quality songs. "Overs," for example, reworks "The Dangling Conversation" situation, but it replaces the literary allusions with more appropriate stale jokes and stale images and prosey lines and bad puns: "No good times, no bad times, just the *New York Times.*" A good song, better even than "The Dangling Conversation" precisely because it is flatter, prosier.

Then there's "Punky's Dilemma," the recorded random thoughts of a young man confronting the first really crucial decision of his life: to stay and get drafted, or split for Canada. "I wish I was a Kellogg's cornflake," Punky thinks, or an English muffin, or a boy named Sue, or anything but a kid about to get drafted. If I become a lieutenant, Mary Jane might put my photo on her piano. Don't wanna be no faggy draft-dodger. Hmmm. Simon leaves him strung out, pondering boysenberry jam and South California (point of embarkation for Vietnam). A subtle lyric in the way it hints lazily at its subject.

And then, of course, there's "Mrs. Robinson," a more popular but less successful song than many of the others on this album. It manages some splendid images ("put it in the pantry with your cupcakes") and one very functional allusion to Joe DiMaggio, the All American wholesome kid (who married the All American pin-up girl . . . who subsequently committed suicide) the likes of which Mrs. Robinson just don't find no more. "What's becoming of the children?" somebody wanted to know in "Save the Life of My Child"; what's becoming of the parents? But "Mrs. Robinson" really isn't a subtle song—even without *The Graduate*—and the sarcasm about Jesus and salvation is a trifle heavy-handed, and the nut-house business in that first stanza never really integrates very well with the rest of the song, and . . . well, perhaps we've just heard it too many times for its own good.

The gems, the real pearls of *Bookends,* are "America," "Fakin' It," and "A Hazy Shade of Winter," three first rate dramatic monologues that will stand up to anything else in rock poetry. "Fakin' It" shows Simon's facility with the vernacular and his observation of thirty-three-year-old self-conscious dead-ends. Moreover, it's remarkably free of metaphor and imagery, except for the fallen vines and the tailor. Two fresh, well chosen images are, however, preferable to a fistful of trite, pretentious images, and the tailor in particular epitomizes a life of tedious, trivial, pointless labor: "I own the tailor's face and hands, I am the tailor's face and hands." Way in the background of that song I detect A. E. Housman, the polished poet of colloquial English, understatement, and the metaphor-free poetry of statement. Nor is "Fakin' It" in any way inferior to most of Housman's own lyrics.

Like "Fakin' It" and several other songs on *Bookends*, "A Hazy Shade of Winter" treats the problem of time and aging. "Time is tapping on my forehead . . . rattling the teacups" wrote Simon in "Overs"; this lyric expands those lines to a full song, beginning with time, time, time pounding on the speaker's brain, reminding him that he's not getting any younger, wondering just what's to be done: what are the possibilities? This is one of those songs from "the dry patch" of 1966-67, but it's a song *about* dry patches and thus very, very honest. And it's richer than most of the lyrics on *Bookends:* Simon uses the seasons as a metaphor for man's life, the Salvation Army band as a reminder of coming old age, patches of snow in winter and falling leaves of fall—indeed, the entire tapestry of the seasons—as images for the passing of time. It is not a long, long while from May to December, Simon discovers. And all the imagery works first because it's appropriate and well chosen for a song on this theme, and second because it's well suited to a speaker who is sitting musing over "manuscripts of unpublished rhyme" sipping a drink and wondering how things came to this. Simon's thirty-three-year-old woman went after a suntan, a diet, and tennis; this character decides he'll pretend it's spring, that his hopes are young and fresh, that he's a kid once more. But nobody is deceivin' nobody; in the end there's that nervous, insistent beat pounding out time, time, time, and a furtive glance over the shoulder at autumn's falling leaves and a patch of snow on the ground that warns of the inevitable and very imminent winter. "A Hazy Shade of Winter" gives us a perfect sense of what it's like to be thirty-three in America's youth-oriented society. All this from twenty-five-year-old Paul Simon, no less.

Bookends closes with what at first appears a throwaway: "At the Zoo." Simon's personification of the animals creates a counterpart for the gallery of characters he's painted throughout the album: the skeptical, the insincere, reactionaries and missionaries all off looking for America. Yes, this is a cute throwaway, but yes it has a point. And the point, if you will, is to throw away the entire album on "What a gas!

You gotta come and see at the zoo.'' Here is a denial of high seriousness and morose satire that undercuts those old folks on side one and Mrs. Robinson on side two. It undercuts the lofty moral standards that allow us to look askance at the crowd of ''Save the Life of My Child'' and the great aspirations that allow us to denigrate the losers of ''A Hazy Shade of Winter'' and ''Fakin' It.'' But there's an affirmation here too, an acceptance of human limitations and foibles, a legitimate sentimentality that allows us to forgive ourselves and each other for being merely human. You gotta come and see at the zoo!

Bridge Over Troubled Waters was Simon and Garfunkel's last album together. It's a good album, no denying that, but it's not *as* good an album, and that makes it a bad album. Or at least a come-down. The title song, for example, is romantic gush, over-written and over-produced. And it's a mixed metaphor to boot: you can be either a bridge over troubled water, or you can be a boat sailing right behind on the water, but you can't be both at once. And, like ''Mrs. Robinson,'' it comes apart: ''Sail on Silver girl'' doesn't quite fit with the rest of the lyric. The melody is strong and well suited to some of Simon's lines, but over-production weakens it considerably. From James Taylor we might expect this stuff; from Paul Simon we demand more. The same might be said of ''Only Living Boy in New York'': a superb melody slightly over-produced, on which are hung lyrics so subtle as to lose their meaning. Just what *is* this song about? Art Garfunkel's movie roles? A dope dealer ''flying down to Mexico''? Or what? Or is this a song like others on this album, ''Cecelia'' and ''Baby Driver'' and ''Why Don't You Write Me?'' that really don't mean too much and don't pretend to mean too much and shouldn't be taken as meaning too much? I'm not sure, and I think I ought to be able to be sure, especially in a song from the creator of *Bookends*.

The album has its moments, though, most notably ''El Condor Pasa,'' ''The Boxer,'' ''So Long, Frank Lloyd Wright,'' and—even though it lies—''Song for the Asking.'' Paul first heard the melody to ''El Condor Pasa'' in Paris in 1965, and it hung in his head for half a decade until the poem appeared. Even though the sound track is the original recording by Los Incas, Simon has managed an almost perfect synthesis of lyric and melody and performance; the clean, almost textbook images, carefully segregated one per stanza, fit the understated, delicate melody, and sound themselves very much like genuine folk lyrics.

''The Boxer'' is a first rate protest song: understated, subtle, psychologically sound, pointed. It's overproduction, moreover, is partially legitimized as the ''lie-la-lie'' refrain builds to a threatening crescendo (sooner or later all those lies and jests we keep unloading on these people are gonna be comin' home to roost), then subsides almost comfortably into passivity and gentility. And the boxer—scarred, punch-drunk, but always flailing away and therefore always potentially dangerous—is a most appropriate image for the poor boys, the down-and-outs, the bottom round of America's ladder of success.

"So Long, Frank Lloyd Wright" may be a trifle presumptuous on Simon's part—I've never been impressed by his songs the way I've been impressed by Wright's houses, and certainly the singer doesn't dominate his field the way the architect dominated his—but the conjunction of music and art in Simon's song is fortuitous, the compliment to Wright well turned, the melody pleasant, the performance professional. Like Simon's performance in "Song for the Asking." Or his performance in the good old-time rock-n-rollers on this album, "Bye Bye, Love" and "Baby Driver." In fact, when you get down to it, "Baby Driver" is a pretty fair modernization of the old rock-n-roll automobile metaphor ("I wonder how your engine feels"—hmmm), an exciting song, up tempo, unselfconscious, a rocker in the best fifties tradition. All it lacks is weight.

And that, in the final analysis, is what the lyrics of *Bridge Over Troubled Waters,* with the exception of "The Boxer" and "El Condor Pasa" and "So Long, Frank Lloyd Wright," lack: insight, seriousness, profundity—a charge you'd not have expected to be leveled at Paul Simon, incidentally. Certainly, early Simon was filled to a fault with profundity, and the nonsense of "59th Street Bridge Song" was refreshing at the time. And the cute frivolity of "At the Zoo" was necessary affirmation capping an otherwise nervous and depressing album, like "I'll Be Your Baby Tonight" at the close of Dylan's *John Wesley Harding.* But enough of this is too much, as Dylan and the dissociated Beatles and rock of the early seventies discovered. You knew Simon was headed in the wrong direction with this album.

And he was. Now Jon Landau and *Rolling Stone* magazine have never much liked Paul Simon, mind you, and you wouldn't expect them to jump up and down over a rock poet of his ilk. So maybe you disbelieve it when Landau titles his *Rolling Stone* review of Simon's first solo album "Everything Put Together Falls Apart." But Landau was right: Simon just didn't get it off on this album, and nothing is more indicative of that fact than Landau's reaction. The review depressed Simon, who felt misunderstood; "A lot of the lyrics they *[Rolling Stone]* thought depressed and pessimistic are really ironic and funny," a Columbia records spokesman told a New Yorker reporter interested in meeting Paul "to clear up some of the lyrical confusion." Well, the album confused Landau, and it confused the *New Yorker,* and it confuses me . . . so maybe it's just a confused album. "Armistice Day," for example, strikes me as protest—protest in the style of early Phil Ochs. Not so, says Simon; "'Armistice Day' is *not* a protest song—protest songs are a little trite at the moment." And I thought "Mother and Child Reunion" was a witty, wistful, impressionistic throw-away; turns out it's about a death. "Seems to have confused a lot of people," Simon admitted. And who knows what "Me and Julio" is about? Other lyrics like "Paranoia Blues," "Run that Body Down," "Everything Put Together Falls Apart" and "Congratulations" seem too personal by half, far too personal to involve me, far too personal to be interesting. I'm reminded of some of those lyrics on Dylan's *Another Side* album, but Simon is not Bob Dylan and he just can't pull it off. "Duncan," a dramatic monologue spoken by a young lad from the Maritimes who discovered sex with a Jesus freak, is psychologically and poetically thin—none of the depth of "The Boxer" or "A Hazy Shade of Winter." I think, in short, Paul Simon was drifting in 1971-72, along with the rest of the country and virtually every other important pop song writer. Everybody's entitled to one bum album.

How else can you explain somebody who created the lyrics of *Bookends* before and lyrics like "Kodachrome" and "Loves Me Like a Rock" and "American Tune" after? Because those three songs, on the *There Goes Rhymin' Simon* album, justify all the mediocrity and confusion of Simon's first solo effort, they justify that dry spell of the early seventies, they justify Simon's claim to being a professional song writer.

This is, admitted, an uneven album, with its share of personal songs ("St. Judy's Comet") and simple nonsense ("Was a Sunny Day") and its patent failures ("Something So Right"), but "Kodachrome" and "Loves Me" and "American Tune" are unquestionably first class, capturing the mood of America in the early seventies, producing fine rock poems by turning sterility into the subject of a song just as "A Hazy Shade of Winter" turned a dry patch upon itself and into fine art. "With the farming of a verse/Make a vineyard of the curse," W. H. Auden once said.

"I have a photograph," sang the old folks on *Bookends*; in "Kodachrome" Simon expands that line into an entire song built on one simple metaphor: my mind to me a camera is, coloring the pictures it takes with the greens of summer, making all the world a sunny day. Time it was, oh what a time it was. All the girls I knew when I was single . . . don't take those memories away. A generation turning thirty? The early seventies nostalgia boom? An exhausted, conservative American reaction to the heady sixties? I don't know, but we've seen a lot of nostalgia lately, and this song is both a part of and an explanation of that nostalgia. And it's a fine metaphor.

151

"Loves Me like a Rock" is, I think, Simon's most successful satire since "A Simple Desultory Philippic," because it's a subtle song. There is the saved and the damned, the angels and the devil, and who do you think you're foolin', confusing one with the other? That is exactly the way Richard Nixon saw things, of course, and that is exactly the way Senator Sam Ervin saw things, and weren't it a rip?

But it's "American Tune" which most impresses me on this album; in fact, "American Tune" may well be the most important single song to come out of rock in the last four years—with the possible exception of Dylan's "Forever Young." It hits the seventies exactly on the head, it's dead serious, it's well chosen both in imagery and melody (the first half of Simon's A melody in stanzas 1, 2 and 4 is taken virtually note for note from the Christian Good Friday hymn "Oh Sacred Head Now Wounded"). Lyrics and melody are perfectly integrated; performance wavers between resigned understatement and guardedly optimistic overstatement; rhythm and rhyme are clean and fascile. It is, in short, a flawless rock poem, as fine a lyric as Paul Simon ever produced on any album.

"American Tune" begins with the admission that Simon just may be mistaken, he's been mistaken before, and confused and forsaken and misused. Could be mistaken now too, but he is really feeling bummed out and "so far away from home." Again the motif of the exile ("I Pity the Poor Immigrant") in 1970s rock. The second stanza generalizes Simon's own feelings: we're all battered, all our dreams have been shattered (the Rolling Stones will pick up on this same vibration at the end of the seventies on their *Some Girls* album), and you've got to wonder what the hell went wrong. Somewhere Simon's life took a wrong turn. Somewhere the decade took a wrong turn. Somewhere the American dream made a right when it should have made a left, and, in a vision, Simon sees a great and tragic vision of overwhelming proportions: the Statue of Liberty, sailing away to sea. There it all goes! There it all has gone.

In the final stanza Simon links the Pilgrims landing on the new world and the astronauts landing on the moon, and the uncertainty of both hours, and implies that everything hangs in the balance. Here is "the nation's most uncertain hour," surely. (Simon's conclusion wavers between resignation and hope, resignation and hope.) When I hear this song, I look at the decade of the sixties in retrospect, and what has become of my country in the seventies, and I sometimes cry.

"This, then, is the death of the American," wrote Phil Ochs on his Rehearsals for Retirement album back in 1969. By 1972 Paul Simon had lived to see this death: dreams battered, everybody up tight, the populace weary and cross, the Statue of Liberty sailin' away to sea. "How the hell did we get into this mess?" he asks. "Well, you can't live the good life forever," he answers. "Still, something must have gone wrong somewhere." The age's most uncertain hour—Paul Simon knows it and laments. But he also offers just a hint of hope: tomorrow's another working day, and maybe this weariness and uncertainty is just a good rest. Get some sleep, and the blood will be running again. Carrion comfort? Perhaps, but the only comfort available to America in 1973, except for the greatest comfort of all, the return of America's artists, Simon among them, after a period of exhaustion and dormancy. If you can't find reassurance in the song's content, you can certainly find reassurance in the song's being: when the artists begin stirring, you know spring can't be far off.

CHAPTER X
PHIL OCHS

When Ralph Gleason was talking about lyricists as poets on the back side of Simon and Garfunkel's *Parsley, Sage, Rosemary & Thyme* album, he had in mind more singers than Paul Simon: "an elite which includes Bob Dylan, Phil Ochs, John Sebastian, Marty Balin, Dino Valenti, Tom Hardin, Al Kooper, Smokey Robinson, Mick Jagger, John Lennon, Paul McCartney." The list looks about right, even at the remove of a decade and a half: all the heavies with the possible exceptions of Pete Townshend and Jim Morrison. But a couple of those names will furrow the brows of second generation rock fans. Dino Valenti. Al Kooper. And who is this Phil Ochs fellow?

There is, Phil's hundred or so faithful keep telling themselves, no just reason that Ochs never made it as a first class, bona fide, twenty-four karat star. Oh, there may be plenty of reasons, but none of them are compelling. "He couldn't sing," somebody charges, "even before the attack which damaged his throat in Algeria." Well, he sang neither better nor worse than the young Bob Dylan. "He tied himself to protest, and when the great ship went down, he sank right along with it," reasons somebody else. But many of Ochs' songs suggest other options: the art song, for example, or a Paul Simon-Leonard Cohen style of serious pop. "Fifteenth-rate topical songs by a tenth-rate journalist," sneered *Little Sandy Review* of Ochs' early work. "Too bad his guitar playing would not suffer much were his right hand webbed," jeered *Esquire* in its usual snotty manner. Maybe it was that last album which finally did Phil in (and god! it was awful), except that it contained two very fine lyrics which might have signaled a new, post-Lincoln Park Ochs, working with a little rock-nproll and a lot of fine art. There was the abortive recasting of "The State of Mississippi" into "The State of Richard Nixon" in late 1973, that hit top forty stations with all the force of a firecracker on the moon. There were a few nights on the coffee house circuit in '74, more in the Village in '75, with Pete Seeger and Joan Baez and Peter Yarrow at the "War is Over" celebration, with Dylan and Baez and Ginsberg and Joni Mitchell and the Company gearing up for the Rolling Thunder Review. And there was the bitterness when Thunder rolled without Ochs. And there was the suicide of April 9, 1976, a week before Good Friday, and a (brief, and not very sympathetic) obit in the *Rolling Stone,* and a memorial concert by friends, and now there are indeed no more songs.

And yet, there at the dawn of the sixties was Phil Ochs, a name, a force, number two in the Village right behind the great Bob Dylan, making it, a crucial part of the folk revival and of the nascent Movement. By 1962 Ochs was publishing topical songs in *Broadside Magazine;* by 1963 he was part of the Newport Folk Festival; by 1964 he had a couple of albums to his name, not to mention some pretty important songs: "I Ain't Marching Anymore," "There But for Fortune." You would have bet the mortgage to your house on this porcupine kid from El Paso, Texas.

It was protest material, topical stuff, the kind of lyrics that were going then, and Ochs was very good at it. Mixed with these topical protest songs were a few more traditional numbers—"Power and the Glory," which closely resembled Woody Guthrie's "This Land Is Your Land," and very fine musical versions of Poe's "Bells" and Noyes' "The Highwayman"—but nobody was paying any attention to all the artsy-craftsy stuff, and all young folk singers bore the impression of Guthrie and Seeger, and obviously topical protest songs were where it was all at anyway. It was a role that Ochs found comfortable and appropriate to his age and to the times in general.

Ochs always was a prolific writer, and an even more prolific performer. "We've printed about 30 or 40 Ochs songs," wrote Agnes Cunningham of *Broadside* in 1963, "and probably have as many others scattered around simply because we haven't the room for them or the manpower even to prepare them for the mimeograph machine." And Ochs sang everywhere, from the coffee houses to Gerde's hoots to the long, grey line of Moratorium events. Little escaped his notice or his pen, and he whipped off songs on the loss of the U.S. Thresher, the Cuban Missile Crisis, Medgar Evers, William Worthy (a reporter who ran afoul of the U.S. government when he visited Communist Cuba), Lou Marsh (a ghetto priest who died stopping a gang fight in New York City), migrant workers, the U.S. invasion of Santo Domingo, Christianity, liberals, students, cops, automation, the Civil Rights Movement, the Vietnam War, the Civil Rights Movement, the Vietnam War, the Civil Rights Movement, the Vietnam War. He even wrote a ballad for Joe Hill, the IWW protest singer of the thirties in whom Ochs obviously saw something of himself.

Being topical, most of Ochs' protest songs died with the causes which occasioned them. Who today recognizes names like Lou Marsh or William Worthy? Who among the young can recall the Cuban Missile Crisis or the sinking of the Thresher? And probably it is best that Ochs' protest songs died quietly: they suffered from the defects of their genre—pointed fingers, easy moralizations, shallow psychology, long rhetoric and short melody. "Whe was a death ship all along,/But she died before she had a chance to kill," Ochs sang of the Thresher; "William Worthy isn't worthy to live here anymore," he sang of the reporter. "His melodies are about as inventive as the average Tibetan chant," said *High Fidelity,* and with respect to Ochs' topical songs it was not far from wrong. In retrospect they appear cliche-ridden, self-righteous, and vaguely hollow in their naive revolution and utopianism.

In a building of gold with riches untold
Lived the families on which the country was founded.
And the merchants of style with their vain, velvet smiles
Were there, for they also were hounded.
And the soft middle class crowded in there last,
For the building was fully surrounded.
And the noise outside was the rhythms of revolution.

With the Movement dead and Richard Nixon twice elected president, a song like "Rhythms of Revolution" is bound to lose its punch, no matter how great it may have sounded in 1965.

All the News That's Fit to Sing, I Ain't Marching Anymore, Phil Ochs in Concert—those three early albums—is there anything there to justify the argument that Ochs really truly deserved recognition? Yes, I think, although it's not the stuff that first attracts attention. For one there is commitment: remarkable commitment of remarkable energies which you knew must one day mature into something ripe and solid. And there is technique: facility with rhyme and imagery and alliteration. "In a building of gold with riches untold" may be cliched, but it has a regular rhythm and clean internal rhyme that remind you of the young Dylan. Third, there are a couple of pretty fair melodies: "The Bells," "Bracero," "When I'm Gone." And finally there is the undercurrent of artiness which would blossom into things like "Crucifixion" and "Pleasures of the Harbor" and "William Butler Yeats Visits Lincoln Park and Escapes Unscathed."

Ochs' best work is contained in his mid-to-later sixties albums: *Tape from California, Pleasure of the Harbor,* and *Rehearsals for Retirement.* In them he combined art with topical protest to form a style similar to and second only behind (here the name again) Bob Dylan. In most cases the self-righteousness that characterized earlier songs was absent ("I Kill Therefore I Am" being a conspicious exception), and brilliant imagery and alliteration insure the lyrics a permanence beyond their immediate subject matter. Ochs' natural prosiness is tempered, turned when apparent to advantage in long ballads like "Joe Hill," where it performs the prosey function of narrating a story. And Phil widened his thematic range a bit, avoiding purely topical material in favor of more general problems: war, cops, human insensitivity and indifference.

"Outside of a Small Circle of Friends," for example, had its genesis no doubt in those all too common stories of women raped and robbed on New York City streets, observed by dozens, even hundreds of city folks from the secure detachment of their apartment windows. But Ochs moves beyond specific incidents to comment on the broader matter of human indifference: "Maybe we should call the cops and try to stop the pain, but monopoly is so much fun, and I'd hate to blow the game." This may not be profound, but it's clever. So too is the irrepressibly high spirited honkey-tonk accompaniment. And other stanzas contain equally impressive, witty lines: "But we've gotta move, and we might get sued, and it looks like it's gonna rain," or "But demonstrations are a drag, and besides we're much too high." Internal rhyme and alliteration: the staples of Ochs' mature work.

The same things you find in "Miranda," also from the *Pleasures of the Harbor* album. Like Leonard Cohen's Suzanne, Miranda is something of a cross between Salvation Army lass and good natured lady of the streets, a dancing girl who will dance your problems to oblivion or trip you off on a tray of pot-filled brownies. As a character, she's attractive; but what made the song was Ochs' wit: "In the bar we're gin and scotching, while the FBI is watching . . ."

In other protest-art lyrics, Ochs did it with imagery as well as or instead of wit, rhyme, and alliteration. "The Flower Lady," for example, distills its statement to a focusing symbol of love and communication, the flower peddler ignored by an army of angry, petty, blind, self-righteous and very quarrelsome antagonists. Millionaires and paupers, quarreling lovers, old folks and poets—each in his own isolation, none buying the flowers that represent communication, understanding, healing. Only in its final stanza does the lyric falter—and then not into anger or ego, but into sentimentality. "Tattered shreds of petals leave a fading trail. . . ."

Imagery and rhyme and alliteration. Combined, and with just a dash of metaphor, Ochs produced some of the sharpest commentary on the sixties. Like "White Boots Marching in a Yellow Land." Casualties rising like the falling of rain, mountains of machinery, old whores following tired armies (a loan, perhaps from Eliot?)—very graphic imagery and some rather clever rhetoric. And in Ochs' final stanza some devastating ironies: "We're fighting in a war we lost before the war began, We're the white boots marching in a yellow land." Not even Dylan at his best outcolored Ochs in this song. The flashes of rhetoric, of imagery, of rhyme and alliteration, of metaphor are all justified. Ochs has a point to make, and it's a valid point, and the art supports it. There's no self-righteousness, and there's no sentimentality. "White Boots Marching" is a topical protest lyric propelled beyond the confines of its genre, turned into a piece of rock poetry by the raw talent of its composer.

The same might also be said of Ochs' other great anti-war song, "The War Is Over." Again the art, again the statement on war, but here the suggestion of something more subtle and more profound than "White Boots Marching": the numbing of our sensibilities by newsreel carnage, our conditioned acceptance of violence as an American way of life, the peculiar way jobs at home can excuse murder abroad, and—perhaps most insightful of all—the realization that a man is no more or less than his beliefs. Ochs inventories the various surrealisms of the war, comparing it all to a bad movie or a bad dream: a mad director, cardboard cowboys, tattooed sons of tattooed mothers, one-legged veterans whistling marches as they mow their lawns. "The gypsy fortune-teller told me we have been deceived," Ochs sings. And "just before the end even treason might be worth a try." And "You only are what you believe, and I believe the war is over." "The only way this war is gonna end," David Crosby once told an interviewer, "is for everybody to look at it and say 'Fuck it,' and just walk away." That is essentially what we get in "The War Is Over": Phil Ochs, unilaterally declaring the Vietnam conflict—all conflict—over and done with. "On Saturday, November 25," he wrote in the *Village Voice* in 1967, "we are going to declare the war over and celebrate the end of the war in Washington Square Park at 1 p.m. . . . Everyone who comes should try to do something creative on his own—make up a few signs like 'God Bless you Lyndon for Ending the War,' wear clothes appropriate to the re-enactment of VE day, wave a flag and mean it, invite a soldier along, form a brass band to play 'When Johnnie Comes Marching Home,' bring extra noisemakers and confetti, drink beer, kiss girls, and give thanks this weekend that the war is over."

I can think off hand of four other major Phil Ochs protest lyrics, each a brilliant combination of imagery, alliteration, witty rhyme, and vituperation: "The Harder They Fall," "I Kill Therefore I Am," "Pretty Smart on My part," and "The World Began in Eden (But Ended in Los Angeles)." They are mordant commentaries on various aspects of contemporary American life, not as particularized as Ochs' earlier work and therefore longer-lived.

"The Harder They Fall" borrows from nursery rhymes both in form and content, creating a dark, Lenny Bruce irony that is half absurdity, half black comedy: "From the dragon to the Viet Cong, Fairy tales have come along." And they *have* come along: Jack and Jill (she with pills) off looking for a thrill, Mary making it with a lamb, all the people running around yelling for their crown ("They are not fooling around," Ochs warns us). We've turned from sexual, social, political revolution to sexual, social, political perversion. The disease is universal. "In the prison of our dreams we die," Phil sings. And again, with an eye to Shakespeare's *MacBeth,* "Only the witches recall, the bigger they are the harder they fall."

Less transcendent of specific issues and the limiting perspective of the middle sixties is "I Kill Therefore I Am," an exceptionally (even for Ochs) vitriolic piece of abuse, made all the more caustic by its alliteration, the metaphor central to all its stanzas, and the sexual inuendo Ochs takes little pain to disguise. Descartes' man thought, and thereby proved his existence; Ochs' cop kills, thereby proving his being . . . and his courage and his masculinity and a couple of other things as well. Traditionally, of course, you shoot first and ask questions later. This is the wisdom of the frontier. But Ochs' "King of cowboys," brandishing his phallic pistol up there on his pale pony, is wiser yet: "He shoots first, he shoots later." "I'll show those faggots that I'm not afraid," he promises, busting black heads and white students.

Trouble is, the cop is not brave: he finds his courage in chemistry, his machismo is a gun, his myths in Hollywood movies, his self in childhood fantasies. Bob Dylan, perhaps too kindly, saw the cop as but another tool in the hands of the power elite. Phil Ochs, perhaps too unkindly, views him as the archenemy, the quintessence of the American disease.

The psychological hang-ups of insecure Americans were also the subject of "Pretty Smart on My Part," Phil Ochs' version of "For What It's Worth." Paranoia is creeping everywhere here, striking deep into our waking and sleeping consciousness. Phil began the jacket notes to *Rehearsals for Retirement* (from which this song and "I Kill Therefore I Am" both come) with these observations:

This then is the death of the American,
imprisoned by his paranoia
and all diseases of his innocent inventions
he plunges to the drugs of the devil to find his gods
he employs the farce of force to crush his fantasies
he calls conventions of salesmen and savages
to reinforce his hopelessness.

"Framed in fantasies and drugged in dreams," he sang in "The War Is Over"; "Through out fantasies we fly,/In the prisons of our dreams we die," he told us in "The Harder They Fall." In "Pretty Smart on My

Part'' Ochs focuses on the roots of those fantasies: paranoid fear of strangers, of women, of thieves, of subversives. Hunters shoot geese, Ochs observes, to defend themselves from imagined burglars threatening constantly to break into their homes, steal the silver, rape the wife. Men hate women because they fear their own inadequacy; they join the John Birch Society because they're up tight about people who talk funny. They hear about the Communist Chinese, so they run out to assassinate the president.

In many lyrics Ochs uses music as an ironic counterpoint to the message of his poetry. "The War Is Over" springs immediately to mind, casting a poem that deals with war by the rather impractical expedient of ignoring it to a melody that recalls war by sounding like a march, by employing military cadences, by echoing "March of the Toy Soldiers." "The World Began in Eden" works just this way: to a purely Las Vegas tune, Ochs sets a morose narration of the debasement of the American dream, from the setting out of the Pilgrim fathers to the westward development of progress to the end point of Los Angeles. Setting out from the old world, desperate to escape social and political pollution and hoping for another chance, another place to start, the founding fathers (and mothers) landed in "the coldest of their colonies." So they got it rolling, and the thing snowballed into highways on top of the houses on top of the homesteads, and before you knew it the new world was every bit as polluted as the old. "It happened that way heading west," Ochs sings with mock enthusiasm. The whole nightmare localizes itself appropriately in Los Angeles, "City of Tomorrow."

Ochs once commented to Marc Eliot,

> This is America. If I had a wounded Viet-Cong, and he asked me, "What are you here for, in my country, fighting, I want to know what America is," I would put him in L.A. You don't breathe carbon monoxide, you breathe jet exhaust. You can hear the cops giving testimony. "I pulled my gun, and shot him in the left shoulder. The first bullet entered his left shoulder. The second bullet pierced his heart. It appeared the suspect had a weapon in his hand, and later on it was discovered to be a piece of paper."

Now you can only take so much of that jet exhaust, or those king-sized cowboys, or the whole perverse scene, and then you can't handle it any more. Jim Morrison discovered just that: he wrote "L.A. Woman," then split the country and ODed. Ochs did not leave the country; in fact he never really left the Movement, and I don't think he really wanted to retire from the record industry or from life. But he stayed in New York, and he hung himself. He had long before cooled his engines.

161

The Poetry of Rock

The events of 1968 especially sapped Ochs' energies. "He was depleted then, tired, and very pessimistic," said one disc jockey who met him after the Democratic Convention and the Lincoln Park riots. Och's depletion, his exhaustion, his hardening cynicism show through his next to last album, *Rehearsals for Retirement*. It's a schizophrenic album, really: the half of it protest in the arty style we've been discussing, the other half dark commentary on the events of Lincoln Park: "William Butler Years Visits Lincoln Park and Escapes Unscathed," "Where Were You in Chicago?" "My Life," "Rehearsals for Retirement." "The days grow shorter, for smaller prizes," he noticed in the title lyric; "I am a stranger to all surprises." To judge from these songs, from the album's title, this was Ochs' farewell to protest. To judge from his next (and last) album, such a supposition was largely correct.

The jacket of *Rehearsals for Retirement* features a tombstone, complete with a picture of the deceased (Phil himself, totin' a rifle and posing in front of an American flag), and bearing a simple inscription:

Phil Ochs
(American)
Born: El Paso, Texas, 1940
Died: Chicago, Illinois, 1960

"I'll paint your memory on the monument of my rehearsals for retirement," Phil sang to America, his only love, his fancy. Clearly he was calling it quits, or threatening to, worn out by the struggle which ultimately served only to secure the Presidency to Richard M. Nixon. Ochs traces the struggle, the hopes and the disappointments, the despair which would one day drive him to suicide, in the song "My Life." His life was first a joy, growing in all directions at once, constantly, magically. Then his life was a toy, as he wound it and found it ran away. Then a myth, like the drifter (Dylan's drifter?) "with his laughter in the dawn; and now a death, as the repression of the late sixties closes in around a paranoid rebel. "Take everything I own, take your tap from my phone," Ochs begs, just leave my life alone.

"Might have known the end would end in laughter," Ochs commented in "Rehearsals for Retirement." "Still I tell my daughter, it doesn't matter." He takes his tattered colors from the lists, slips quietly out of the tournament. You hate to say it, but the bastards seem to have gotten the best of Old Phil.

Even in the album's most optimistic Convention-influenced song (and I say optimistic because of the analogy it draws between the Movement and another, successful revolution), Ochs seems strangely detached, alone, isolated, willing to retreat. In "William Butler Yeats Visits Lincoln Park," Phil casts himself as the Irish poet, committed to the cause

162

of Irish independence and madly in love with the beautiful revolutionary Maude Gonne, throwing himself and his art into a fever of political activism. In images and symbols borrowed from Yeats' own poetry, Ochs projects his personal future: "I'll go back to the city where I can be alone."

And Ochs did in fact retreat. His last album joined the rest of the pop music community—indeed the rest of the country—in retreat to the Nixon-Eisenhower fifties. There was one weak attempt at protest ("Ten Cents a Coup," recorded at the fall moritorium in 1969), but even that worked as much off the rock-n-roll automobile as the used cars Dick Nixon sold. In later coffee house appearances Ochs liked to let on he had a political point to make by appearing in a gold lame Elvis Presley rock-n-roll style outfit and doing new golden oldies—but whatever the political point may have been, it was largely lost on Ochs' audiences. *Greatest Hits* was rock-n-roll and country trivis, bad songs carelessly produced, and lost on the generation of the seventies. "I'll be around," Phil promised at the album's conclusion—but he wasn't.

It should have been clear from the last song on the last album that Phil Ochs released that this time he was sayin' good-bye for good. "No More Songs," it was called, a hauntingly beautiful melody, and an apology of a song for the fact that there are/were no more songs. The ashes of the dreams can be found in the magazines, Ochs sang, and it seems that there are no more songs to sing, no more songs to write, just plain no more songs. Not that anybody would care, Ochs thought. He pictured himself, perhaps self-pityingly and being slightly derivative from Dylan as a ghost without a name standing ragged in the rain. Marc Eliot recounts Phil's Westbury Music Fair Concert on August 4, 1969: Ochs is unsure of himself and tired; promotion for the concert is almost non-existant; fans are sparse and uncertain. It is an unfortunate end to what should have been a brilliant career.

Somebody, in a college campus next winter, when the snow has effectively seized the building, will discover a roommate's record collection, and will hear "I'm Going to Say It Now" for the first time. Who is this Phil Ochs, he will ask. Does he write his own stuff? Is he still around?

I last saw Ochs in January of 1974, still around, playing Bryn Mawr's The Main Point to two shows of a couple of hundred fans each, on the eve of Bob Dylan's Philadelphia appearances (in the Spectrum, in front of 22,000). He was largely unrecognized genius, introduced as a singer of high quality, slightly dated protest songs. The Philadelphia *Inquirer* called him "a real trooper."

Things need not, however, have come to this. Ochs did not have to die with the Movement, because he was capable of things other than high quality, slightly artsy protest songs and personal farewells to Lincoln Park and to life. Not the country or the rock-n-roll of *Greatest Hits,* but the art allegory he had developed concurrently with his art protest, beginning with *Pleasures of the Harbor* and continuing right through "Bach, Beethoven, Mozart and Me" and "No More Songs" on *Greatest Hits.* Here was an undercurrent which might have been made a main channel.

I like to call them allegories, although in the strictest sense they are not. Perhaps "Pleasures of the Harbor," "The Scorpion Departs But Never Returns," and maybe "Crucifixion." The rest are vaguely allegorical, throwing off a surrealism similar to what you find in Leonard Cohen's *Songs of Love and Hate* or Jackson Browne's *Late for the Sky.* Phil had done art songs as early as his first album, with that version of Poe's "Bells," but his own art lyrics did not appear until the later sixties. On the jacket of *Pleasures of the Harbor* he wrote,

I've been away for a while but I hope to be back soon.
I'll return with a tune to show all was not lost on the naked moors.
From the razor's edge of a Louvre of loveless beds a tone tossed across
  an ocean of seas, pass the body please.
Some might mistake it for a coin it sparkles so over the waterless waves.
others might suspect a falcon to attack their own flagellant flying
  saucers.
now who would be that depraved certainly not the children of Chaucer's.
  but it's only a filament of fantasy diffused through the stained glass
    window of the haunted whorehouse
    the last desperate laugh of a fool's passion
  to say I have been faithful to thee Cyrana in my fashion.

This may have been heavy and pretentious, but it was surely an indication of new directions. Ochs has been away for awhile, and he's back now with something new: art allegory.

There are three on this album: "I've Had Her," "Pleasures of the Harbor," and Ochs' most ambitious project ever, the ten-minute "Crucifixion." None is protest, even art protest. All are lush in both poetry and music. All are quite beautiful songs.

The first is a surrealist love song (or anti-love song) vaguely reminiscent of Bob Lind's "Elusive Butterfly of Love"; across a seashore landscape Ochs pursues his mysterious lady, symbolic of all his aspirations and dreams, knowing that he's had her and she's nothing, impelled nevertheless to rush on. 'Tis the human condition: always off chasing something. To reach, to pursue, to dream—perhaps one day to discover a dream which does not turn to ashes in the mouth.

"Pleasures of the Harbor" is also a sea song, turning a voyage and brief port stop into an allegory of man's journey through life: long hours of labor and straining at the oar, broken only by brief hours of leisure spent in wine, women, and laughter. The lyric paints a delicate picture of one mate's visit to one of them there houses of ill repute ("The fingers draw the blind, a sip of wine, the cigarette of doubt, 'til the candle is blown out, the darkness is so kind"), juxtaposing against it an honest glimpse of some sailor bar and a strong sense of timelessness and universality. Life as a journey from sea to occasional harbor and back to sea is a metaphor as old as the oldest English poetry; Ochs here is working within well defined conventions. But his handling of tradition is effective: the delicate vignettes of shore life, a magnificent melody that waves and swells along with the sea, the cyclical effect achieved by repeating first stanza as last stanza—all make this a very fine art song.

"Crucifixion" is the artiest of the art songs on this album, thanks mainly to Ian Freebairn-Smith and Joseph Byrd's arrangement and Larry Marks' production. The lyric, frequently anthologised as a poem, narrates the crucifixion of Christ-the-rebel, allegorizing it into a treatment of the love-hate man feels for his leaders, divine or human, political or social or theological. The hero of this game is Christ in one sense; he is also Socrates, John Kennedy, anyone who speaks the truth, leads his people, pays the price. Probably Phil saw not a little of himself here.

The lyric opens with a birth of cosmic importance: planets are paralyzed, mountains amazed, all glowing brighter from the brilliance of the blaze. The child grow, attracts a following, and becomes thereby a threat: "the giant is aware that someone's pulling at his leg, and someone is tapping at the door." The mass of men, their emotions a mixture of love and hate, turn as they turned on Christ, on Socrates, on the Who's Tommy, and this hero is crushed by the losers he vanquished so magnificently. Time passes, memories fade, the threat is refined "to the safety of sterility," to codified religion, to the secure patriotism of a dead Lincoln or Kennedy or Tom Paine. The people settle to their complacency, until disturbed by another birth, a new hero, another sacrifice. Ochs repeats his first stanza as his last.

"Crucifixion" had everything: imagery, symbolism, alliteration, rhyme, a splendid melody, and a full orchestra of atonal and thoroughly cosmic production. It was the high point of Och's art song, and a very important piece of music, well ahead of its time, before *Sgt. Pepper's* and Van Dyle Parks' song cycle. Understandably, Ochs backed off a trifle in his next album.

The art lyrics of *Tape from California* were less successful than what Phil had attempted earlier: "When In Rome" and "The Floods of Florence" are dense and obscure, neither as clean as "Pleasures of the Harbor" nor as carefully developed as "Crucifixion." Only "Tape from California" approaches the success Phil had known earlier, but it walks a thin line between allegory and protest. Ochs has been influenced by Dylan some in this lyric, but just as clearly the surrealism of the landscape owes much to the allegories of *Pleasure of the Harbor*. And the lyric looks forward to a couple of songs on subsequent albums.

"The Scorpion Departs But Never Returns," not the sort of song that impacts loudly upon a listener's soul with first hearing, may in fact be the quintessential Ochs lyric. It is both allegory and protest, filled with the riches of imagery, metaphor, alliteration, and melody that mark Ochs at his best. In it Phil returned to his first album and a song called "the Thresher" for his central symbol: the nuclear submarine that simply vanishes from the observable universe. The death ship comes to symbolize a new lost generation—the Vietnam exiles, the Watergate dropouts—which looked around, realized that for them at least the war was over, and split. "Oh captain, my dead captain," Ochs begins, echoing deliberately the well known school poem by Walt Whitman, "we are staying down so long. . . ." The radio begs them to return, promising reconciliation and forgiveness and anything else they want, but the only answer is "the silence of their sinking." And the generation, perhaps the last and brightest hope of the country, simply disappears; the phantom ship sails on forever. This sort of art-protest lyric is as alive today as it was in 1969, and will be around for a long, long time to come, after the music of the sixties has been sorted and sifted, listened to and listened to again. It is nearly an anthem for a generation.

Ochs was good at the art lyric, mixed with protest or otherwise, and he continued to produce art lyrics right up to his last album. "No More Songs" is in some respects an art allegory, as is another song on that album: "Bach, Beethoven, Mozart and Me." Here Phil's bitterness begins to show: the end is come, he's feeling old and neglected, remembering the past and the way things used to be, still trying to outdo himself and Bob Dylan, failing, retiring into himself. "Just me and a couple of other musicians hangin' out here away from David Bowie and Alice Cooper and all you other heavies of the seventies," Ochs seems to be saying. "Of course we're not much, as the fans know, but if you get interested, stop around for some tea. We're here: Bach, Beethoven, Mozart, me, a few other ordinary folk." Here in his retirement Ochs leads the most mundane of existences, thinking of the past, reading the newspaper, talking, drinking wine, making calls and receiving guests. It's a regular old folks' home.

Such an atmosphere must have been intolerable to the flaming radical of the sixties, to the bundle of energies that was Phil Ochs in his twenties, especially because Ochs' retirement was as much a forced retirement as a self-imposed exile. He was not an old man, not at thirty-five. The causes may have been dead, the words may not, as those who remained to do his explaining for him claimed, have been there in '75 and early '76. And perhaps he would never outdo "Crucifixion" or "No More Songs" or "The Scorpion Departs" or "Pleasures of the Harbor." But it was a tragedy when Phil Ochs imposed upon himself the ultimate retirement, a tragedy greater than the almost imperceptible media rumblings suggest. For now there are indeed no more songs. And one scarcely knows how to interpret the silence of his leaving.

A DISCOGRAPHY

II. Some Basic History and a Few Middleweights

Joan Baez, *Come from the Shadows*, A&M SP 4339.
The Beach Boys, *Close Up*, Capitol SWBB 253.
—, *Pet Sounds*, Capitol DT 2458.
Chuck Berry, *Chuck Berry's Golden Decade*, Chess 2CH 1514.
Big Brother and the Holding Company, *Cheap Thrills*, Columbia KCS 9700.
Buffalo Springfield, *Retrospective*, Atlantic SD 33-283.
The Byrds, *Greatest Hits*, Columbia CS 9516.
The Coasters, *Greatest Hits*, Atlantic 33-111.
Leonard Cohen, *Song of Leonard Cohen*, Columbia CS 9533.
—, *Songs from a Room*, Columbia CS 9767.
Cream, *Best of the Cream*, Atlantic SD 33-291.
Crosby, Stills, Nash & Young, *Deja Vu*, Atlantic SD 7200.
The Everly Brothers, *The Everly Brothers Original Greatest Hits*, Barnaby BGP 350.
Woody Guthrie, *The Greatest Songs of Woody Guthrie*, Vanguard VSD 35/36.
Buddy Holly, *Buddy Holly: A Rock and Roll Collection*, Decca DXSE7-207.
B. B. King, *Live at the Regal*, ABC Paramount ABC S-509.
Joni Mitchell, *Clouds*, Reprise R 6341.
Little Richard, *Little Richard's Grooviest 17 Original Hits*, Specialty SPS 2113.
Peter, Paul and Mary, *Peter, Paul & Mary*, Warner WS 1449.
—, *In the Wind*, Warner WS 1607.
Pete Seeger, *We Shall Overcome*, Columbia CS 8901.
—, *Dangerous Songs?!* Columbia CS 9303.

The Weavers, *Traveling On,* Vanguard VSD 2022.
Woodstock, Atlantic SD 3-500.

III. The Beatles

Meet the Beatles, Capitol ST 2047.
The Beatles' Second Album, Capitol ST 2080.
A Hard Day's Night, United Artists UAS 6366.
Beatles '65, Capitol, ST 2228.
Help! Capitol SMAS 2386.
Yesterday and Today, Capitol ST 2553.
Rubber Soul, Capitol ST 2442.
Revolver, Capitol ST 2576.
Sergeant Pepper's Lonely Hearts Club Band, Capitol
    SMAS 2653.
Magical Mystery Tour, Capitol MS 2835.
The Beatles (The White Album), Apple Records
    SWOB 101.
Abbey Road, Apple Records SO 383.
Let It Be, Apple Records AR 34001.

IV. The Rolling Stones

The Rolling Stones, London PS 375.
12 X 5, London PS 402.
Rolling Stones, Now, London PS 420.
Out of Our Heads, London PS 429.
December's Children, London PS 451.
Big Hits (High Tide and Green Grass), London NPS 1.
Aftermath, London PS 476.
Got Live If You Want It, London PS 493.
Between the Buttons, London PS 499.
Flowers, London PS 509.
Their Satanic Majesties Request, London NPS 2.
Beggars Banquet, London PS 539.
Through the Past, Darkly, London NPS 3.
Let It Bleed, London NPS 4.
Get Yer Ya-Ya's Out! London NPS 5.

Sticky Fingers, Rolling Stone Records COC 59100.
Rolling Stones Hot Rocks 1964-1971, London 2PS
    606/607.
Exile on Main Street, Rolling Stone Records COC 2900.
More Hot Rocks, London 2PS 627.
Goats Head Soup, Rolling Stone Records COC 59101.
Some Girls, Rolling Stone Records COC 39108.

V. The Doors

The Doors, Elektra EKS 74007.
Strange Days, Elektra 74014.
Waiting for the Sun, Elektra EKS 74024.
The Soft Parade, Elektra EKS 75005.
Morrison Hotel, Elektra EKS 75007.
L. A. Woman, Elektra EKS 75011.

VI. The Who

The Who Sings My Generation, Decca DL 74664.
Happy Jack, Decca DL 74892.
Tommy, Decca DXSW 7205.
Live at Leeds, Decca DL 79175.
Who's Next, Decca DL 97182.
Quadrophenia, MCA 2-1004.

VII. The Jefferson Airplane

The Jefferson Airplane Takes Off, RCA LSP 3584.
Surrealistic Pillow, RCA LSP 3766.
After Bathing at Baxter's, RCA LSP 4545.
Crown of Creation, RCA LSP 45058.
Volunteers, RCA LSP 4238.
Bark, Grunt FTR 1001.
Grace Slick and Paul Kantner, *Blows Against the Empire*,
    RCA LSP 4448.
Grace Slick and Paul Kantner, *Sunfighter*, Grunt FTR 1002.
Long John Silver, Grunt FTR 1007.

VIII. Bob Dylan

Bob Dylan, Columbia CS 8579.
The Freewheelin' Bob Dylan, Columbia CS 8786.
The Times They Are A-Changin', Columbia CS 8905.
Another Side of Bob Dylan, Columbia CS 8993.
Bringing It All Back Home, Columbia CS 9128.
Highway 61 Revisited, Columbia CS 9189.
Blonde on Blonde, Columbia C2L 41.
John Wesley Harding, Columbia CS 9604.
Nashville Skyline, Columbia KCS 9825.
Self-Portrait, Columbia C2X 30050.
New Morning, Columbia KC 30290.
Planet Waves, Elektra-Asylum 7E 1003.
The Basement Tapes, Columbia CBS 88147.
Blood on the Tracks, Columbia PC 33235.
Desire, Columbia PC 33893.

(Dylan has been bootlegged more than he's been released legally. For a detailed study of unofficial Dylan albums, see Paul Cable, *Bob Dylan: His Unreleased Recordings,* Schirmer Books, 1978.)

IX. Paul Simon

Wednesday Morning, 3 A. M., Columbia CS 9049.
Sounds of Silence, Columbia CS 9269.
Parsley, Sage, Rosemary & Thyme, Columbia CS 9363.
Bookends, Columbia KCS 9529.
Bridge Over Troubled Water, Columbia KCS 9914.
Paul Simon, Columbia KC 30750.
There Goes Rhymin' Simon, Columbia KC 32280.

X. Phil Ochs

All the News That's Fit to Sing, Elektra EKS 7269.
I Ain't Marching Anymore, Elektra EKS 7287.
Phil Ochs In Concert, Elektra EKS 7310.
Pleasures of the Harbor, A & M SP 4133.
Tape from California, A & M SP 4148.

The Poetry of Rock

Tape From California, A & M SP 4148.
Rehearsals for Retirement, A & M SP 4181.
Greatest Hits, A & M SP 4253.